Daughters of Suburbia

Daughters of Suburbia

Growing Up White, Middle Class, and Female

LORRAINE DELIA KENNY

RUTGERS UNIVERSITY PRESS
New Brunswick, New Jersey, and London

Library of Congress Cataloging-in-Publication Data

Kenny, Lorraine Delia, 1961–
Daughters of suburbia : growing up white, middle class, and female / Lorraine Delia Kenny.
p. cm.
Includes bibliographical references and index.
ISBN 0–8135–2852–6 (cloth : acid-free paper)—ISBN 0–8135–2853–4 (pbk. : acid-free paper)
1. Teenage girls—New York (State)—Shoreham. 2. Whites—New York (State)—Shoreham. 3. Socialization—New York (State)—Shoreham. 4. Kenny, Lorraine Delia, 1961– I. Title.
HQ798 .K47 2000
305.235—dc21

00–028087

British Cataloging-in-Publication data for this book is available from the British Library

Manufactured in the United States of America

Frontispiece: Christina Mezzalupo

For my daughter, Simone Lena Kenny Robbennolt:
May your life be filled with many stories worth telling.

Contents

Acknowledgments

Many people supported me through the research and writing of this book. In particular I would like to thank members of the University of California-Santa Cruz community. Those who influenced my work most during my tenure there include Nancy Campbell, Steven C. Caton, Deborah Connolly, Teresa de Lauretis, Giovanna Di Chiro, Virginia Domínguez, Joseph Dumit, Julia Erhart, Donna J. Haraway, Susan F. Harding, John Hartigan Jr., Galen Joseph, Yvonne Keller, David Schneider (now deceased), Sheila Peuse, Joan W. Scott, Victoria Smith, and Anna Tsing. All of these people contributed in direct and indirect ways to this book.

Daughters of Suburbia would not have been possible without the participation of the students and staff at the Shoreham-Wading River (SWR) Middle School. I thank them all for letting me into their classrooms, their circles of friends, and their personal lives. In particular I would like to thank Ross Burkhardt for sharing his students with me. And I am especially grateful to Diane Little Burkhardt, who supported me and this project in more ways than I can possibly enumerate. Thanks also to Emily Heinrichs for sharing her story one more time and trusting me to represent it fairly.

Martha Heller's enthusiastic and careful reading of a draft of the manuscript was invaluable. I'd like to thank her and other members of the Rutgers University Press editorial staff for their help in completing this project, including Marilyn Campbell and Susannah Driver-Barstow for her expert copyediting. Special thanks to David Myers for taking over this book and pushing me to finish it in a timely manner after Martha left the press to pursue other interests. In addition, I'd like to thank the manuscript's readers, including Ruth Frankenberg, David Roediger, and Kamala Visweswaran. Their insightful queries helped me clarify my positions and strengthen the coherency of the argument as a whole. I appreciate the time and interest they took in reviewing the original manuscript.

In this regard, I would like to acknowledge a second set of readers, a group of "natives," the SWR book women, Diane Burkardt, Eva Iacono, Corinne Milmoe, Toni Thorn, and Anne Westover. They allayed any fears I may have had that my perspective was completely idiosyncratic. I want to express my appreciation as well to Christina Mezzalupo for working closely and patiently with me to produce the illustrations for this book. As a daughter of suburbia herself, Christina deftly complements my analysis through her drawings.

This work was funded in part by a 1994–95 Woodrow Wilson Dissertation Grant in Women's Studies. I thank the foundation for its continuing interest in my work and for its commitment to building a women's studies community that reaches across generations of scholars. In this vein, I would also like to thank my former colleagues at the National Council for Research on Women, especially Mariam Chamberlain, whose years of dedication to producing and mentoring women's studies scholarship remain an inspiration.

I am indebted to the students I've worked with at Sarah Lawrence College and at Eugene Lang College. Some read and commented on parts of this manuscript; all taught me to be a better writer and teacher. Their ongoing interest in my work let me know in no uncertain terms that I had to complete this project. In part, *Daughters of Suburbia* is for them and their peers throughout the country.

I am grateful to my parents, Mary Margaret and James Thomas Kenny, for letting me move back into their home while I conducted fieldwork at the SWR Middle School, and for the hours of babysitting they did so that I could write. Without their selfless support through this and other endeavors throughout my life, this book would never have been possible.

Finally, thanks are due to Ray Eduardo Ochoa Robbennolt, who sustained me and our daughter, Simone Lena, throughout the many stages of this project. In addition to all the day-to-day details that he took care of, his unswerving belief in my work kept me focused and committed to completing what I had started. Simone and her young vision of the world reminded me why I began this project in the first place. This book is for her.

Daughters of Suburbia

Introduction

Truth or Dare

Home once interrogated is a place we have never before been.

—Kamala Visweswaran,
Fictions of Feminist Ethnography

THIS BOOK is filled with stories: narratives about white middle-class teen girlhood, about suburbia as an historically specific place, about Long Island as a prototypical suburban landscape, and about Shoreham, New York, a small town seventy miles east of New York City on the north shore of Long Island. Since I am a "native" ethnographer, these are my stories, as much as they are the stories of the girls I returned home to study. I grew up in Shoreham, was educated in its schools, and, to a large extent, took its culture for granted. I argue throughout this book that white middle-classness thrives on not being recognized as a cultural phenomenon. Its culture is a culture of entitlement in which the Self does not question its position within the dominant, normative group and instead accepts all the privileges of race and class that seem to naturally come her way. I returned home to write an account of the socialization of Shoreham's current teenage daughters so that I could examine that which I had heretofore learned to take for granted and thereby begin to articulate white middle-classness as a cultural practice with broad social consequences.

Daughters of Suburbia is part ethnography, part memoir, and part cultural study. It is an autobiographical ethnography or, more succinctly, an autoethnography, which is the term I use throughout the book. In writing this autoethnography, I am playing my own version of Truth or Dare, a game that girls I studied told me they played with each other after school or at sleep-overs. As the game goes, one girl asks for a "truth" or a "dare." If she picks truth she has to confess something about herself; if she picks dare, the other girls get to ask her to do something outrageous. One time, through a gale of giggles, a close-knit group of girls told me about daring their friend Maureen to run around the outside of her house in a bra and panties.[1] Apparently, much to their surprise and delight, Maureen took them up on their challenge. The act of telling white-middle-class girls' stories takes on the challenge of both revealing a truth and facing a dare. In examining white middle-classness as it manifests itself in the lives of its teenage daughters, this book attempts to speak a kind of truth, one that necessarily dares to disrupt the silences that engulf a life intentionally taken for granted. For it is these silences that constitute white middle-classness as a cultural norm. And it is these silences that do not want to be spoken or analyzed by a native or even nonnative ethnographer.

I garnered teenage girls' stories in part from fieldwork I conducted among eighth-grade girls at my adolescent alma mater, the Shoreham-Wading River (SWR) Middle School, during the 1993–94 school year. I sat in classrooms with girls, roamed the halls, visited the playing fields, went on overnight trips, shopped at the mall, ate lots of Big Macs and pizzas, and attended school plays, after-school private dance lessons, movies at the nearest multiplex, and the end-of-the-year graduation ceremonies, among other activities. While I did not interact only with the girls—SWR is a co-ed public institution—in writing this account, I mainly focus on girls' stories.

Girls are members of the white middle class in bad or at least precarious standing. As females in a world that still largely places males and masculinity at its center, white middle-class teen girls can make the limits of normative culture visible in ways that white middle-class boys don't often do, or are not supposed to do. When I began this work, the media were fixated on (white) girls and the trouble they can get into and cause. Mainstream, academic, and political minds alike worried about girls and their waning self-esteems, girls and their eating disorders, girls and their promiscuous sexual activity, among other socially transgressive or self-destructive behaviors. In addition, the media had recently sensationalized the stories of several white middle-class teen girls who had gone "bad," or, in other words, turned violent or broken the codes of middle-class femininity in some overstated manner, for example by killing abusive fathers, wayward lovers, or people they perceived as sexual rivals. Instead of turning in on themselves and their bodies, these girls had lashed out, making their anger external rather than internal. If white middle-class girls should be seen and not heard, normal girls turned bad definitely make themselves seen *and* heard. In the telling and retelling of their tales, the media vividly render the racial, classed, and gendered preoccupations of the culture at large. As a result, these girls' stories give SWR girls' lives a broader context, so some of them are also among the stories examined in this book.

It was not until the late 1990s, with its spate of deadly school-yard shootings and reports of steroid abuse among male high-school athletes, as well as the "discovery" of other equally horrific and disturbing trends, that the white middle-class suburban boy began to usurp his female counterpart in the national imagination as a cultural liability, or what amounts to a threat to the status quo of normative suburban life (see, for example, Gurian 1998, Garbarino 1999, Hall 1999, Kindlon and Thompson 1999, LeBlanc 1999, Pollack 1999). Notably, these stories suggest that when boys turn violent they project their anger out onto a generalized target—jocks, kids who actively uphold religious beliefs, teachers (not necessarily a specific teacher)—before turning their literal arsenals of destruction on themselves. Boys seem to conceive of themselves on a grand scale, while girls don't venture far beyond the boundaries of their families and friends—attacking their aggressors, or perceived aggressors, specifically. The difference underscores the divergent social positions girls and boys occupy in relation to normative whiteness, with girls caught in an internalized rather than a public world of struggle. While both boys' and girls' stories point to the notion that something is terribly wrong in the mainstream's housing subdivisions, I turn to girls' stories to explore white middle-classness specifically because as girls they are always already outsiders within the normative suburban world they inhabit.

Girls occupy an ambivalent and at times contradictory position in relation to the norm. They are what I call throughout this book "insider-Others." Insider-Others are figures who are both insiders *and* outsiders. At times they can appear fully ensconced on the inside, but upon closer examination there is something not quite normative enough about their identity or how they carry themselves in a normative world. As almost-insiders, almost-outsiders, insider-Others offer a perspective on the otherwise deceptively perspectiveless culture of white middle-class America. Ordinarily, the normal goes unnoticed. It is a silent and invisible yet powerful social category. It derives its potency precisely from its muteness and invisibility. To call attention to the normal is to make it strange and to question its authority as a self-evident idea and practice. Historically, the norm in the United States has been defined in terms of whiteness and middle-classness. This is not to suggest, however, that the norm *is* white middle-class America, but that the culture at large imagines it as such. Relegating something to the imaginary in no way diminishes its effect. In fact, to a great extent it increases its capacity to shape, albeit with little critical reflection, anything from public policy to popular culture to everyday social relations. But locating something within the imaginary also makes it abstract, hard to pinpoint, and difficult to perceive, analyze, or critique. Insider-Other girls give the lie to the perspectiveless world of normative culture. As young females, white middle-class girls have, wittingly or not, a partial perspective on the norm. Therefore they offer a window through which to catch sight of this otherwise intentionally elusive category. In the end, they demonstrate that not having a perspective is indeed a perspective, a socially dominating one at that.

The teen girls of this book are not its only insider-Others. As an autoethnographer, I am one of the daughters of suburbia here. I am literally a daughter of SWR; my family moved to the community in 1965 when I was four—fleeing a more congested and increasingly socially diverse area north of New York City—and my parents still live there, as does one of my older siblings and her daughter, also a graduate of the local schools. SWR is a very familiar and familial place to me, as is its culture of whiteness and middle-classness, or what I identify as its culture of silence and avoidance. However, as a prodigal-daughter ethnographer I return to my home with the critically trained eye of the social scientist and the cultural analyst. In addition, though I carry the effects of my girlhood with me in my daily life, I am no longer a teen girl. As such, I am necessarily an insider-Other in relation to my subject. I do and do not fit into this suburbia and the teen-girl culture it sustains.

This became painfully obvious to me on one of my first days in the middle school. Gym had just ended and I was walking down the hall to go to an English class. A group of boisterous girls made their way just ahead of me. Though I had only been in the school three weeks, I knew these girls constituted a socially powerful clique among the eighth graders at SWR. They were tougher than some and not as tough or scholastically inclined as others, yet they possessed the authority to demarcate social boundaries and hierarchies. One girl in particular, Kerri, carried herself as if it was her responsibility to deem other girls worthy of inclusion or exclusion. She made me nervous. She was the kind of girl—focused more on her social life than on academics—I was never friends with when I was growing up. Consequently, I felt ill equipped to reach her inner circle as an ethnographer. I was still an "egghead," though this time I was completely on my own. As a thirteen-year-old walking these very same halls, I at least had had a group of "smart kids" with whom to hang out. Even if I had been curious about girls like Kerri back then, I hadn't needed their approval; I hadn't really needed to know what their world was like. This time around, I wanted to find out what made Kerri's world tick, so I was acutely aware of being on the outside.

On this particular day, my longing for acceptance was complicated by the fact that I was not alone in the hall with Kerri and her followers. Another girl, Elizabeth, walked ahead of me and behind them. Elizabeth, I had already noticed, was always alone. I had tried to introduce myself to her a few days earlier in art class, but she seemed unable or unwilling to respond to my attempts at small talk: "Hi, I'm Lorraine, I don't think you were in English the day I introduced myself. I'm writing a book about being in eighth grade, about growing up in Shoreham." Silence. No eye contact. "What are you gonna make in here? That's a nice drawing." Silence.

Despite our earlier encounter, I had not given up on Elizabeth. I could tell that she was aware of me watching her and the popular girls. I found myself in a panic. If Kerri and her entourage saw me talking to Elizabeth, I would never get a chance to hang out with them. On the other hand, I felt for Elizabeth and I wanted to reach her as well. In some grandiose and very likely misguided way, I imagined that my attentions could help bring out Elizabeth's "true self," could boost her "self-esteem," assuming her lack thereof was the source of her withdrawal from the clamorous world of the middle school and from my own inquisition. But that day in the hall with Elizabeth and Kerri, I spoke to neither. The peer culture prevailed; Kerri had her way with me, maintaining her sovereign control over this social space. Being between the inside and the out was a feeling I would come to know well and a position that I would learn to understand better through the course of my fieldwork and the writing of this book.

As it so happened, the line between inside and out of the local teen-girl culture ended up being the least of my problems. I quickly found a way into the worlds of both the Elizabeths and the Kerris of SWR. Most girls, as I explore in depth later, thrive on having a story to tell and an audience to tell it to. It wasn't long before they figured out that I was all ears and that my position as an anomalous adult—neither teacher nor parent—could at times serve their purposes well. (I could take them places, legitimize their presence in others, all without the heavy hand of parental or pedagogical authority. I was not there to teach them, discipline them, or judge their individual lives. I was just there to listen and take note of all the cultural stuff, significant and seemingly insignificant, that filled their days.) The culture of inside and out that would prove more difficult to straddle would be that of white middle-classness. This was a culture that did not want to speak its name and that I myself inhabited with sometimes less-than-critical eyes.

Most studies of race in the United States focus either on sites of racial conflict and difference or on communities that are stigmatized as racially Other to mainstream whites. This is understandable. Difference and conflict can help clarify social positions. Conflicts force definitions based on negations: I am white because I am not black; I am a middle-class white because I am not "white trash." This is the model of identity construction that permeates most accounts of race in America. The Self can name itself only by recognizing what it is not, its Other. I avoided this comparative approach and chose instead to rejoin my community of similarity—in 1994 the SWR Middle School was roughly 95 percent white—to study normative white femininity not simply because it was literally the site of my own white-girl origin story but because I knew that I had grown up in a place where my racial identity was not formed through a social system of racial or class differences, but rather propagated in what I liken later in the book to a social greenhouse, a closed system, one that feeds off itself feeding off itself, an insular community that doesn't see too far beyond its present conditions and boundaries. At the turn of the millennium, the suburban greenhouses of Long Island and SWR appear to have outgrown the resources—ample space, uncongested roadways, and well-funded public educations—they once heedlessly consumed and took for granted. The result is a suburban ecosystem in a state of decline and disrepair. My main concern here is with how the daughters of this book make their way through the social landscape that all this unbridled consumption has wrought.

Suburbia fosters a lack of racial, class, and cultural self-consciousness in that it consists of towns where girls can grow up and see mirror images of themselves and their families in their neighbors, and where they never—or rarely—have to encounter directly people of different racial and class standings. Though at the beginning of the twenty-first century, suburbia, including Long Island's suburbia, is finding itself sharing the local supermarket or nearest warehouse chain store like Price Club or Cosco with more and more nonwhite and even poor immigrants (Mahler 1995), many communities are still, for the most part, the lily-white enclaves that the post–World War II generation settled and consolidated in the decades after the war. What racial differences exist in a place like Long Island are still largely relegated to segregated communities (Brown 1994). It is the founding history of white flight from urban diversity to suburban homogeneity and its continued resonance in today's suburbia that has led me to call the geographic location of my study "the anti-OtherAmerica"—a place intentionally built on imposing distance between white America and its Others. By choosing the negative appellation, I intend to call attention to this constitutive relationship. Though suburban white America does not necessarily see itself as a racialized place—indeed, the culture of suburbia largely dodges addressing the issue of race, its or anybody else's—nevertheless, by identifying suburbia as the anti-Other America, I am insisting that there is a fundamental racial (as well as classed and gendered) component to suburbia, one based on the exclusion of the Other and the denial of this practice (see also Lipsitz 1995).

While I was growing up and still later when I was doing fieldwork, my suburban home was a place where white middle-class, largely Christian families lived among other white middle-class, Christian families and where the majority of the sons and daughters of teachers, doctors, lawyers, bankers, and physicists left town to matriculate in college and become professionals themselves. The community never presumed or imagined other lives for their offspring. For example, while in the field I attended a high-school orientation meeting for eighth-grade students and their parents, which took place six months before eighth-grade graduation. In the course of this evening, a high-school administrator exhorted the eighth graders to "take challenging classes, develop personal qualities, and be as involved in high-school activities as you can." Later, a guidance counselor informed us that 95 percent of SWR graduates go to college and the remaining 5 percent go to BOCES (Brookhaven Occupational Center and Educational Services), a public vocational school that students can attend on a part-time basis while they are still in high school. In case we missed the point, he went on to say that "when people at BOCES ask me why SWR doesn't send more students to their program, I tell them that our students prefer to go to Harvard, West Point, or a community college after graduating from SWR." In a somewhat rare moment for a culture based on silences and denials, these public figures delineated some of the normative values that define, at least in theory, white middle-class, suburban life. As a girl who had grown up in this community, I also knew that this white middle-classness comes with a specific set of gendered expectations as well. And I knew that my girlhood experiences were neither unique nor idiosyncratic, but by-products of post-war, anti-Other suburbia, with its history of exclusion and investment in constructing a normative, homogeneous, and heterosexual familial culture.

Studying whiteness in the context of suburban teen girls makes clear that whiteness is not only about race. Nor is race simply about skin color. I use the term *race* as an historical and cultural concept. Historians have underscored that race is more than skin deep by demonstrating that not all groups who are now considered white in the United States were always treated as such (see Domínguez 1986; Roediger 1991; Ignatiev 1995; Jacobson 1998; Brodkin 1999). Italian, Irish, and Jewish immigrants, for example, *became* white only after they assimilated economically, educationally, and culturally into the U.S. mainstream. By these accounts, whiteness is also, among other things, a classed position, tempered through and recognizable as "cultural capital" (Bourdieu 1984): the ability to have access to and make optimum use of things like higher education and the learned social graces, vocabularies, and demeanors that allow one to prosper among the elite or at least compete within the dominant culture. In this regard, I define class not merely in terms of one's economic resources but with equal, if not more, emphasis on one's culture and upbringing. For example, though I may not reproduce my parents' middle-class economic standing in my lifetime, as a college-educated professional raised in white suburbia, I will always be on some fundamental level middle class. I will think, act, and talk middle class. I will feel entitled to certain privileges and accept that I am denied others that are still clearly out of reach in a middle-class life. Since I am speaking of whiteness as a normative concept, I am referring to white middle-classness, to the ability to fit into institutions like suburbia and corporate America, to see oneself reflected in broadcast media, and to feel relatively unencumbered by the existing legal and penal systems, to name a few primary sites producing and reproducing the norm. Such are some of the (unspoken) privileges of mainstream whiteness. But it is important to note that not all whites are the same. Poor whites, for example, do not as seamlessly enjoy the same advantages that middle-class whites do (see Wray and Newitz 1997; Hartigan Jr. 1999). Likewise, wealthy, dynastic families travel in a world that barely resembles their middle-class counterparts' (Marcus with Dobkin 1992; on the middle class more generally, see Newman 1988, 1994; Ehrenreich 1989; Ortner 1991). To speak of whiteness alone, therefore, makes little social sense. But because it is awkward to continually write "the white middle class" (or some version thereof), there are instances in this book where I will just use the term *middle class* or just use the terms *whites* or *whiteness*; the reader is advised to keep in mind that I intend these race and class terms to be linked throughout this text. Similarly, when I use the term *normal* or its derivatives (*normative, normalizing, the norm*), I am referring to the white middle class, and I am investigating not reasserting this group's normative status.

Working within a community of similarity and a culture of avoidance makes the process of naming normative whiteness nearly impossible, especially when the researcher can also count herself among the researched, or at least one of their descendants. As an autoethnographer without a ready-made comparative field to study, I decided that one way to get a perspective on my hometown would be to turn to media stories about notoriously bad, white middle-class, suburban, teen girls, and about Long Island girls in particular. I focus on "bad" girls' stories because those are the narratives the media proffer. There's no sound bite or TV movie-of-the-week in the life of a "good girl" (that is, a normal teen who is following the rules). Her existence, as the SWR girls insist, is "sooo boring," "sooo normal," sooo without a story worth telling unless she in some way takes a turn for the worst. These bad girls are the girls the media and the viewing public love to hate. Normal girls gone bad, and hence what I deem unlovable subjects: girls the mainstream cannot turn its back on or cannot *not* love precisely because normative culture depends on redeeming them and bringing them back into the fold. They are after all one of its own. However, by being bad and deliberately defying the prevailing codes of white middle-classness, they make the rules and values of this culture perceptible. And therefore make my job as a student of white middle-class femininity much easier. I find my larger-than-life unlovable daughters in the media, and I find tamer versions of them among the SWR girls.

More generally, the media stories are the stories that precede me into the field. In this sense, they are precursor ethnographies (Limón 1991). Though they are not technically ethnographies—most are media extravaganzas—they do, to one degree or another, tease out some of the everyday details of life as a girl on suburban Long Island. They impart a sense of place and culture—however sensationalized that may be—that lingers beyond the particular stories at hand. They are the narratives that shape public perceptions and understandings of teen girlhood, suburbia, and Long Island. They are the stories SWR girls and their parents know. And beyond that, they engage the national imagination in ways that can have direct and indirect consequences for the girls I encountered in the halls at SWR. Moreover, intentionally or not, these media productions have turned the unrepresentable into a palpable representation. In following the narrative twists and turns of these public bad-girl tales, I am able to show white middle-classness in the process of constructing itself. What these stories highlight, what they identify as a problem or aberration, as well as what they choose not to represent or call attention to are the keys to breaking the silences surrounding middle-class whiteness. But these stories do more than give normative whiteness substance; in their plot developments and viewed in relation to prominent stories about social Others, they also reinforce the norm. The media form one of the white middle-class institutions responsible for defining and sustaining a normative cultural order. They do this, in part, through the telling and retelling of suburban bad girls' stories. Because the media are a prime component of the greenhouse they are also among the main players and subjects under scrutiny in this account of growing up normal.

In framing the stories of unlovable teen girls, television, film, and print productions tend to rely on stock characters (the all-American teenager, good girls, and bad girls) politically charged figures (teenage moms and white supremacists), and conventional story-making genres (boy-meets-girl stories, ethnic and racial parodies, and tales of redemption). The everyday stories that clutter the lives of SWR girls pick up on and recycle fragments of these popular stories. Sometimes, girls literally retell media stories, discussing in detail the latest plot twists in *Melrose Place* or *Beverly Hills 90210* (both popular TV shows among SWR students while I was in the field). Other times, they seem to reenact, if unconsciously, their own mini-serial dramas, replete with betrayals, rumors, and petty jealousies. The parallels between these two worlds of story making—the media and the every day—give one pause: Who is retelling whose stories? Girls tell their stories in the course of making a place and identity for themselves among their friends, family, and the outside world. Sometimes this practice is about fitting in; sometimes it's about deliberately marking oneself as different, though not too different; and other times it's about the failure to fit in. Regardless, it is always about the making of a life within a social context.

Rather than splitting my story in two—first half textual analysis, second half ethnography, a solution that would have followed the narrative conventions and progressions of more traditional ethnographies, at least in part—I chose a more collagelike structure, one that replicates the overlapping and symbiotic alliance the media and my ethnographic subjects live out on a daily basis. Some readers may want to know more of the ethnographic girls' stories; some may want to know once and for all how the media affect girls' body images, emotional lives, and future aspirations. *Daughters of Suburbia* refuses to oblige these habits of reading and asks instead that the reader pay attention to the texture of the relationships among the various kinds of stories in the book. It is here that the myths of white culturelessness and the normalcy of being normal begin to break down. Likewise, it is here that traditional notions of the ethnographic field dissolve as a place with identifiable boundaries to which ethnographers travel and from which they return. My field is my home, my past, my present, as well as my subjects' presents and futures. Moreover, my field is the media and the stories my subjects generate, as well as the SWR Middle School and the stories it facilitates and tolerates, and over which it sometimes loses control.

Through this hybrid approach, the white middle-class, suburban, teen girl emerges as a complex figure who lives a specific kind of whiteness and girlness, both in local and broader contexts. Naming the unnamable is risky business. But it is a practice the daughters of this book, SWR girls and their media counterparts, take on despite their personal desires in most instances to fit in and go unnoticed. They do this by being unlovable and making trouble, all kinds of trouble. For the most part, however, girls' irruptions sustain and fall within rather than outside the status quo. The conflicts of white middle-class teen girls are already subsumed within the suburban greenhouse. Antagonisms between parents and their adolescent daughters are practically de rigueur in suburbia, considered part and parcel of growing up, a notion continually reinscribed by the mass media from the classic *Rebel Without a Cause* (1955, directed by Nicholas Ray) to contemporary TV sitcoms and melodramas like the critically acclaimed, but short-lived, *My So-Called Life* (an ABC drama that ran for two seasons beginning in August 1994). The latter, often, revolved around a teen girl's conflicts with her mother.[2] When girls break the rules adults get the opportunity to reinforce the codes of normalcy and thereby set their daughters more firmly on a path toward a life of privilege. So while I do rely on the social struggles that emerge in relation to and among white middle-class teen girls to frame my analysis, I do not see these conflicts producing identities in opposition as much as reproducing greenhouse subjects. All is not lost, however. Although their efforts may not have been aimed at bringing about cultural change and in many instances do precisely the opposite, in the end, girls' rebellions are not random. By looking at what they act out against, what kinds of stories they tell or provoke the media to tell, *Daughters of Suburbia* gives substance to the culture of privilege and in so doing, undercuts its ability to continually unself-consciously replicate itself in its daughters. It is in this spirit that this book recounts girls' stories, big and small.

Chapter Outline

Each chapter in *Daughters of Suburbia* tells a particular piece of the story of white middle-classness, and suburban teen girlhood. Each includes and in most cases revolves around one or two insider-Others, or unlovable daughters.

Chapter 1, "Raising Teenage Girls: Suburban Landscapes and the Culture of Privilege," serves as my ethnographic "arrival story"—or as the case may be, my story of return. I use myself and the predicaments of my homecoming as a way to begin to articulate the culture of suburbia that defines life in Shoreham-Wading River. From my perspective, my reentry into this community was not a smooth one on many levels, some more public than others. By imagining and then later finding myself back within this community, I quickly came face-to-face with some of its more prominent cultural features, namely, its culture of avoidance, by which I mean a culture based on social indirectness, moral ambiguity, and the historical and everyday silences that sustain SWR's normative and hence privileged life. To contextualize this personal experience and the SWR girls' stories that surface more fully in later chapters, "Raising Teenage Girls" presents a history of the towns of Shoreham and Wading River as told through the rise and fall of the Shoreham Nuclear Power Plant. As the biggest local story to surface in the area over a good part of the last three decades, a period not coincidentally corresponding to the boom and bust of the SWR school district, the demise of the nuclear power plant and the community struggle it engendered magnifies the character and tenor of this suburban enclave. It reveals the limits of the community's penchant for isolating itself, avoiding conflict, and looking out for itself at the expense of others. In the end, the things most jeopardized by these practices are SWR daughters' futures.

In the next chapter, "Amy Fisher, My Story: Learning to Love the Unlovable," I turn to the story of the quintessential unlovable Long Island teen girl, the one and only (one can hope, anyway) Amy Fisher, the "Pistol-Packing Long Island Lolita" whose story swept the tabloid nation in the 1990s, putting Long Island teen girlhood on the national cultural map. While Amy's story predates my arrival into the field, it had a long media shelf-life and made a lasting cultural impression of what that land mass jutting out from the mainland of North America, east of New York City, with its endless strip malls, parking lots, and manicured lawns, holds in store. Amy's suburban saga—a convoluted tale of extramarital sex between a teen girl (Amy) and a Svengali-like married man (Joey Buttafuoco) that ended when Amy shot Joey's wife (Mary Jo Buttafuoco) on the doorstep of her suburban home, paralyzing one side of her face—has all the dramatic qualities of a made-for-TV movie; so much so that the major networks produced and broadcast with much fanfare three different and competing movies about her. These, however, would only be the icing on the media cake, so to speak. Amy alone generated an entire greenhouse industry, replete with books, touring theater productions, T-shirts, Amy Fisher mock postage stamps, an Amy and Joey comic book, endless newspaper, magazine, and TV news stories, and countless hours of television talk shows. This chapter asks, Why all the fuss? What kind of cultural daughter is Amy? What can be learned from her story about the role white middle-class teen girlhood plays in the cultural imagination? Moreover, how does the nation perceive of Long Island when it takes Amy Fisher to be its poster child?

In writing this chapter, I also felt compelled to explore my own interest and stakes in Amy's story. As a Long Island daughter, I count myself among the viewing public here. As such, I have to ask why I'm drawn to a girl like Amy, and how I can responsibly read her story without producing yet another sensationalized account. I name this attempt to critically and productively interpret Amy's story as "learning to love the unlovable." In many ways, Amy is the girl who taught me just how important the unlovable subject is to the reproduction of the status quo, and moreover how important it is to find a way to engage her. Though I may have an obvious personal connection to Amy, as a national story, Amy's story is everybody's story to one degree or another, whether you are a white suburbanite or an African American city dweller, or anything in between or beyond these two stereotypical examples. She is the thing of darkness we must embrace on some level as our own, even when we actively disregard her as meaningless media rubbish and think she has nothing to do with our individual lives. We all live in a media-driven world, even those who spend their lives setting themselves apart from popular culture. Not turning on your television is an act already framed within a media-dominated culture. We are always already caught up in the greenhouse, whether we like it or not. Learning to love the unlovable is a model for interpreting within the greenhouse in a critical and responsible manner. It is about owning up to one's position in and relation to the greenhouse. It is about engagement. It is about acknowledging one's perspective and hence producing partial accounts that go against the grain of normative culture and on some level beat the greenhouse at its own game. Throughout this book I am attempting to love the unlovable. I invite my readers to join me in this process.

Chapter 3, "Justify My Love: The Heterosexuality of Teenage Girlhood," analyzes the stories of two other unlovable girls—Cheryl Pierson, an incestuously abused Long Island teen who hired a classmate to murder her father, and Dora, the adolescent subject of one of Freud's most revisited cases. Both girls' stories show the toll a normative culture of avoidance can take on its daughters. While Dora is clearly not a contemporary Long Island girl, her story represents a foundational moment in the historical construction of normative teen girlhood. In this sense, it is as much a part of SWR girls' lives—even if they don't know it—as are the Amy Fisher story or the television programs they watch religiously. Dora's case history defines normative teen girlhood directly in relation to heterosexuality, and it defines heterosexuality as a bourgeois patriarchal institution. Here, I am distinguishing between the practice of heterosexual sex, which is not necessarily an institution, and the cultural (and what turns out to be political) construct of heterosexuality as the predominant social paradigm. Again, this discussion is about the imaginary, about how heterosexuality is defined and understood by the normative culture, and about what effect this construct has on teenage girls' lives. This is where Cheryl comes into the picture. The media portray this modern-day suburban girl as the seemingly happy-go-lucky, all-American cheerleader. On the surface she appears every bit the normal suburban adolescent. But this icon quickly unravels, and what remains in the ruins of normality is a heterosexual patriarchy gone terribly wrong. Interestingly, both Dora's and Cheryl's stories focus on what is left said and unsaid by the girls and their respective social contexts. Thus they show how normative culture is invested in certain silences and threatened by others, especially those pertaining to the mainstream heterosexual order.

"Among Friends: Stories that Make a Normal Life Possible," chapter 4, further explores this investment in girls' talk (or the deliberate lack thereof), by listening to the stories that SWR girls fabricate and circulate among themselves. SWR girls' stories demonstrate the paradoxes of being normal. While Dora is identified as abnormal by Freud because of her hysterical psychological symptoms—things like losing her voice for no apparent medical reason or wetting her bed well past the point that most children could reasonably be expected to have control over their bladders—I find in the SWR girls' collective hysterical talk the social mechanism for producing these girls as normal. In this context, I use the words hysterical or hysteria in their colloquial as opposed to diagnostic senses, meaning that SWR girl culture can appear somewhat out of control, ridden with anxiety, and highly volatile and emotional without there being any real cause for alarm. SWR girls fill their otherwise storyless (or cultureless) normal lives with wild stories that get fashioned and refashioned as they make the rounds among select groups of girls. The girls who participate in this seemingly chaotic practice in the end are the ones who are most fully ensconced in a normal life, while the girls who appear unremarkably normal or even prototypically normal—who don't join their peers in turning their everyday lives into collective serial dramas—are the ones who linger too far on the edges of what counts as normal. They are the ones, like Cheryl, who are in real normative trouble.

The final two chapters focus directly on questions of whiteness or, more specifically, the racialization of middle-class girls. "I Was a Teenage White Supremacist" retells the story of Emily Heinrichs, a former white supremacist and teen mom who has gone public with her tale of extremist hate-filled beliefs and eventual redemption. Unlike the other chapters on girls the media adopted as their own—Amy and Cheryl and in a slightly different public venue, namely academia, Dora—Emily's is based on an interview I conducted with her as well as on analyses of media representations of her story. Emily and I both talk back to the media here. In the process, the media clearly emerge as a white-making institution. Emily's story shows how public narratives deliberately manipulate girls' stories in the name of maintaining a mainstream white middle-class heterosexual order. As a white supremacist, Emily filled her normal white life with a big story to tell, but her story does not become interesting to the media until she renounces this bad-girl life. Only then can white supremacy become a foil for producing mainstream whiteness. Through Emily, white supremacy arises as an insider-Other, something the norm can define itself against while not having to actually acknowledge its racial Others or its own racial positioning. Normative whiteness stands as racially neutral to Emily's former extremist whiteness. But in analyzing Emily's stories these two expressions of white identity (or anti-identity as the case may be for the mainstream) emerge as relational and, at times, even converge around certain narrative threads and figures, especially around images of the teenage girl and the middle-class nuclear family.

The final chapter, "Learning to Tell White Lies: Living with the Other in the Anti-Other America," turns back to SWR and looks at how differences emerge and function within this community of similarity and how its daughters shape and reshape these practices in their everyday lives. If one needs an Other to define one's Self, what happens to girls in a virtually Otherless world? More specifically, given the whiteness of SWR and its culture of avoidance that mandates a "don't ask, don't tell" policy, how are girls racialized in the absence of difference? Regardless of the overriding myth of suburban homogeneity, communities of similarity are not without their Others. The greenhouse is not always airtight. In addition to its insider-Others, SWR also accommodates girls who are more outsiders than insiders, white girls lacking in economic and cultural capital. (While there were some SWR eighth graders who were not phenotypically white, as I will discuss later in the book, the few nonwhite SWR girls among my subjects functioned through their mastery of local cultural practices closer to the mainstream than not. Therefore, I do not count them in this context as culturally meaningful Others or outsiders.) Though these bona fide outsiders are rare among the SWR middle schoolers, they nevertheless have an impact on how the majority of girls are socialized to be part of the norm. Namely, no one acknowledges what difference these outsiders make. Class and racial disparities are hardly, if ever, spoken of directly. Instead girls express these and other differences in other vocabularies. For example, Amber, a lower-middle-class white girl, is called "muscular" or "big," and she is, for the most part, avoided. The one difference that can be named is gayness, though the SWR girls rarely use the term to refer specifically to a gay person. Instead it is a catchall, identifying anyone and anything that makes insider girls uncomfortable. More often than not these differences are internal and hence in some ways more threatening than those that the nearby outsiders pose. The girls' practices of deflecting difference and fabricating internal Others—gayness—demonstrate how race works in the anti-Other America by showing the lengths a community of similarity will go to deny their Others and thereby themselves. In the end, not talking about something like race, class, or gender doesn't render it meaningless; on the contrary, the silences can make it all the more consequential and culturally effective. This book attends to these effects.

Chapter 1 Raising Teenage Girls

Suburban Landscapes and the Culture of Privilege

SHOREHAM-WADING RIVER is a fairly typical suburban community, albeit a middle- to upper-middle-class one. The streets are tree lined, the houses almost all well-kept colonial-style ranches or two-storied single-family dwellings with two-car garages, and many of the household incomes are in the six figures. Despite the fact that SWR is located on the shores of the Long Island Sound, many of these homes have backyard pools, which keep the beaches underpopulated during the hot summer months of July and August. When they're not playing video games or watching TV, or when they haven't managed to convince their parents to drive them to the mall or the nearest multiplex, kids ride their bicycles around the neighborhoods or play on soccer teams or attend dance classes at a commercial school in a nearby strip mall. The school district—with its three elementary schools, middle school, and high school, which also houses the local public library—is the heart and soul of this community. It is one of the few resources most residents have in common; it is the place where neighbors meet neighbors on a regular basis as they attend meetings, theater productions, track meets, or baseball games. Aside from a few delis, bagel shops, and pizza parlors, the schools are all the local teenagers have within walking distance, and with very little public transportation to speak of, walking distance matters.

The one thing that really sets SWR apart from most other suburban communities is the now abandoned Shoreham Nuclear Power Plant, which occupies a large section of the beach on the border between Shoreham and Wading River. Proposed in the late 1960s and decommissioned in the early 1990s, the large, obtrusive facility stands as a symbol of how far a community will go to obtain and maintain privilege. In return for living with a nuclear facility in their backyards for the good part of two decades, the SWR community enjoyed low property and school taxes while the utility basically subsidized the local school system. As a result, the story of the power plant is a fulcrum both within the community and within this chapter on the culture of privilege. Here, I offer a sketch of the suburban landscape the white middle-class girls of this book traverse directly and indirectly throughout their lives. By looking closely at the town both before and in the wake of the demise of the nuclear power plant, I trace the history, economics, and racialization of SWR, demonstrating how the town itself was crafted through a series of decisions that excluded some and included others, and how the different layers of this suburban story both reflect and enact a culture of avoidance that serves as the bedrock of white middle-class privilege. It is a privilege not to have to deal directly with many social and economic issues and to avoid conflict whenever possible. The SWR community has developed complex ways of practicing this privilege and passing it on to its daughters. This chapter starts to examine this process, and the rest of the book follows suit.

Though race itself or, more specifically, whiteness, is not the major focus of "Raising Teenage Girls" (see chapter 6 for an in-depth discussion of the whiteness of this community), since it is one of the fundamental registers of privilege operating at SWR this chapter introduces whiteness as a concept and looks at how the community's understanding of whiteness fits into and builds upon the culture of avoidance that constitutes its temperament in general. Through a brief analysis of local discussions, or lack thereof, of race, it becomes clear that SWR largely sees itself (a misrecognition at best) as a community without race and thereby attempts to bypass the issue all together. Hence avoidance characterizes whiteness at SWR. In a world where race neutrality is prized over specific racial identities, by sidestepping race the community actually positions itself and its offspring firmly within a culture of racial privilege. In the end, the avoidance of race is not really an option as much as a smoke screen.

As a daughter of this community, I am part of this story of privilege. I have internalized many of the values of this culture and have learned to take its privileges for granted. Therefore, I use myself as one of the layers in this analysis. At times, I am the prodigal-daughter ethnographer struggling to see what I have been taught not to notice by this culture of avoidance. At other times, I am the thirteen-year-old girl roaming the halls of the middle school or watching the bulldozers plow through a nearby estuary to make room for the soon-to-be-erected nuclear power plant. I analyze my own responses to and reflections on these events in an effort to identify the culture out of which they arise. However, I am only part of the story and ultimately a means to an end. What matters most throughout this autoethnography are the teenage girls. I use myself as a ground upon which their story can be told in greater detail. But the ultimate question remains: What effect does the culture of privilege have on SWR girls' lives?

The ethnographic process is somewhat mysterious and certainly limited in its ability to grasp a culture in its entirety. I decided to write an autoethnography because I wanted to foreground the role that the ethnographer plays in the making of (partial) cultural knowledge and to explore the lines of responsibility and vulnerability the researcher must face in undertaking a cultural study, especially a cultural study of race, class, and gender relations. Initially, I found clues to understanding SWR girls by attending to the ways the local suburban culture affected my sense of Self and understandings of who counts as an Other, or an outsider, in this largely homogeneous community. Below, I begin by working out from the personal to find a way into SWR's white middle-classness. When all is said and done, *Daughters of Suburbia* will not tell the whole story of SWR and its teenage girls. But it will offer a set of stories that conveys in part what it means to grow up white, middle class, and female. Again, I am not so much interested in my story per se as I begin this autoethnography, but in how SWR's and the girls' stories can be read through my own responses and susceptibilities. As an insider-Other attempting to reposition myself in this community, I had to relearn many of the cultural codes that undergird this culture of privilege. Here, my body literally stands as ethnographic ground zero.

Expectant Arrivals and Moral Minimalisms

Two weeks before I was to move back in with my parents and start eighth grade all over again at my adolescent alma mater, I found out I was pregnant. Once I recovered from the initial shock of seeing the home pregnancy test come up positive rather than negative, as I had complacently assumed it would—I had after all been "careful" and nothing like this had ever happened to me before—my thoughts began to turn to the field, my hometown. Single women weren't supposed to get pregnant and have babies in this mostly upper-middle-class, white, 46 percent Catholic, overwhelmingly Christian community. And if they did, they certainly weren't supposed to hang out with the town's thirteen- and fourteen-year-old daughters. I was, to say the least, a bit panicked and consumed by a confluence of conflicting emotions and rational and irrational thoughts.

In part, I felt as if I had prematurely "gone native." At thirty-two years old, I was about to become a teenage mother of sorts. I was in a relationship with someone who was reluctant to make a commitment to me and, as it turned out, who adamantly did not want to be a father. I was faced with becoming a single mother with no immediate means of supporting myself or a child. Moreover, I feared that the school and community would deem me an unfit role model for their daughters, that I would become a local scandal and thereby visit shame upon my family and jeopardize my fieldwork. Similarly, I wondered how being pregnant would affect my ethnographic relationship with the girls. How would they position me within their social order? How would they make sense of my life as I grew increasingly visibly "with child"?

Even without knowledge of my pregnancy, SWR students seemed particularly concerned with my marital status. They would often ask me questions about my life outside of the middle school. Was I married? Did I have a boyfriend? Did I have or want children? How old was I? And so on. Kids who already knew the answers to these questions, who had asked me earlier, would ask me again in other contexts. It seemed that they needed to place me in relation to local categories of adulthood and childhood. When they found out I was in my thirties, they couldn't or wouldn't believe I was as "old" as some of their parents. How could I be? I wasn't married, didn't have children, didn't own a house or a car, didn't have a job, and I didn't have a familiar role in the world of their suburban community and school. Their discomfort with my anomalous status began to demark the limits and homogeneity of this suburban community: one was either a parent or a child, or an adult teacher or a young student. I was none of these things.

When a group of boys found out how old I was and that I had gone to high school with parents of some of their classmates, they parodically started calling me "mom." Actually, they alternated between calling me mom and "Lorena Bobbitt," the woman who for most of the year preceding my field research had occupied headlines for cutting off her abusive husband's penis with a kitchen knife in the middle of the night. I assumed I earned the latter moniker simply because of the phonetic similarity between Lorena (pronounced lo-rain-a) and Lorraine; nevertheless, I found the semantic weight of the mom/Lorena dichotomy hard to pass off as just part of the vagaries of thirteen-year-old boy humor. In setting up a virgin/whore figuration, the boys consciously teased me and struggled to position me within their social (psychosexual) order, while they seemed to be unconsciously naming their anxieties about their relationship to older, socially undefinable women at a time when their own sexualities hung in the balance. One of these boys had a steady SWR eighth-grade girlfriend; one said he had a girlfriend in another town and held many of the SWR girls at bay sexually while engaging them quite intimately and affectionately as friends; another had an SWR eighth-grade girlfriend for less than a week; and two others were best of friends to each other, spending very little time with girls during or outside of school. The girls also struggled with issues of heterosexual dating. Here I served more as a confidant than a source of sexual tension (some boys openly flirted with me; girls did not), though my nebulous status seemed to make them anxious over issues of disclosure. Was I like them, and hence privy to the details of their sexual desires, fantasies, and experiences? Or was I more like their mom or a teacher, and hence potentially disapproving of this aspect of their lives? No doubt, being a pregnant ethnographer would factor into my interactions with

SWR boys and girls, though in gender-specific ways. Would the girls find my predicament threatening or would it actually help them open up to me about their sexualities? Would my pregnancy allow the boys to fix me in their mom/Lorena dichotomy or would it make me more of an anomaly in their eyes? Whatever the effect, I was quite certain that my pregnancy would not go unnoticed by SWR students or adults. What kind of a mom/Lorena Bobbitt was I?

On an ethnographic and emotional level, I began to wonder how much of my anxiety, ambivalence, self-doubt, and despair over my unplanned pregnancy had to do with my Self and how much with the collective subject I was studying—suburban, white, adolescent girls—and the epistemological process I was engaging as the prodigal-daughter ethnographer. How much of the powerlessness I felt had to do with my decision to reconstitute myself as a white middle-class teenage girl living with her parents, unsure of what the future would bring and unable to assert her own desires and values with self-confidence and without fear of recrimination or abandonment? These were not questions I could explore openly at SWR, but they were concerns that were as much about the culture I had come to study as they were about my personal psyche.

My unwed pregnancy was surely not going to simplify my homecoming or research into teen girlhood, but it would make visible and visceral the moral order of this community and position me squarely within the culture of silence and avoidance that characterized its public and private lives. There were many things in this suburbia that were not discussed or challenged openly. Most conflicts were avoided through a practice that M. P. Baumgartner, in her study of another affluent New York suburb, termed "moral minimalism": tolerating or doing nothing at all about disturbing behavior, abandoning contentious matters, avoiding annoying individuals, approaching offenders in a conciliatory fashion, or complaining secretly to officials (1988, 10–11). In other words, doing everything in one's power to ward off face-to-face confrontations, while working the system, when necessary, to one's advantage. The place unwed pregnancy held in SWR's moral minimalism became more explicitly clear when two eighth-grade girls "confessed" to me that they had figured out that their mothers were pregnant before they married their fathers. In one case, the girl herself was the product of an unplanned pregnancy, in the other, the girl's older brother was. They told me these family secrets in hushed yet thrilled voices: they knew something "bad" about their parents that they weren't supposed to know and that they certainly weren't supposed to be telling me. Their sotto-voce-told stories let me know that single pregnancy and motherhood were not uncomplicated things in this town. In fact, the only single mothers (i.e., women raising children without a father, divorced or otherwise, in sight) among the eighth-grade parents were women who were clearly not insiders in this community. They lived in the small pocket of lower-income homes on the outer edge of Wading

River, just barely within the confines of the SWR school district, or in the army houses turned public-assistance housing across from the local high school, tucked back on a short dead-end street off the main, local, east-west intertown artery, 25A, in Shoreham. Most of these families were far from permanent or visible members of the SWR community, and their children, girls like Amber and Penny whose stories will appear in later chapters, did not easily fit into the school's peer culture.

Because I was an educated, middle-class, white woman raised as an insider in this culture of silence and avoidance, I could not see single motherhood as a clearly viable choice for me or my impending offspring. I had very clear expectations for myself and my future family; in fact, my social position as an SWR daughter had led me to believe that becoming pregnant would be a choice and not an accident. The world was not working the way it was supposed to. My choice was not whether or not to become pregnant but whether or not to carry this pregnancy to term and become a single mother. The biological reality, the emotional rush, and the moral implications of being "with child"—the father's preferences notwithstanding—did not allow me to dismiss the possibility out of hand, while the social pressures of reentering the world of middle-class teen girlhood in my hometown did not make the option immediately preferable.

While the public culture at SWR did not actively accommodate or recognize teen pregnancy or single motherhood as a local issue—for example, there were no programs in the high school to assist girls who might find themselves "in a family way"—I knew that this probably didn't mean that the situation did not exist among SWR daughters. Current rumors and past memories told me so. I knew for a fact that one of my own classmates had gotten pregnant our senior year of high school. She mysteriously disappeared from school. Subsequently, she married the father of her child, had other children by him, and moved into her own home in the SWR school district. These developments reconstituted her as a legitimate and visible member of the community; without them she might have remained a banished insider. Moreover, my ongoing research on teenage girls had told me that at the time I was in the field at SWR white teenagers accounted for over two thirds, or 68 percent, of all adolescent births in the United States and over half of the births to unmarried mothers. About one million teenagers, or 40 percent of all female adolescents, became pregnant at least once before they were twenty. Half of these pregnancies ended in abortions. In terms of Long Island, Suffolk County—where SWR is located—had the second highest rate of teen pregnancies in the state of New York, second only to New York City. And 80 percent of the pregnant white teenagers in Suffolk opted to have abortions (Lawson and Rhode 1993; Henry 1994, sec. 14, 1,10). Such figures suggest that single pregnancy and abortion were common and presumably acceptable white middle-class behaviors on Long Island; my experiences growing up there and later as an ethnographer indicated otherwise. Teen pregnancy and abortion were not regular or comfortable topics of public conversations; the SWR girls' hushed-voiced revelations to me about their own families and my former classmate's "disappearance" clearly demonstrate the scandalous nature of this phenomenon and the degree to which this community believed that some things were better left invisible and unsaid.

In an effort to break the silence and find out more directly what the SWR girls thought about teen pregnancy and abortion, I staged a semipublic discussion on the topic in an English elective on girls' diaries that I offered as part of my "payback" to the school. Upon the recommendation of one of the eighth-grade English teachers, I assigned excerpts from *The Diary of Latoya Hunter: My First Year in Junior High*. Latoya, the book tells us, is a "real" teenage girl, a Jamaican immigrant growing up in the Bronx. Despite my misgivings about the racialization and urbanization of teen pregnancy that such a book reinforces, I welcomed the opportunity to broach the subject with the girls. Likewise, given its insider status as a book an SWR teacher might assign, it seemed very much a part of the local discourse on teen pregnancy—such as it was—and hence an ethnographically useful and appropriate text. I included the following entries among the readings:

> February 1, 1991
>
> Dear Janice,
> It's the first day of February. I hate this month. It just seems so long. I think it'll be really boring. It's getting closer to the wedding though. I'm really happy about that. There's a girl in my school who actually had a baby already. She's in the ninth grade, she's probably around 15. My friends were talking about her today. I feel really sorry for her, it's too early! She is only in Junior High! I wonder how it happened. I mean, I know how it happened, but how could she let it? Her mom must have been so upset. I would never do that to my mother. This really makes me thing [*sic*] about this whole sex business. I wonder if that girl was ready. I know I talked about a person feeling that they're ready and doing it. Maybe she thought she was and still knows she is but just isn't ready for a child. I think being ready for sex and ready for a child are two different things. To be ready for sex, you must have the ability to fall in love and feel close to the maximum to the person you are with. To be ready for a baby, you should be able to take care of yourself and the child and know what's right and what's wrong. You should be able to devote yourself to the child in every way possible. The thing I would say should have been taken care of by that girl is protection. Ready or not ready, she should have thought about that.

March 6, 1991

Dear Janice,
The world is so sin-corrupted. I guess this is coming from my new religious awareness but it's really true. These days no one thinks about God or following his rule. People kill, back and forth, even those who think they have a right. Like mothers who kill their unborn child. They give it a fancy name—abortion, but I think murder is a much better word for it. The child may be unborn but it is still a person who has the right to a life. If the mother doesn't want to be a part of it why doesn't she give it up for adoption or give it to a home that will care for it? I think it's a very sinful act and it sickens me to hear about it. The number one argument these people keep saying is it's their body. Well, to me, the baby inside them is the one who should say that. Who gives the mother the right to terminate its life? (Hunter 1992, 69–70, 80–81)

The girls' responses to these excerpts ran the ideological spectrum. In the course of a single small-group discussion, one girl, Christine, initially declared that "abortion is murder." She then decided that "it should be up to the mother," and, still later, she dismissed my attempts to get her to clarify her position with "I'm just glad I don't have to think about it now." Unbeknownst to Christine, her shifting convictions and lack of a resolution on the topic echoed my own emotional and moral state. Though unlike Christine, I did have to think about it now. Other girls offered gruesome stories ("totally true suburban legends") about botched abortions, deformed babies, coat-hanger abortions in Connecticut, and welfare mothers who have babies so they never have to work. "It's true, my mom's a social worker. She sees it every day. And their [her mom's clients'] kids are mostly retarded. It's sad," Kathy insisted, while arguing that she agreed with Latoya's anti-abortion position for herself, but that she didn't have the right to make that decision for someone else. While Christine personalized her response, putting herself into the picture, Kathy, in keeping with a culture of avoidance, deflected the issue away from SWR, making teen pregnancy somebody else's problem, namely that of the lower class.

One of the most articulate girls among the diary's readers was also notably the only phenotypically nonwhite girl in the group. Amy was born in Korea and was adopted when she was six months old by a Jewish couple who also happened to teach in the SWR school district. "It would depend on where I was," interjected Amy. "If I was in a place like Shoreham, I would have the kid because I could give it up for adoption and know that the kid would have a good life. But if I was in a place like India, or someplace like that, I would have an abortion." This precipitated a discussion among the girls about Amy's Korean name. "It's pretty," said Megan, "not that Amy Goldberg isn't, but it's sooo

American." Here the girls deftly avoided the abortion debate, practicing a teen-girl version of the town's moral minimalism. This particular group of girls did not like to disagree with one another. On numerous occasions, I had witnessed them prefacing anything that could be construed as a challenge to one of their friends with profuse apologies: "I'm really sorry I have to say this . . . but I don't agree with you. . . . " Not everyone in the room agreed with Amy, so conversation veered away from the abortion question, only to de-ethnicize, or whiten (Sacks 1994), Amy's Jewishness and exoticize her Koreanness. In one fell swoop, the girls' conversation deftly abandoned and literally whitewashed two contentious matters: abortion and their racial and ethnic differences.

I came away from these abortion conversations with my suspicions confirmed: the moral minimalism of SWR left its daughters floundering and especially vulnerable precisely to questions of morality. By avoiding difficult topics and potential sources of conflict, SWR didn't provide its daughters with a clear social framework, one they could adopt or contest. Instead these girls (and this ethnographer) were left with a nebulous sense of what was considered right and wrong and what behaviors would indeed be tolerated and in the end acceptable. But perhaps more disturbing, the moral minimalism of the community also did not delineate the consequences that would befall a girl who did not always live up to the local culture's understood standards of virtue and decorum, leaving girls little room for cultural negotiation and this ethnographer trapped between a rock and a hard place.

Hometown Predicaments

Most ethnographies begin with an arrival story whereby the anthropologist offers a first impression of the physical and cultural landscape she went to study, or she narrates her first notable encounter with her subjects. I begin this autoethnography with what to some may seem an all-too-personal story that would be more comfortably left out of an ethnographic account. Ethnographies are more typically about an outsider gaining access to an insider's view of a distant and often exotic Other culture; ethnographic authority rests on the success or failure of this epistemological journey between Self and Other (Clifford 1988). But autoethnographers do not travel the same distance and direction. The insider-Other autoethnographer already instantiates the very culture in question, yet because she attempts to achieve a critical and analytical perspective on it, she can never exist seamlessly as an insider. She is always on some level both an insider and an outsider, practicing a kind of double consciousness. The autoethnographer constantly moves away from as much as toward her subjects. She attempts to recognize what she has already learned to take for granted. I begin this account with a tale of personal and cultural dissonance in order to locate the reader within the realm of the insider-Other. It is an uncomfortable place. As an autoethnographer of SWR teen girls, I can neither feign distance nor assume belonging; instead I function within an interstitial zone, working from a perspective that is, epistemologically, both a blessing and a curse.

The autoethnographer of the white middle class, however, takes this ethnographic predicament one step further, in that she labors under a double double bind: she takes for granted a culture that takes itself for granted. Recent theorists of race (notably, Dyer 1988; Morrison 1992; Frankenberg 1993) have argued that whiteness in the United States—especially in its middle-class, heterosexual configuration—occupies a position of social privilege precisely because it cannot and will not speak its own name. It is racially unmarked—in most contexts we do not need to say "white" American; the whiteness is assumed, though we are compelled to say Korean (or Asian) American, or African (or black) American, and so on. As a result, whiteness seems to come upon its social standing as the neutral and universal category naturally. From the perspective of those born into privilege, middle-class whiteness is invisible, and its access to power unremarkable. In functioning as a privileged norm, white middle-classness does not appear to be raced or classed in the way that other races and classes are. By this social logic, everyone else has a race except whites and class is reserved for those with and without money, either the very rich or the very poor. In striving to name the unnamable and see the invisible, the autoethnographer of middle-class whiteness works against the very foundations of the culture she both embodies and has come to study. If whiteness is, as Toni Morrison suggests, "mute, meaningless, unfathomable, pointless, frozen, veiled, curtained, dreaded, senseless, implacable" (1992, 59), then the autoethnographer must learn to recognize the social processes that bring about this meaninglessness and unfathomability. The substance of whiteness is the very behaviors and beliefs that make it appear immaterial. It is the silences, the culture of avoidance, and the moral minimalisms, among other things.

When the girls avoided the abortion question only to segue into comparing Amy's "pretty Korean" name to her "sooo American" (read race-neutral) adopted name, they were "acting white" in that they effortlessly and unselfconsciously deracialized the norm. But they also, inadvertently, pointed to the ways in which race is not just a matter of biology. Throughout this study I approach race and class (as well as gender) as cultural practices rather than purely biological or economic designations. I am interested in the cultural capital (Bourdieu 1984) of whiteness and middle-classness, especially as they function in tandem with each other. The biology and economics of race and class are only part of what it means to be white and middle class. What one values or expects from the world, how one communicates, dresses, and is educated, for example, say more about what being white and middle class is all about, than does one's skin color or bank account.

The degree to which Korean-Jewish-American Amy participated in the moral minimalism and the normalizing of race and class at SWR raises the question of just how "white" or "nonwhite" a girl like Amy is in a town like Shoreham. In "Brown-Skinned White Girls," France Winddance Twine (1997) offers a compelling ethnographic account of how racial categories are markers of upbringing and context. Her subjects, biracial women of African descent, identified as white while they were growing up in their middle- and upper-middle-class, predominantly white, suburban communities. It was not until later in their lives—in the wake of puberty with its turn toward heterosexual dating or as students in a multiracial university setting—that they came to see themselves or were socially positioned by their peers and other institutional forces as nonwhites. In the process of analyzing their stories, Twine begins to fill in the blanks of normative whiteness, giving content to this otherwise abstract and formatively elusive concept. To be white in her study is to be color blind, race neutral, and/or to conceive of oneself as racially invisible; it is to possess a certain "purchasing power" or access to the material privileges commensurate with a white middle-class lifestyle; it is to see oneself as an individual rather than as a member of a racial or ethnic community; it is to feel comfortable around white-skinned, middle-class people, to not feel (racially) self-conscious or to engage in self-censorship. The whiteness Twine delineates in her study is clearly class-based and located within a specific social milieu, underscoring the degree to which whiteness is dependent on and intertwined with other social conditions and identity categories, including gender, region, age, generation, class, and upbringing. Whiteness here is only minimally biological; ultimately it is rooted emphatically within cultural practices.

Unlike Twine, I did not systematically study the racialization of the identifiably nonwhite girls in the eighth grade at SWR. Among the core group of students I studied (roughly two thirds of the 1994 eighth-grade class) only two girls would fit into this category. In the entire eighth grade that year, there were only one African American girl and four Asian students, at least two of whom had been adopted by white families. In part I did not single out the nonwhite girls because I was interested in watching white middle-class femininity unfold in everyday exchanges among the eighth graders more generally; the girls of color I observed did not actively deviate from the SWR norm. Amy, in fact, seemed every bit as caught up in the culture of middle-class whiteness as her white girlfriends: she was academically competitive with her peers and socially active; her diary was filled with stories about her weekends spent horseback riding and clothes shopping. One memorable entry included an inventory of all the hair and skin products she had amassed. The list of brand names and her accumulated activities and tastes demonstrated that she lived a life in accord with white middle-class privilege. Though I never asked Amy directly what she thought about this privilege and her place within it, I never asked her (white) peers such questions either. I was there to see privilege in action. The locals practiced a don't ask, don't tell policy. I wanted to identify how this policy functioned not to rewrite its mandates and bylaws, or disrupt its performances in any immediate sense or at the level of my ethnographic encounters. I leave such disruptions to the success of this account and its ability to help its readers scrutinize an otherwise inscrutable culture.

As an autoethnographer of middle-class whiteness I already practiced, to one degree or another, these same policies, and sometimes to the extent that I couldn't recognize them for what they were: cultural rather than natural practices. I had to struggle to identify my own blind spots and self-imposed silences. I needed to see myself as part of a social group with a racialized, gendered, and classed history and culture. I implicate myself in this autoethnography as a necessary critical strategy. Where will my own insider perspective take my subjects' worldviews for granted? And how can I use these moments, when I perceive them, to speak through the unspeakable?

While occupying both a privileged (insider) and disadvantaged (can't-see-the-forest-for-the-trees) position vis-à-vis her subject, the autoethnographer also shoulders added degrees of accountability and vulnerability to her community of study. My unplanned and unwed pregnancy illustrates how a hometown ethnographer cannot claim a comfortable cultural or moral distance from her subjects. Throughout this account of white teen girlhood, I am both subject and object of my inquiry, but only insofar as my Self can refract my community. "The autobiographical," Kamala Visweswaran argues, "is not a mere reflection of self, but another entry point into history, of community refracted through self" (1994, 137). Though I literally returned to my growing-up place to do fieldwork, and I deliberately write myself into this account, at times situating myself in the history of this community and at other times foregrounding the way my own ethnographic knowledge unfolds, my ethnography is not simply autobiographical. Instead, it uses autobiography as an ethnographic tool, a way to articulate contexts, histories, moral and cultural orders, relationships, and situated knowledges (Haraway 1991). I am one of the grounds upon which white middle-classness operates, and my story is just one of the many daughters' stories that get told throughout this book.

But theories of autoethnography only tell half of why I begin this account of my white middle-class suburbia with such a profoundly personal revelation. The confusion, shame, and resounding silence that engulfed me upon my ethnographic homecoming brings forward the culture of silence and avoidance that drives this community and, moreover, demonstrate the consequences this silence has on its daughters, past and present. Significantly, unwed pregnancy and motherhood would not constitute the only walls of silence and avoidance of conflict I would encounter throughout my fieldwork. But they were the things that began to make tangible the ways that silence and avoidance operate to secure a life of privilege. With regard to my unplanned and inauspiciously timed pregnancy, I decided to practice my own version of avoidance. I ambivalently chose to have an abortion, and I guarded that decision at all costs during my tenure in the field. I no more wanted the SWR community to know that I had consciously terminated a pregnancy than I wanted them to know me as a single mother. My silence and isolation in this matter enabled my homecoming, helping to usher me back into an advantaged life, however dubious those advantages may sometimes feel.

The rest of this chapter offers a brief history and cultural analysis of SWR as they pertain to the making and unmaking of white, middle-class, suburban privilege. Here I begin to calculate the economies of community that founded and maintain the suburban life of my subjects and that make the avoidance of teen pregnancy and single motherhood a possible collective response. It is a tale that reveals the machinations as well as the vulnerabilities of social privilege, while it describes the range of cultural practices that foster this social position, namely: misrecognition, silence, deflection, deferment, rationalization, and avoidance. In narrating this history and analyzing these practices, I am attempting to give myself and my subjects a racialized and class-conscious story we can no longer take for granted as daughters of privilege.

A Community without Race

Silences about race and especially whiteness were among the most resounding and salient I encountered at SWR. As I readied myself to leave for the field in August of 1993, a couple of weeks before the school year was to begin, I encountered what turned out to be an enduring and pervasive public fantasy: SWR was a community without race. In arranging this project, I had met with the principal of the middle school, Dr. Williams, and the superintendent of SWR schools, Dr. Clark, earlier that summer. Both took an interest in my study, especially as it pertained to gender—at the time, both were fathers of girls in their teens or young adulthoods. In addition, Dr. Williams was the only African American administrator in the district and one of the few nonwhite teaching or nonteaching staff members in the middle school: of the forty-eight teachers in the sixth through eighth grades that year, three were African American women; the rest were understood to be white, as were the school secretaries, maintenance workers, paraprofessionals, and teachers' aides. After our individual meetings, Drs. Clark and Williams agreed to let me come into the schools in September and to make the necessary public announcements to the community and their teaching staffs about my plans. Dr. Clark asked me to write a brief description of my project that he and Dr. Williams could use to facilitate this process. In my initial discussions and correspondences with both administrators, I had explained that my research focused on how girls grow up white, middle class, and female in suburbia. However, I later realized that Dr. Williams had not fully understood my interest in issues of white racial identity formation until he had read my formal written proposal. He responded to this document by sending me a letter that expressed grave reservations about my study. He wrote:

> I am bothered by several statements that you make in your written proposal. For example, on Page 2, you write: "I have consciously located my study in a white, middle class, suburban community." By describing Shoreham-Wading River as a "white . . . community", what message are you giving to students and staff of color who live and work here? With a stroke of your pen, you have, it seems, eliminated the non-white segments of our community.
>
> You further state that "Most research (on adolescents) focuses on troubled and/or trouble-making kids: on poor kids, urban kids, African-American or Latino kids . . . " At the risk of being oversensitive, here I see you designating "poor, urban, African-American or Latino kids" as those adolescents who are troubled or trouble-makers. Later in the same paragraph you ask a question: "How do girls learn to be white . . . ?" I don't understand what this means! Aren't girls born white? What kind of questions would you be asking to determine how kids "learn to be white" and might not these questions be offensive to girls of color? Later in your proposal, you refer to the white middle class as the "cultural norm" in America. The "norm?" From whose perspective? Certainly not mine and other African-Americans!
>
> Given the focus of your research on white girls, how would you plan to interact with girls of color whom you would encounter in our 8th grade? These students already too often feel left out of many school and community social activities and your presence in the building might only further increase their feelings of alienation. Here in the Middle School, over the last 14 years, we have made a concerted effort to bring students of different backgrounds together. Why would we now want to pull them apart?
>
> In summary, the more I think about it, the more inappropriate it seems to conduct racially-based research on students in a public school setting. (Personal correspondence, 20 August 1993)

Once I got past the initial shock of receiving his letter, I replied:

> Dear Dr. Williams:
> Thank you for your detailed response to my research proposal. From the concerns that you have raised, it has become clear to me that I did not adequately describe my research plans and I fear, as a result, you have misunderstood the intent of my project. I apologize for my lack of

clarity and would very much like the opportunity to address your concerns.

I have absolutely no intention of creating any racial divisions in the school or community. I understand that Shoreham is not a homogeneous white community. While it is clearly true that people are born into a race, we learn to attribute specific meanings to racial categories. I am particularly concerned with how white girls in overwhelmingly white suburbs have a hard time noticing that not everyone in the world enjoys the same privileges they do. This point was brought home to me this past December when my niece, [Jennifer], who was born and raised in Shoreham came out to California to visit me. While she was here we spent time with one of her friends whose family had recently moved to the Bay Area from Shoreham and was now attending a racially diverse high school. [Jennifer's] friend started talking about racism in Shoreham and about how kids in Shoreham don't see how their ideas about the world are very much influenced and limited by the relative homogeneity of the community. [Jennifer], who is a fairly astute observer of the world, did not quite get what her friend was talking about. It occurred to me that the difference between [Jennifer] and her friend was that her friend had moved to a community where she could no longer take her race privilege for granted, and consequently she had begun to understand something about how race works in America.

I do not believe that white, middle-class people should be considered the "cultural norm." But I do see many powerful political and social institutions operating on this assumption. When I wrote that "most research focuses on troubled and/or troublemaking kids: on poor kids, African-American, and Latino kids . . . ," I did not mean that these kids are troubled/troublemakers, but that the dominant culture often treats and represents them as if they are bad kids. I think it is telling, for example, that pregnant teenagers are more often than not portrayed as girls of color in newspaper articles and on television programs (Bill Moyers's "The Vanishing Family" is a notorious instance of this), when more white girls become pregnant than girls of color.

It is popular understandings of race, class, and gender that I want to study. The fieldwork side of my project focuses on the day-to-day way in which girls who are born into the dominant position often learn to assume they are the cultural norm. I do not think it is possible to come right out and ask girls questions around these issues. They don't think about their lives in this way. But somehow they learn to value certain ways of being in the world over others. I do not think that a place like the middle school or a community like Shoreham sets out to teach girls to be racists or to think that being white means that they occupy some kind of naturally privileged position in the world, instead I think numerous cultural and social phenomena influence girls and teach them things about themselves and about the world at large.

> I do not plan to leave anyone out of my study. I would imagine that the girls of color in the eighth grade probably have a more articulated understanding of the racial structure of the community if only because they are, as you point out, "often left out of many school and community social activities." Similarly, I am sure that the less affluent girls are also more aware of how class operates in a community like Shoreham than do girls who do not have to think about money. Again, I do not plan on asking students these kinds of questions directly, rather I plan on observing how they work out these differences on their own.
>
> The intent of this project is to contribute to an understanding of how race, class, and gender work in America. . . . Though in this letter I have focused on the racial questions embedded in my research interests, I do not intend to single out racial issues in my fieldwork or [ethnography]. In general, I am interested in the overall process by which girls form their identities and understandings of the world. Race, class, gender, geographic location, and religious affiliations, among numerous other social and cultural factors play a significant role in this process. I think it is important to study these concerns as interrelated. . . . (Personal correspondence, 24 August 1993)

My explanation satisfied both administrators. Dr. Williams wrote back stressing that his "concern was not with my research in general, but rather with how it could be carried out in a public school setting if [I] were only planning to be involved with white students" (Personal correspondence, 14 September 1993). Given the racial makeup of the school, I still wondered how I could do otherwise. Between 1982 and 1993, the SWR school population went from being 98 percent to 95.9 percent white (Brown 1994, A35). These numbers do not bode well for interracial research. Regardless, neither of us mentioned the "misunderstanding" again.

Unwed pregnancy aside, the above exchange left me wary of the kind of welcome I would receive in the school and the community, and it taught me to keep my interests in white racial identity formation to myself. It was my first ethnographic lesson in managing conflict and difference in a culture of silences and sameness. And it was a lesson I expanded upon when I finally did return, three months later, as the secretly pregnant, unwed, prodigal-daughter ethnographer. To my surprise, upon entering the middle school on my first day of fieldwork, Dr. Williams greeted me by asking if I wanted to take over the vice principal's advisory, SWR's version of homeroom. He explained that the vice principal had become seriously ill a few months earlier and the school did not know when or if she would be able to return to work. The school had reassigned her five students to other eighth-grade advisories, but given the intimacy of the advisory program, Dr. Williams wanted to reconstitute the original group. Advisory consists of about five to ten students paired with a teacher or administrator.

They meet every morning for fifteen minutes at the beginning of school; they eat lunch together for fifteen minutes at noon in their respective classrooms; and advisors meet with students individually throughout the year and with the students' parents on parent-teacher conference days. The advisory system makes each student someone's priority, so the school can keep track of the kids academically and socially, intervening when appropriate. Despite being hesitant about having an official role in the school, I knew that being an advisor would help me get to know girls quickly, so I agreed.

Though Dr. Williams's initial letter directly challenged my position and hence went against any notion of moral minimalism this community might uphold, his subsequent use of me as an acting advisor, placing me in a socially sensitive and visible role with students and their parents, one in which I represented the school in a professional capacity (albeit without the remuneration), seemed to overcompensate for his earlier lapse of local decorum. The fact that we never mentioned our differences again fits well within the boundaries of a culture of avoidance. However, I would not soon forget the underlying tenor of Dr. Williams's letter: race, especially whiteness, is not an "appropriate" topic of discussion at SWR, and white girls naturally come upon their social standing as members of privilege, and hence do not need to be studied by some ethnographer, even if she is a prodigal daughter. In this sense, Dr. Williams's letter worked for, not against SWR's moral minimalism, reinserting me into its economies of silence and avoidance, teaching me to manage my relationships with girls, their parents, and the middle school staff with care and obliqueness.

While I learned the hard way not to talk too directly about issues of race, I also came to realize that the kids would rather not know I was studying *girls*, and their parents and most teachers only wanted to know I was observing gender differences with a focus on girls. When Dr. Williams had me introduce myself to a parent liaison group, mainly made up of mothers, they responded enthusiastically to my presentation and wanted to talk about girls and self-esteem, girls and math and science, and girls and the messages they get from the media: all prominent topics in popular magazines and television talk shows in the late eighties and early nineties. On the other hand, when I introduced myself to a class of students for the first time, they became visibly and audibly uncomfortable when I explained I was studying how girls grow up in a white middle-class community like SWR. The boys giggled and the girls looked a bit horrified. The teacher advised me to tell future groups I was studying how kids grow up in SWR in general. This was the approach I adopted henceforth.[1]

The community's various reactions to my way of naming who they were, or naming which parts of who they were mattered, underscored the degree to which white middle-class femininity did not want its name spoken here. Consequently, I needed to note the degree to which the girls and the adults in their lives deflected this identity, manifesting and expressing its properties indirectly and euphemistically (see especially chapter 6). I also began to listen for their enforced silences, track the ways in which they struggled over community problems, and analyze the social history of the town itself in order to identify larger cultural patterns. I pieced together SWR's past from recent newspaper accounts, documents haphazardly saved in the local public library, materials in my father's personal archive of news clippings collected over his more than thirty years of residency in Shoreham, and my own memories of what this community was and impressions of what it had become. The portrait of the town that unfolds from my readings of these community situations and artifacts sets the stage for the SWR girls' everyday exchanges that I explore at greater length later in the book. Girls didn't construct elaborate scenarios about women on welfare having more and more "retarded" babies nor turn questions of race and ethnicity into matters of aesthetics and fashion just because it was more fun than grappling with their own moral ambivalences and social differences (such that they were). They did these and other similar things as fledgling members of the white middle class. The town's story that I render below is as much a part of who they are as is their parents' civic (mis)behavior or the school district's struggle to survive a precipitous loss of tax revenue. Such stories give an otherwise elusive and ineffable identity—white middle-classness—tangibility and materiality. They are among the local stories that school SWR girls into their lives of privilege.

The Good Life: Manicured, Precise, Almost Too Pretty

The early stages of my work at SWR taught me that my terms of analysis (whiteness, middle-classness, and femininity) mattered so much in this community that they were not open for discussion, let alone interpretation. Interpreting the norm denaturalizes it and undercuts the seamlessness of privilege. Privilege built on a foundation of silence and avoidance. The moment one calls attention to privilege it begins to unravel. No, girls are not just born white. Whiteness, middle-classness, and femininity are cultural processes that are made and remade over time and across social conflicts or the avoidance thereof. The social history of SWR rests on acts of avoidance, be it of outsiders or of difficult social and moral questions and choices.

For the most part, this practice of avoidance has served the community well. Shoreham and Wading River are still places where white middle-class families can set up house, relatively secure in the knowledge that their children can safely play in a neighbor's backyard or find "like-minded" friends with whom to hang out. And up until recently, they could also send their children to well-regarded public schools that offered a range of extracurricular activities and educational opportunities that surpassed those of most schools on Long Island, if not in the country. Regardless of appearance, this life of middle-class privilege did not come naturally. Home-owning residents of Shoreham and Wading River had to draw purposeful lines around themselves and their property, choosing their words carefully as they fought to keep some outsiders at bay and bending the rules to let other, more desirable, insider-Others in. But perhaps most significantly, they had to be willing to live with a nuclear power plant in their backyards, a choice that eventually came back to haunt them. How they went about fighting for some projects and against others demonstrates not only the way that social privilege operates through a series of exclusions, denials, silences, and avoidances, but also the toll it takes on a community and the limited capacity of privilege to sustain and reproduce itself within the middle class (see also Ehrenreich 1989). Below, I mine the town's public life for signs of the precariousness and at times hypocrisies of this privilege.

In the summer of 1994, soon after I finished my fieldwork, the *New York Times*'s Sunday real estate section featured Shoreham in its weekly "If You're Thinking of Living In" column; it limned an image of an idyllic suburban enclave on the wooded hills of the Long Island Sound—idyllic, that is, if you can afford a home costing between $120,000 and $500,000. The article reported that Shoreham residents enjoyed a median household income of over $70,000 and a tax rate of $2,838 on a median-priced, one-family home.[2] "For the last 75 years," it asserted, "the biggest [Shoreham] village event has been an annual Fourth of July parade. Paraders assemble at the community center where a band entertains and refreshments are served" (Kellerman 1994, R5). This is the kind of place, the *Times* led its readers to believe, where the biggest civic problem revolved around how many hot dogs to throw on the barbecue at the Fourth of July festivities. This image, it turns out, was not in keeping with the everyday reality of the local taxpayers and school board members; practicing its own moral minimalism, the *Times* only alluded to these more consequential troubles.

Instead of exploring the more dicey subject of local politics, the article touted the wonders of the school district, which at the time educated about two thousand students systemwide, noting that 90 percent of the graduating seniors in 1993 went on to higher education;[3] 50 to 75 percent of the district's students participated in the extracurricular music program; 75 percent of SWR's middle- and high-school students played interscholastic sports; the high-school newspaper had won the Columbia Journalism Award; and the annual literary magazine had received national recognition. The most negative comment in the article came from one resident who observed: "From late spring to late fall, the walnut and pine trees are so full, you can't even tell there are people next door. . . . [But Shoreham] does suffer from not much to do without a car." This from a research associate in biology at the nearby Brookhaven National Laboratory, whose wife is an assistant professor at Suffolk County Cornell Cooperative; together they undoubtedly own at least two cars. Imagine if you're a teenager too young even to have your learner's permit: with hardly any public transportation and with very little commerce to speak of, Shoreham doesn't offer many options for its daughters outside of school-, neighborhood-, and family-related activities, and even then, most of the time parents have to be willing to transport them to and from places.

The *Times*'s feature was full of statistics and tidbits of information about the town and its history, which it dated back to 1671 when several farming families bought land from the Montauk Indians and settled what they called Long Chestnuts. In 1906, the town was renamed Shoreham when the Long Island Railroad extended its service, connecting Shoreham to New York City via roughly two hours of rail travel. The railroad discontinued this route in 1939, deadending its North Shore line in Port Jefferson, which is a twenty- to thirty-minute drive west of Shoreham depending on traffic on the strip-mall-lined Route 25A. A stone-and-mortar trestle stands over a Shoreham village street as the only vestige of the railroad left.

In addition to this physical isolation, the *Times* narrated a history of social exclusion: in 1913 the village of Shoreham incorporated itself, establishing a parochial form of governance that assured homeowners against excessive or unwanted growth; and in 1920, fearing that others would want to move to the area, residents protested when an oil company put the town on its service stations road maps. My own perusal of clippings in the SWR public library turned up similar incidents dating from a more recent era: in 1971, residents and county executives opposed a proposed 805–garden-apartment complex, stating "apartments would disfigure the rustic environment of the community [though apparently a nuclear power plant wouldn't], . . . an influx of children from apartments would place a burden on the school system, . . . and [the complex] would not be in the best interest of the town or the community of Shoreham."[4] In 1977, a similar neighborhood debate ensued after the Suffolk Association for the Help of Retarded Children proposed an intermediate-care facility for "multiply handicapped retarded" persons in Wading River, the first such facility on Long Island and one of the first in the state.[5] Local opposition to both these projects prevailed. As a result, SWR remained ostensibly middle to upper-middle class and able bodied.

While the above examples could suggest that SWR was simply against any kind of growth, the power plant notwithstanding, the local records show otherwise and hence demonstrate just what was at stake in the battle over the housing complex or the home for the mentally or physically challenged. The community was not categorically against the idea of special or restricted housing, as long as what counted as special remained within the bounds of or in some way benefited the white middle class. In 1971, Shoreham and its contiguous neighbor Ridge became the site of the first retirement community on Long Island, Leisure Village. An article in the local newspaper introducing the new development, "Village Designed to Exclude Worry," deemed Leisure Village a "new life-style for the elderly—an instant life-style . . . [Leisure Village] is low and flat, like its North Shore landscape. It is manicured, precise and almost too pretty. It looks exactly like a brochure."[6] What the article failed to note, however, was that Leisure Village is also overwhelmingly white and middle class. While the people who live there may not be SWR's literal grandparents, they certainly could be, making Leisure Village a welcome or at least tolerable anomaly among the two-story, one-family colonials that make up most of SWR's neighborhoods. The Leisure Village set constitutes a group of insider-Others and as such, appears mostly innocuous when it comes to the local suburban culture.

An estimated two thousand residents live in the 1,500 units—one-to three-bedroom, single-floor condominiums—that make up Leisure Village. By 1995, other "leisure housing complexes" had sprung up in the immediate vicinity, including Leisure Glenn with 392 two-bedroom, two-bath condos and Leisure Knoll with nearly 800 individual single-family homes. Located on the southern perimeter of Shoreham, wooded areas, the Catholic church, the middle school, a sod farm, and 25A physically separate this senior-citizen village from most of the town's other residents. This is a gated and planned community in the most literal sense. People under fifty-five cannot legally live there, and there appears to be very little interaction between Leisure Village denizens and members of the surrounding neighborhoods. Leisure Village didn't often come up in conversations among the eighth graders, though once a year a group of Leisure Village residents, members of the Ladies Auxiliary of the American Legion, sponsor an essay contest for SWR eighth graders. The year I was there, Teresa, one of the most academically inclined girls in the class, won first prize, a check for $150, for her essay on the Bill of Rights. On the evening Teresa and the second-, third-, and fourth-prize winners accepted their awards, a group of SWR students, their English teacher, and some of their parents got dressed up and attended a ceremony at Leisure Village in honor of the essay-contest winners. As far as I knew, this was the only official contact the eighth graders had with Leisure Village seniors that year.[7] The only other times I witnessed any student interest in Leisure Village were when I drove small groups (usually two or three students) to have lunch at the nearest McDonald's or Taco Bell, about ten to fifteen minutes south of the middle school. The drive there took us right past Leisure Village's main complex and security gates. Often seniors would be playing golf inside on the fenced-in green or walking their dogs along the outer perimeter. One group of boys who I went to lunch with frequently—they were quite adept at convincing me that they just "had to have a break today" or needed to "run for the border"—had a way of getting fairly silly on our excursions and would sometimes focus their teen-boy humor on the retirees, calling out harmless though definitely rude comments as we drove past. Though the activity made me uncomfortable, in the spirit of ethnography, I let it slide, only scolding them in a teasing fashion. They seemed to delight in this response as if we were all willingly participating in a charade of typical middle-class adult-child relationships. This was, after all, the same group of boys who also insisted on calling me mom/Lorena. Leisure residents never responded to their taunts. I assume they couldn't hear them sufficiently as we whizzed by. Even in this more direct encounter, the boundary between Leisure Village and SWR remained sacrosanct.

Though, on a day-to-day basis, Leisure Village and SWR exist in their more-or-less separate middle-class orbits, the retirement complex has had an impact on the social and economic landscape of the surrounding community. Leisure Country, comprising Leisure Village, Glenn, and Knoll, is a sign of the inability of suburbia or the white middle class to incorporate its elderly into its nuclear family life. It is part of the culture of avoidance that operates on both sides of the complex's fences. Young and middle-aged families don't have to confront their futures and the aged don't have to mourn their pasts. While Leisure residents may appear fairly well off and taken care of, what happens to those elders who are not as financially solvent or physically able? Suburbia does not offer much by way of community or mobility. The local paper explained the retirement village's isolation in functionalist terms: "[The residents] don't see younger people going off to work, so they don't miss it." My father, a retired mortgage officer, suggested otherwise, when he told me that while he was still working at a nearby bank, a couple from Leisure Village came in to inquire about their mortgage and the costs of moving. The husband played cards with his neighbors, and he had grown weary of the fact that an ambulance came into the complex almost nightly; they kept losing card players from their circle of friends. Furthermore, my father noted that the local Catholic church had a funeral for a Leisure resident almost daily. Apparently, this generationally homogeneous community does not turn out to be the picture-perfect living environment for everyone.

Likewise, though Leisure Country houses the white middle class, essay contests aside, the retired residents do not have an immediate and sustained stake in the local schools, arguably the lifeblood of the middle class. As Barbara Ehrenreich has noted, "We may be born into the middle class, but we are expected to spend almost thirty years of our lives establishing [through education] ourselves as members of that class in good standing" (1989, 76). In other words, the middle class is made in and through education. With all of Leisure Glenn and seventy units in Leisure Village located in the SWR district, the elder insider-Other faction plays a significant role in placing limits on a given year's educational spending, by regularly voting against proposed budgets and voting for fiscally (and educationally) conservative school-board members. Clearly, the school district is not one of their primary concerns. Though SWR initially found the middle-class retirement community an acceptable use of Shoreham property, it turns out that fences do not always make good neighbors and not all conflicts can be avoided, especially when a community takes its privileges for granted for too long. This became even more apparent when the wider SWR community, as a result of the closing of the Shoreham Nuclear Power Plant, was forced to become more financially cautious themselves. The fallout from this event was anything but minimal.

Residual Radiation

During the spring and early summer of 1994, Leisure Country turned out to be the least of the school district's worries when the community at large voted down the proposed school budget twice, finally settling on a budget of $32.2 million, down $6.5 million from its highest point, in 1991–92. The new budget eliminated 42 teacher, civil service, and administrative positions from the approximately 200 jobs remaining in the district, making cumulative staff reductions due to layoffs and early retirements tally in at over 100 jobs since 1992; increased the remaining faculty's instructional responsibilities in the middle school and high school by one period a day; reduced staff development funds by 90 percent and transportation costs by $300,000; and raised the typical homeowner's school taxes by $19 per month, increasing taxes by about 17 percent.

In a district known for maintaining one of the lowest teacher-student ratios and one of the highest per student spending rates—in 1993, 9.7 and $19,308 respectively, compared with Suffolk County's average of 14.2 and $10,789 (*Long Island Almanac 1993* 1994, 26)—as well as one of the lowest tax scales on Long Island, the public battle over the 1995 school budget called into question SWR's standing as a middle-class community committed to giving its children the best possible education and accustomed to maintaining civil or morally minimal relationships with each other.[8] Residents on both the spend and cut sides of the budget question made their positions known during the district's weekly school-board meetings and, albeit often anonymously, in the "Letters to the Editor" column of the local weekly, the *Community Journal*.[9] At times, the tenor of the discussion was rancorous, coming to a head when the president of the school board publicly campaigned against the first board-approved budget by driving around town with antibudget placards on his car and leafleting the neighborhoods with a letter calling on the community to vote "NO" on May 11. A week before the first vote, the *Community Journal* ran a letter by the board president, in which he accuses the SWR administration and school board of being "credit card addicts." His letter is joined by two unsigned (apparently conflict is okay as long as you don't own up to it), vitriolic responses against an earlier statement published by the SWR Teachers Association that had equated turning down the budget to "giving up on the children of SWR." Objecting to teacher sabbaticals and in-service training, the letter from "Sleepless in Shoreham" claims: "It's obvious to me the Teachers Association is focused on their needs and their agenda over our children's needs. . . . It's the people, the families and commitment to our children and one another, that makes this community so special" (*Community Journal* 1994, 7). In public discussions, however, the antibudget contingent never fully articulated how they intended to manifest this commitment to their children. Instead, they focused on taking programs away and imposing a "job speed-up" on the teaching staff left after downsizing, ostensibly disregarding the effect these cuts and punitive measures would have on their children's educations and the community's overall well-being.

Nothing was sacred in the battle over the budget: residents called for either the wholesale demise or piecemeal reduction of programs like the science museum, the middle-school farm, the annual district calendar featuring students' artwork, the elementary schools' Peacemakers initiative that trains students in conflict-resolution techniques (an activity that would seem to fit well within this culture of avoidance), teen recreation (a supervised program the district ran on Friday and Saturday evenings that gave students a presumed safe place to socialize and play games like basketball and volleyball together), summer music-education classes, the district's bus contract, and even the middle school's acclaimed advisory system. As a child in this district, I was among the first group of students to benefit from many of these programs. I knew firsthand some of the personal and educational rewards that many of them carried with them. For example, as part of our math-science curriculum, my eighth-grade class started the farm. I witnessed students who otherwise did not excel in a traditional educational setting designing and building chicken coops, shelters for goats, and vegetable gardens, among other farm-related activities. The tasks required research, mathematical problem solving, patience, and perseverance. In the end, we were proud of what we had accomplished both individually and collectively. Two decades later, it was with personal regret that I watched the school board essentially close the gate on the middle-school farm. An act that did not take into account the educational and social value of the program.

Similarly, at the board meeting that decided the fate of the district's long-standing relationship with its bus company, one resident stood up and pleaded with the board to maintain the bus contract in the name of the children's safety and the community's economic stability: "Eighty percent of the bus drivers who service SWR live in the district; if we get rid of our present company, these people will be unemployed" and our children, the speaker went on to imply, will be driven to school by outsiders who know neither the local streets nor the local families. Another resident concurred, pointing out that "you can always get something for less, but you get what you pay for." The board voted in favor of finding a new bus company, "strangers," to transport the district's children to and from school. The bottom line was money and not their children's safety or their neighbors' livelihoods.

Meanwhile, as the teachers in the district feared for their jobs or mourned the loss of programs that helped make SWR a model middle school (e.g., Maeroff 1990) and administrators carried the weight of all this on their shoulders as they tried to find the least invasive ways to accommodate the newly slashed budgets, the school made an effort to buffer students from all this upheaval and the resultant bad feelings by not discussing with them what was going on. For the most part, staff silences worked, though enough eighth graders had some inkling as to what was going on behind the scenes and began circulating rumors about this or that teacher leaving. In the end, many of the younger and oftentimes more enthusiastic teachers, people students were generally quite fond of, were the first to lose their jobs under a last hired, first fired type of policy. Though even when exact information about who was going to be "let go" was made public, the situation was not collectively, officially acknowledged between middle-school students and staff. It was only at the year-end staff meeting, after the students had gotten on the buses to go home for the last time that school year, that the staff came together, paid tribute to those leaving, and collectively bereaved the school's losses.[10]

Living with Risks

The battle over the budget extended far beyond the local context, culminating almost thirty years of county, state, federal, and corporate deal making in relation to the Shoreham Nuclear Power Plant and the U.S. nuclear industry in general. In 1994, SWR's budget crisis could be counted among the nuclear wastes that still needed to be disposed of properly in the wake of the 1989 agreement between New York State and the plant's owners, the Long Island Lighting Company (LILCO), to abandon the recently completed facility.

But the nuclear power plant is as much the result of SWR's culture of privilege as it is its architect. When LILCO first proposed erecting a then state-of-the-art nuclear facility in Shoreham, the combined towns of Shoreham and Wading River contained acres of untouched wooded areas and fallow potato and sod farms that were ripe for development—or at least the kind of development that would complement the town's vision of what their suburban landscape should encompass. This was a middle-class community on the verge of expansion, the last frontier of the post–World War II suburban sprawl that had bulldozed Long Island into an assortment of white middle-class housing developments, a string of strip malls, and, in later years, a conglomerate of multiplexes and corporate complexes. (See chapter 2 for a more in-depth discussion of the suburbanization of Long Island.) The power plant was to be a part of that bright and nuclear (in both its familial and technological senses) future of the white middle class.[11] During my fieldwork, that future was rapidly becoming a thing of the past. What kind of past was this? And what kind of future had it wrought?

For the SWR school district, the story of the nuclear power plant began in 1968 when LILCO applied for a permit to construct an 840–megawatt generator on 499 beachfront acres on the border between Shoreham and Wading River. I remember the colorful brochures LILCO sent to the community introducing the plant in architectural renderings that made the complex look pristine and community friendly. My father kept a file on the plant in the basement. As a young girl, I occasionally looked through these papers; my curiosity was piqued; I knew my father thought the plant was a good idea, but something about the whole enterprise left me mistrusting the wonders of technology, "progress," and my father's judgment. I worried about what a nuclear future would bring to Shoreham-Wading River. Did my father know best? Was nuclear energy really safer and cleaner than older forms of energy production? The Nuclear Regulatory Commission (NRC) issued a construction permit in 1973, the same year Shoreham opened the doors of its first institution of secondary education, the SWR Middle School, and the same year that the United States endured the inconveniences of the Arab oil embargo. From this context, it was easy for the residents of SWR to trust that the power plant—a rich source of tax revenue for the town—would help the community prosper and liberate them from "foreign" interests. I don't recall any of this being discussed openly within SWR classrooms when I was a girl. I knew what I knew, in large part, from my parents' dinner-table conversations and my subsequent "research" through my father's files.

I spent the summer of 1974—the summer between seventh and eighth grades—"scientifically" exploring the salt marshes that serve as a transitional ecosystem between the Long Island Sound and the scrubby woods surrounding and dividing the manicured lawns of Shoreham and Wading River. I was participating in a school-sponsored summer marine biology program for students in the district. We met each morning at the newly dredged harbor and boat launch along the eastern perimeter of what was fast becoming a looming turquoise-and-gray concrete eyesore on the shores of the Long Island Sound, the Shoreham Nuclear Power Plant. In preparing the area for the plant, LILCO constructed two boulder-and-concrete jetties that reached out into the water further than I felt comfortable swimming, despite the fact that I was a strong and well-trained swimmer. In time, however, an expansive sandbar formed between the massive rock structures keeping the water in the area unnaturally shallow and warm. As we waded through the marshes and combed the nearby beaches identifying marine life and fauna, no one in the science class seemed to pay much attention to this monstrosity of technology breeding in our midst. Why should we? Our town was burgeoning—a new middle school had just opened and the district's first high school was under construction, set to spare my classmates and me the disruption of being bussed fifteen miles to go to high school among kids we didn't know in Port Jefferson. Though the power plant never looked very appealing or reassuring, and LILCO's decision to locate it in this ecologically rich and unique shoreline habitat never made much sense, the community didn't seem too disturbed. Taxes promised to remain low while the school district continued to expand its facilities and resources. Shoreham-Wading River, in a sense, had become the utility's company town; for the next two decades, the power plant would underwrite this middle class's rather extravagant way of life and state-of-the-art education system.

When LILCO proposed the plant in 1968, it estimated that it would cost $271 million and would go on-line in four years. Over two decades and $5.5 billion later, in February of 1992, New York State bought the reactor from the utility company for one dollar, putting the administrative responsibility for the plant in the hands of the Long Island Power Authority (LIPA), a six-year-old, state-government-created, tax-exempt agency. The deal removed the power plant from the district's tax rolls, threatening the solvency of the local school district, which had come to rely on the power plant for more than 90 percent of its yearly revenues. Between 1976 and 1991, LILCO expended $676 million on school, town, and county taxes to cover the assessed value of the plant.[12] LIPA started decommissioning procedures in June of 1992, transporting more than five million pounds of radioactive waste material from the plant to licensed waste burial and volume reduction facilities in South Carolina and Tennessee. After 353 truckloads, LIPA completed the job in October 1994. It was the first time in the history of the U.S. nuclear industry that an NRC-licensed commercial nuclear facility had been decommissioned and dismantled. The entire process took place with little fanfare from the surrounding communities.

Ostensibly, the Shoreham plant (colloquially referred to as just "Shoreham" or "the plant") began to meet its demise in 1979 when the Three Mile Island nuclear accident in Pennsylvania brought the threat of nuclear mismanagement to the forefront of the nation's imagination. In the wake of Three Mile Island, Congress determined nuclear utilities cannot be licensed to operate unless they devise and implement emergency evacuation plans covering the ten-mile area immediately surrounding a plant. The New York State Legislature upped the ante by insisting that LILCO figure out a way to evacuate safely and efficiently residents living within twenty miles of the nuclear site. Given the geography of Long

Island, the density of the population, and the limitations of the local roadways, the task proved insurmountable, at least in the eyes of the legislature. While LILCO completed construction of the plant in 1984, conducted low-power tests between 1985 and 1987, and received a full-power operating license from the NRC on 21 April 1989, it could not meet the state's evacuation standards. The NRC amended LILCO's jurisdiction over the plant to a possession-only license in 1991, revoking the utility's authority to operate the plant, and the state took over from there.

Though the plant had faced some opposition since its inception, in large part this did not come from local SWR residents. Historically, the area had accommodated numerous technological and military projects, beginning with Nikola Tesla's Electrical Lab of 1902, where Tesla attempted to send electrical signals from Shoreham to Mars, and including the Grumman Corporation aerospace manufacturing plant in nearby Calverton, which, in its heyday, manufactured the lunar module that enabled the first humans to land on the moon in 1969,[13] and the Brookhaven National Laboratory, less than five miles south of Shoreham on the William Floyd Parkway, a preeminent scientific and nuclear research facility equipped with its own reactor.[14] SWR is home to numerous scientists who work at the lab or the nearby state university, SUNY-Stony Brook, a campus that includes SUNY's largest downstate medical research facilities and teaching hospital. Given the historical and current concentration of scientific, medical, and military production in the area, it is perhaps not surprising that the SWR community valued technological advances that offered immediate perks like better schools and lower taxes over imagined apocalyptic futures that popular films like *The China Syndrome* (1979, directed by James Bridges) and *Silkwood* (1983, directed by Mike Nichols) fostered elsewhere in the country over the same period. This is a community that either has a direct faith in science or is focused on short-term tangible gains. For most, the power plant made good economic sense. As a community SWR neither fought nor feared the nuclear facility.[15]

In June of 1979, when word got out that a large antinuclear protest was about to descend on what we saw as our "sleepy" community, my best friend and I decided to bake several batches of oatmeal cookies, which we called "No Nuke Cookies," and our slogan was "Get Them Before They're Radiated." We set up shop on the beach, greeting hungry protesters with our home-baked antinuke goodies. We were a hit among the political crowd. Some asked us where the profits went; we smiled and said ourselves. They appreciated our candor and proceeded to buy more of our sugary, fiber-rich fare, turning what could have been an early lesson in nonviolent political and civic-minded protest into my first lesson in successful marketing. Our economically opportunistic approach to the nuclear situation in our town mirrored that of the adults in our lives.

The local community had both rationalized away and capitalized on this potential technological nightmare in their backyard. And their children clearly followed their lead.

Back in Shoreham as an ethnographer, I noticed that SWR kids still didn't seem too concerned about the power plant. Though the threats of meltdowns and radiation leaks were no longer a factor in 1994, the power plant clearly affected life in this community. In fact, in its current state of demise, the plant had a greater impact, especially on the community's children. However, the battle over the state of education at SWR did not seem to concern most eighth graders. It was not a topic of conversation among peers or, as noted earlier, discussion within classrooms, despite the fact that students were beginning to have to live with the effects of budget decisions on a day-to-day basis: after-school and valued extracurricular programs were disappearing, class sizes were growing, and popular teachers vanishing. When I asked Sarah, a recent SWR graduate and the older sister of a current SWR eighth grader, about this seemingly large gap in consciousness, she replied, "I didn't feel that I knew enough about what it [the nuclear power plant] was, and how much danger was involved. I felt that there was a lot of political stuff that was going on that was distorting a lot of the truth. I think my parents supported it. My dad, being a scientist, sort of felt that it was pretty much, pretty safe. So . . . " When I asked her if she ever worried about living near the plant as a girl, she said:

> No, I'm sure it crossed my mind a couple of times like what it would be like to get off the Island, and I would pretty much just die [laughs], but it wasn't something I was always worried about. I was more worried about a war or something than the nuclear power plant. . . . Maybe by the end of high school, people [her classmates] wanted it [the power plant] closed. When there was talk about it closing, people sort of talked about it, but it was more like the teacher would say something in class, so there would be a little discussion there. It wasn't something people were really concerned with socially. We were all getting ready to leave Shoreham. We were thinking more about getting out than about anything that was going on in Shoreham. (Interview with SWR graduate and Princeton undergraduate, 6 May 1995, Princeton University)

Sarah had lived through the greatest transitional period in the life of the power plant. Regarding the safety of the plant, she echoes her parents' and the community's lack of concern. In terms of political consciousness, she mirrors the current set of students' lack of focus on local community predicaments. However, Sarah's memories of life at SWR indicate not so much her own limitations—as a young adult, she was clearly politically informed and had a commitment to issues beyond her own well-being—as the community's desire to deflect conflict and shelter its children from having to think about anything greater than their own good. Unlike Sarah, the SWR eighth graders of this ethnography have only experienced the plant as a moot issue. They would have been between three and seven years old when the plant conducted its low-power tests and eight or nine years old when the plant closed. Regardless, they were living through the most intense period of educational retrenchment (or reform, depending on your political perspective) that the relatively young district had ever undergone. Like Sarah and her classmates, they were mostly uninvolved in the debate, neither encouraged by their parents or teachers to participate nor actively interested on their own. (See chapter 4 for a delineation of the kinds of issues that occupied the girls' imaginations.)

Limited Privileges

The publicness of the battle over the school budget and the demise of the nuclear power plant are symptoms of a moral minimalism that has outlived its effectiveness. The community can no longer maintain its silences. It doesn't have the resources to look the other way anymore. Its citizens made a pact with the devil when they chose to look no further than the immediate benefits they would derive from the power plant and when they took their middle-class lifestyles and educational system for granted through the more than two decades that the plant was under construction. But unlike their daughters, who flounder to find some moral compass to anchor their opinions in relation to, for example, teen pregnancy, while still brushing off their ambivalences as something they don't have to deal with right now, the parents can no longer defer the inevitable. The SWR community's years of perfecting its silences and calculating its exclusions and inclusions have left it civically devoid, unable to work through its differences and unclear about its commitments. Where does its bottom line lie: with its children's educations or its tax rates and electrical bills?[16] While these concerns are not necessarily mutually exclusive, at SWR, the years of leaving their privileges unexamined have rendered them irreconcilable. The community must choose, and in working out its choices the limits of maintaining a code of silence and avoidance become all too apparent.

Yet, despite all the upheaval in the school district that has resulted from not dealing with or thinking about the consequences of one's actions, the warning signs can still go unheeded. For example, the principal's letter to me clearly delineates that there are still things that are believed to be better left unsaid. When it comes to race, the results of this misrecognition and avoidance can be devastating. In chapter 5, I look at what happens to a girl who goes to extremes looking for a way to articulate herself racially.

As this chapter comes to a close, I am still relearning what not to say in order to fit in and successfully carry out my ethnographic, prodigal-daughter role in the white middle-classness and Christianness of this place I call home. I am learning not to speak about the school budget or the nuclear power plant to the community's daughters. I am learning to be careful about telling people I am studying white middle-class girls. And I am caught in the silence and aloneness of my own moral uncertainty about my decision to terminate my unplanned pregnancy and thereby avoid the consequences of going public with either my pregnancy or my abortion.

In addition to learning not to say some things, I am also looking for the words to explain what I know I am witnessing, what I know I have already internalized: the ineffableness of white middle-class femininity. And I am beginning to understand that my inarticulateness reflects the culture I am here to study. Not naming certain things, not recognizing others, and maintaining community silences that protect the "innocent" and disavow underlying truths or at least unpleasant possibilities are part of how this community of white middle-class, nuclear families fashions itself. The heart of this autoethnography lies in trying to identify those things and analyze their effect on the daughters of this suburbia.

When a class of eighth graders read Langston Hughes's poem "What happens to a dream deferred?" they mostly understood it in terms of their own lived experiences. They talked about their "dreams" to become architects, lawyers, basketball players, marine biologists, pediatricians, photographers, veterinarians, chiropractors, and physical therapists. One girl said she wanted to "get a job that helps people," while another replied, "I don't know what I want to be." A few seemed to understand that Hughes's poem reflected on race and racism in the United States. One girl, Elizabeth, mumbled something about the civil rights movement. When the teacher asked her to elaborate, Elizabeth replied: "I don't know." Teacher: "You do know." Elizabeth, in a very soft voice: "I know, but I don't know how to explain it."

Elizabeth's "I know, but I don't know how to explain it" is not about her own personal limitations, but about the ones she is being taught to internalize as a white, middle-class, suburban girl. This autoethnography is in search of the words to understand what the white middle class does not or will not explain about itself. It is in the deferred and hushed articulations that I find my analysis. I hear the silences, disavowals, and rationalizations as the markings of privilege, the things carefully constructed as "taken for granted," the things that go unsaid and unnoticed. This is an autoethnography about privilege, where dreams do not have to be deferred so much as left unexamined. My role as an ethnographer and cultural critic necessarily crosses paths with this way of being. I am doomed to remain the wayward daughter, an insider-Other, looking to say what cannot be said in an effort to help girls like Elizabeth say what it is they know about themselves and their futures, but are in the process of learning to silence, defer, and misrecognize. Such is the landscape and culture of privilege.

In the next chapter I turn to another wayward daughter, Amy Fisher, the "Pistol-Packing Long Island Lolita," who in turning suburban codes of avoidance and decorum on their head, put white middle-class, suburban Long Island girls on the national cultural map. I look at the telling of Amy's story to examine how Long Island and its teenage daughters are understood (or misunderstood as the case may be) on a larger scale. Amy's story and later Cheryl Pierson's (the focus of chapter 3) are precursor ethnographies (Limón 1991) to my autoethnography. While they are not ethnographies in the formal disciplinary sense, I include them here because in the glut of media representations of Amy's and Cheryl's real-life dramas, I read certain cultural preoccupations with and delineations of normative whiteness. Their stories define Long Island, suburbia, and white teenage girls in the cultural imagination, prefiguring the ethnographic versions I encountered in the field. SWR girls live with and against these media-fabricated selves, both directly and indirectly. For the most part, I am interested in the indirect effects of such widely circulating stories on how girls grow up white and middle class in suburbia. Who does the culture at large expect them to be and how does that shape their understanding and experience of Self? Moreover, an analysis of the details of Amy's and Cheryl's stories offers another layer to the cultural mix. In the media's fascination with Amy and Cheryl, I find a way to further speak the unspeakable and name the unnamable: the landscape of white middle-class femininity.

Chapter 2 Amy Fisher, My Story

Learning to Love the Unlovable

How Do You Solve a Problem Like Amy?

ON THE MORNING OF 19 May 1992, seventeen-year-old Amy Fisher went to the Buttafuocos' single-family home in Massapequa, Long Island. She rang the doorbell and spoke to thirty-seven-year-old Mary Jo Buttafuoco, the mother of two young children and the wife of a local car mechanic—thirty-six-year-old Joey. According to most media accounts, Amy told Mary Jo she wanted to talk to her about her husband, who she claimed was having an affair with her alleged sixteen-year-old sister. When Mary Jo did not seem inclined to believe her, Amy held up a T-shirt from Joey's garage as proof of her sister's and Joey's intimacies. She claimed that Joey had given the shirt to her sister as a sign of his affection. Mary Jo reportedly responded to the "news" in a dismissive manner, as if she did not consider the pretty teen girl standing before her a credible messenger or a threat to her marriage. When she turned around to go back inside, Amy Fisher shot her in the head.

Amy subsequently testified that the gun went off by accident. She claims that because Mary Jo did not take her seriously, she was enraged, so she impulsively reached out to grab her and hit her (not shoot her) in the head with the gun. *People* magazine's first feature story on the case excerpts the following from Amy's initial ten-page statement to the police:

> I felt she was dismissing me and didn't care about what I was saying. . . . I saw her turn to go back in the house, at which time I took the gun out of my pocket and hit her on the back of the head. I saw her stumble. I had my finger on the trigger. I went to hit her again because I was so angry. I then raised the gun again and it went off. I heard a pop

sound and saw blood coming out of her head. (Treen and Eftimiades 1992, 34)

Regardless of intent, she left Mary Jo lying in a pool of blood on her front porch.

Mary Jo survived the shot, though she was left with a bullet lodged in the side of her head and half of her face paralyzed. While recovering in the hospital, she identified her assailant as a young teen girl with long, violet hair. (Amy had recently dyed her hair, a not uncommon fashion-practice among her peers that season.) Joey Buttafuoco knew who Mary Jo was talking about and subsequently named Amy Fisher for the Nassau County police department detectives investigating the case.

The story that unfolded in the weeks and months following the shooting and the arrest and incarceration of Amy on attempted murder charges and later Joey on a statutory rape count proved fraught with lurid details. Amy insisted she had been having an affair with Joey since she was sixteen and that Joey had put her up to killing his wife. Amy also claimed that early in their relationship, Joey had set her up as an "escort" for a service in nearby Baldwin, Long Island. Initially Joey confessed to the affair but later denied it vehemently to the police and media.

As soon as the story broke, Amy became headline material in the national and regional presses (both in so-called reputable and disreputable venues, from the *New York Times*, *Newsday*, and the *Washington Post* to the *New York Post*, the *Daily News*, *People* magazine, and the *National Enquirer*, among others); she was the "Pistol Packing," "Long Island Lolita," the "Teen Fatal Attraction," and the "High School Student by Day . . . Call Girl By Night." In an unprecedented media event, Amy became the subject of three movies-of-the-week: NBC's *Amy Fisher: "My Story"* (starring relatively unknown Noelle Parker, aired 28 December 1992), CBS's *Casualties of Love: The Long Island Lolita Story* (starring teen-sweetheart Alyssa Milano), and ABC's *Beyond Control: The Amy Fisher Story* (starring the quintessential teen bad-girl both on and off the screen, Drew Barrymore[1]; the latter two were broadcast simultaneously on 3 January 1993). There was much hype surrounding these movies when they first aired; subsequently, they have landed in video stores, where they continue to attract a kind of cult following.[2] In addition, two books were published about the case, Maria Eftimiades's *Lethal Lolita: A True Story of Sex, Scandal, and Deadly Obsession* (1992) and Amy's own version supposedly cowritten with Sheila Weller, *Amy Fisher: My Story* (1993). Amy also became the butt of late-night comedians' jokes, the subject of a traveling theater production, and a recurring feature on talk shows and TV tabloid magazines like *Hard Copy*, *Current Affair*, and *Entertainment Tonight*, to name some prominent examples of how the media became obsessed with the case, aggressively stalked its main characters, restaged its pivotal social conflicts, and exposed its cultural territory: suburban Long Island and white middle-class teen girlhood.

Why did the nation care so much about Amy Fisher as this plethora of coverage suggests? Someone was watching all these programs and reading all these texts. What is at the root of this obsession and fascination with a supposedly typical white middle-class teen girl gone far astray from the expectations of her suburban Long Island upbringing? What can be learned about white middle-class America from her story? About teenage girls and suburban femininity? About Long Island as a cultural place?

This chapter is not about Amy Fisher, but about the representations of Amy Fisher that glutted the information and entertainment circuit of the early-to-mid-nineties. Whenever I use the name "Amy," I am referring to a concept, a media fabrication, an imagined Amy. This imaginary Amy and the imaginary Long Island she inhabits precedes me into the field, into the halls, playing fields, and classrooms at the SWR Middle School. When I write about white middle-class Long Island girls I do so through a cultural filter that stories like Amy's have indelibly colored. As a larger-than-life paradigm of Long Island teen girlhood, Amy reverberates throughout this autoethnography. The seemingly endless stream of accounts about Amy vent an otherwise unspeakable cultural anxiety about white middle-class femininity as it is embodied in the figure of the teenage girl and about conjugal heterosexuality—a major founding principle of the suburban nuclear community. Amy violates the understood terms and conditions of suburban culture, or what essentially stands as the dominant cultural norm. For the media, Amy's story is only worth telling to the degree that it deviates from what counts as normal in white middle-class suburbia. Would the three major television networks really have produced three movies-of-the-week devoted to Amy if she had been, for example, an African American girl from New York City or a Latina from South Texas?[3] I think not. The norm is the ultimate subject of Amy's story. This chapter delineates how the representations of Amy participate in defining, perpetuating, and producing this norm.[4]

Amy is an insider-Other. She is a white middle-class girl who doesn't quite fit in. She is what I am alternatively calling in this chapter an unlovable subject. The unlovable is so desperate for love, she sabotages every chance at love she gets. She puts her need to be loved above all else; she does not trust that she is ever really loved; and she seeks constant affirmation of any love she does receive, essentially procuring her own unlovableness. Amy herself writes in an article for the premiere issue of *mouth 2 mouth*, a teen magazine for "guys and girls," "I prostituted myself, lied to my parents and friends, shot a woman and gave up what could have been some of the best years of my life—all in the name of 'love'"(Fisher 1994, 74).[5] Love and the unlovable are core themes in the Amy Fisher story. But the unlovable subject is also the thing that cannot not be loved.

She is an insider-Other who needs to be attended to, for whom responsibility must be accepted.

To one degree or another, all white middle-class teenage girls are understood to be unlovable. As the stereotype goes, they are moody, lovestruck, hormone-driven, uncooperative clothes horses who spend much of their free time talking on the telephone.[6] In later chapters, white middle-class teen girls will also appear as hysterics, white supremacists, and gossipmongers, among other unlovable things. As unlovable insiders they are marked characters, deviating from or in some way threatening the stability of the norm. But, their threats are finally recoupable. In the end, they remain insiders, and their rebellions and transgressions ultimately help the culture at large reassert the norm. Unlovable insider bad girls can be disciplined back into good middle-class girls. That's what is simultaneously appalling and appealing about their misdeeds and out-of-control behavior. They can be redeemed, at least narratively, if all else fails. And narratives, as Amy's story suggests, count for a lot.

The idea of the unlovable functions on two levels in this analysis. I use the word unlovable not only to call attention to the ways in which girls themselves occupy a fraught social position but also to identify how writing and reading about girls like Amy and other suburban teens demands a certain commitment, passion, and patience that can transcend the knee-jerk dismissive responses the unlovable can provoke. Like the SWR girls and the other daughters of this book, Amy piques my interest and at times my sympathies and compassions. She can even delight and amuse. But she also infuriates. She lies and obsesses over (bad) men and material possessions. She manipulates the people who love her and desperately try to help her. She does not say what I want her to say. Her remorse sounds rehearsed, her eventual critiques of Joey, insincere. In the end she says what her lawyers, social workers, and mother, as well as the public, want to hear. Even in her final appearances before a judge and a parole board in the spring of 1999, after nearly seven years behind bars, Amy's tearful apology to Mary Jo and her later statement that "I won't let [the media] affect my life. If I don't want to be bothered, I have to tell them I'm not interested and not talk about it and that's it" (McQuiston 1999, 35) do not ring entirely believable. This is not a girl I am inclined to love. Nevertheless, her behavior makes the status quo vulnerable to scrutiny, offering the cultural critic of the white middle class a golden opportunity to articulate what is usually taken for granted: the ascendancy of white middle-class norms and the ambiguous position of girls within those norms. In this sense, Amy opens up a kind of suburban Pandora's box. And for this, Amy is a girl I am hard-pressed not to love.

Writing about (unlovable) teen girls also opens up questions of responsibility. They are, after all, youthful subjects in a culture that legally and socially demarcates them as in need of protection and not fully autonomous. And here,

Amy is no exception. Who is accountable for and to Amy? I name the act of being accountable in this context as learning to love the unlovable. Love serves as a model for interpretation that is about risk, responsibility, and relationality. It is about seeing the world as an interminable balancing act between Self and Other. This is not a romantic love based on boy meets girl, boy marries girl, boy and girl live happily ever after. Instead, it is a love that understands the cultural world as a series of imbroglios and intimate and complex situations and relationships that bear layers of responsibility and bring the gamut of emotions into one's life. It is a world that needs to be engaged and revisited continually; one is never finally done loving someone and to love someone means that you take on a certain ongoing responsibility for and accountability to them. The key here is engagement. Not engaging Amy, staying above the fray, will not make her go away or reduce her cultural significance. In this regard, this chapter is about finding a way to stay engaged in Amy's story, and by implication in Cheryl's, Dora's, Emily's, and the SWR girls' stories of the rest of this book.

Amy and stories of white middle-class teen girlhood in general are too easy to dismiss. Adults deem their world frivolous and trashy, proclaim that they're going through a stage, brand them Generation X, and in the case of Amy, find her beyond hope, or identify her as somebody else's problem daughter. But, dismissing girls like Amy as the unfortunate detritus of contemporary life ensures her reproduction and leaves the status quo—the maker of her predicament to some extent—unexamined, an irresponsible stance for any student of popular culture to assume. And we are all arguably students of popular culture, whether we like it or not. As a cultural critic writing about Amy and as an ethnographer hanging out with eighth-grade girls, I needed to get mixed up in the contents of their culture. I had to engage them, not as a disciplining parent, teacher, or other adult, in the case of my ethnographic subjects, and not as a disengaged cultural critic in the case of Amy. This did not mean, however, that I was going to mindlessly celebrate their cultural transgressions and let them get away with murder, so to speak (or attempted murder, as the case may be). There had to be a middle ground between labeling anyone who thinks there is a socially relevant message in Amy's story a "total idiot," as one prominent commentator did (see below), and elevating Amy (and her unlovable sisters) to the venerable post of rebels with a cultural and feminist cause. I find a more measured approach in learning to love the unlovable. I identify my analytical practice as a kind of love, in part because I want to implicate myself, to foreground my own vulnerabilities and responsibilities to my subjects. By extension, I also want to invite my readers to take note of the cultural significance of Amy's story and to realize that engaging the Amys and other suburban daughters of this text is the only viable option. What is at stake in Amy's story is not just one love-struck white girl's reputation so much as a larger cultural understanding of how white middle-class femininity functions within an intricate system of social hierarchies. We are all positioned somewhere on the continuum. While our locations may differ, and those differences matter, nevertheless we are all insiders here to one degree or another, and as such we need to find a way to engage the Amy Fishers of this world. To engage her in this sense is to love her, for better or worse.

Culture as a Parodic Imbroglio

The array of characters, stories, and institutions involved in the Amy Fisher phenomenon constitute the story as an imbroglio. I borrow the term *imbroglio* from the story itself. In *Lethal Lolita*, Maria Eftimiades writes:

> With the media spotlight on a variety of new characters, Joey Buttafuoco was feeling a bit left out. He still chatted gamely with reporters camped on his front lawn—he even passed out sandwiches one afternoon. But slowly Joey was beginning to realize he didn't exactly look great in this *imbroglio*. It was time to tell his side of the tale, his version of the Amy affair. (Eftimiades 1992, 181, emphasis added).

The Fisher-Buttafuoco imbroglio is a set of overlapping narratives, all of which are tainted with lies and breaches of commonly respected community standards (e.g., thou shall not strike people with loaded guns, thou shall not lead young girls into prostitution rings, etc.). As a contorted and layered drama, it begs its readers to position themselves in the telling and retelling of the tale. Who do you believe more and why? Whose side are you on? Who is the real victim here? In what respect are they victims? In what context? At which moment? Who is culpable or at least more culpable? Why are so many people curious? And what lurks behind the public's interest in this case?

The story is only a story because there is an audience out there to be entertained or disgusted by it and all the attention it garners. Amy's ambiguous positioning within this narrative as well as Joey's audacious lack of integrity and Mary Jo's pathetic credulousness (She can't really believe that Joey is telling the truth?) actively call forth an audience, one that needs to take sides and form opinions, and one that finds itself entangled in a debate on social mores and cultural values. This story cannot be viewed from the outside. There is no outside here. To disavow any interest in or to simply ignore or dismiss this contemporary suburban soap opera is to see the world in separate, hermetically sealed categories and cultural boxes. As Mary Jo's experience demonstrates, to disavow, ignore, or simply dismiss is a dangerous and ultimately untenable position to occupy. Turning your back on this imbroglio will not make it go away; it may only get you more embroiled in it.

Below I turn to a set of parodies of this story to demonstrate how as a tale of intertwined social categories and converging and conflicting narratives it relies on the specificity and demands the accountability of its audiences. As a genre, parodies are at the very least double-voiced texts (Morson 1989). They critically refer to and typically subvert an original narrative or collection of narratives. Parodies are necessarily intertextual and indexical, pointing to other stories and giving themselves and these references a context that exceeds the narrow confines of their own plots and characters. Moreover, parodies rely on an audience of knowledgeable readers who get the "jokes" and who actively read through and around the narrative layers and allusions. Parodies demand an engaged audience.

Though I focus in this section on three fabricated parodies of the Amy affair, the case itself, even without the intentional use of a double-voiced narrative, resembles a parody. The nonparodic accounts of Amy's story also employ overwrought stereotypes of the teenage girl, the philandering husband, and the passive suburban housewife in addition to well-worn narratives with predictable outcomes and familiar plots: the love triangle, the cat fight, and multiple tales of betrayal and forgiveness. It is as if Amy, Joey, and Mary Jo were caught up in a narrative not entirely of their own making. As it teeters on the edge of being its own worst parody, Amy's story is ripe for satirizing and demonstrates just how close lived culture can come to the parodic. In other words, everyday culture is itself referential, multiply voiced, and repetitive.

As unlovable marked subjects, teenage girls also at times appear to participate in a kind of self-parody. They live out stereotypes and restage cultural narratives. A constitutive and prototypical part of white middle-class teen girlhood is being noticed, getting a reaction, positive or negative, from your peers, your teachers, your parents, and other adults in your life. It is seeing how much you can get away with, how much you can please, or how much you can aggravate. It is about setting off a chain of responses from an audience and having an audience that can follow the narrative threads necessarily comprising most social interactions in teen girl life. (See chapter 4 for more about how SWR girls' stories constitute relationships and rely on audience participation, especially the section entitled "Stories of Entitlement and Obligation.") Early on in my fieldwork, I became aware of how good girls are at getting noticed when I taught the English elective on girls' diaries. Despite the fact that they had all volunteered to participate in the class and they knew that I had a special adult status in the school, I quickly experienced girls either defying me or ingratiating themselves with me. By offering an elective, I somewhat naively had positioned myself within the extant dynamics of the official culture of the suburban middle school. Though this was not the type of relationship I wanted to pursue with SWR girls, taking on the role of the teacher for a short time afforded me a frustrating and disconcerting glimpse at how well they knew how to get noticed. It was as if the girls and I, without missing a beat, began to enact a well-rehearsed script; the effect, from my perspective, was nearly parodic.

But the difference between a near parody and a full-fledged one is that successful parodies don't just repeat the stereotypes and reproduce the reference points, they recontextualize them and thereby offer a social critique. Modes for doing this include featuring anachronistic plot elements and characters, mixing genre conventions, and exaggerating or understating particular aspects of the original text (Morson 1989). In this manner, parodies make the familiar strange and foreground that which is most taken for granted. The Amy parodies employ these strategies and in the process call attention to what matters most in her story. Below, I delineate this by looking at what exactly gets parodied in Amy parodies. This process harks back to my analysis in chapter 1 of discovering which identity terms at SWR were up for discussion, which were under lock and key, and for whom. In other words, how are questions of race, class, gender, and region figured and refigured in the Amy parodies just as SWR adults and teens worked and reworked these terms and their cultural significance in their initial responses to my ethnographic project?

In January of 1993, *Saturday Night Live* (*SNL*) devoted a large portion of one of its shows to a series of Amy parodies. The focus on Amy was, in part, presumably inspired by the fact that the Italian-American, New York–accented Danny DeVito, who for most of his career has portrayed working-class characters, hosted the show. The pairing of host and subject bespeaks the degree to which Amy's "ethnicity" (or at least half of it: her mother is Italian American; her father is Jewish) and her regional and class identities figure into popular understandings of this case. Interestingly, Amy's Jewishness is barely acknowledged in any of the representations—parodies or not—of her story that I came across. In part, this lack of attention to any connection to Jewishness further "whitens" Amy in a culture where being a Jewish American can mark one as a stigmatized white or even nonwhite. Though, as historians have documented, non-Jewish European Americans, like the Irish and Italians, were also not always considered white upon immigrating to the United States (see, for example, Roediger 1991; Ignatiev 1995; and Jacobson 1998), the degree to which Amy can be white *and* Italian American in many of the published accounts demonstrates just how white Italian Americans have become. Amy's whiteness is not in question when the media portray her as a "guidette," though it is to a degree made strange. More specifically, in this context, calling attention to Amy's Italian Americanness raises the issue of class more than it does race or ethnicity (see below, "Somebody Else's Daughter"). Only the more sensationalized and parodic versions of Amy's story ethnicize her. For the most part, the media present her as a more ethnically neutral suburban girl. Everybody's daughter.[7] Her Long Islandness usually serves more as her ethnicity than her Italian Americanness.

In this sense, following the stereotype of Long Island, her Long Islandness firmly situates her into the suburban middle class. Indeed, it is precisely her Long Islandness that gives the media a way of indirectly naming what is otherwise an unnamable class position. Long Island becomes a euphemism for the white middle class. In a similar vein, readers of earlier versions of this chapter have insisted that Amy is not middle class but working class. Again, this is a representational problem. Economically there is nothing working class about Amy. At the time her story broke, Amy's family owned its own upholstery business and its own substantially middle-class home in a predominantly middle-class neighborhood. The impression that Amy is working class comes from the ways the media emphasize the trashiness of her tale and the ways in which Amy herself seemed to intentionally go "slumming," hanging out with Joey the auto mechanic as well as with more ethnically and hence class-marked kids in Brooklyn and Queens. With a typical working-class job, Joey is more ambiguously part of the middle class than Amy. His family may own the garage where he works, but Joey is really just an employee, having lost his partner status after he got himself in trouble with drugs and the law long before Amy came into the picture. Nevertheless, Joey and Mary Jo have some of the accoutrements of middle-class life on Long Island, including a waterfront home and a power boat, the *Double Trouble*, made infamous by the media as one of the places Amy and Joey met to carry out their affair. Turning Amy into a working-class girl gone bad is another way of making her somebody else's problem. A more accurate description of Amy would recognize her as a middle-class girl who transgresses the boundaries of middle-class life. That DeVito's ethnicity and his working-class persona—earned, in part, by his years as a scrappy New York City cab driver, Louie De Palma, on the television sitcom *Taxi* (1978–1983)—prompted *SNL* writers to devise an entire episode around Amy demonstrates just how much Amy's case is about social stratification. After all, DeVito, as far as I know, had no other connection to Amy. The *SNL* episode included Amy skits that picked apart, one by one, the different social categories in the "real life" Amy drama, calling attention to the ways in which Amy's story is precisely about the making and unmaking of *white middle-class, heterosexual, Long Island, teen girlness*.

Two skits took on class and race issues by shifting and exaggerating one or the other category in the narrative and by recontextualizing scenes from the "original" Amy story. "The House of Buttafuoco," a spoof on PBS's *Masterpiece Theatre*, featured a gentile, upper-class Amy sipping tea with her parents. In the opening dialogue Amy confesses to her mother and father that she has contracted a case of genital herpes. Early on in Joey and Amy's "real-life" relationship, Amy accused Joey of giving her herpes. When she told her parents, they confronted Joey and threatened to have him arrested on statutory rape charges. Amy retracted her accusation and claimed that she got the sexually transmitted disease from her high-school boyfriend, Rob. The Fishers subsequently didn't press charges. The *SNL-Masterpiece Theatre* Amy sits on a parlor settee, dolled up in a white Victorian lace, high-collared dress. She speaks in an upper-class British accent.

AMY: Mummy, Daddy?
MR. FISHER: Yes, Amy darling.
AMY: I'm afraid I have some rather startling news.
MRS. FISHER: Oh don't tell me, it's not the motor car again?
["Real-life" Amy had numerous accidents in the car given to her by her parents shortly after her sixteenth birthday. Her visits to Joey's auto body repair place, "Complete Auto Body," allegedly precipitated their affair.]
AMY: No, not quite. It seems I've contracted a rather nasty case of herpes.
MRS. FISHER: Genital?
AMY: Yes, I'm afraid so.
MR. FISHER: Genital herpes, how awful for you.
MRS. FISHER: How ever did you catch it, darling?
AMY: A chap named Joey Butt-uh-foo-oh-coh.
MRS. FISHER: Oh, that big, dumb auto mechanic. How could you?
AMY: Ever so sorry, Mumsy.

At which point a contemporary, working-class, Italian-American version of Joey, played by DeVito, enters the scene. He's dressed in a T-shirt, colorful baggy pants, and running shoes, an outfit the "real" Joey Buttafuoco typically wore. Here DeVito functions as an anachronistic intrusion, prompting the audience to notice the already overstated impossibility of an upper-class, Victorian Amy.

The next Amy skit, "Amy Fisher: One Messed-Up Bitch," features black actors from the *SNL* cast. The parody opens with a black Joey and black Amy in "Complete Auto Body's" garage. Joey has just looked over Amy's cracked-up car.

JOEY: That's some serious damage, baby. You got rear ended?
AMY: Oh, not yet. You in-ter-est-ed, Mr. . . . ?
JOEY: Buttafuoco. Joey Buttafuoco.
AMY: [giggles.]
[Throughout the scene this Amy seductively writhes and touches her body while she talks to Joey.]
JOEY: First you gonna have to let me check under your hood.
AMY: Oh, suga. I'm gonna need a fill-up.
JOEY: Damn, you making my Italian blood boil.
AMY: Well if it's boilin', let's cook up that sausage.
JOEY: Baby, your pot ain't big enough.

[Amy turns to leave.]

AN ANONYMOUS AUTO MECHANIC, ALSO BLACK: Yo, Joey, that ho is white. You got a Miss Buttafuoco at home.

JOEY: Baby's got a vish-ass [as in vicious ass].

[Amy leaves the scene with her back to the camera, swinging her hips as she departs.]

The skit then cuts to Amy confronting a black Mary Jo on her front porch. A high-pitched fight takes place between them with Amy insisting that Joey is "stickin her sistah" and Mary Jo repeatedly telling Amy to get her "fat ass outta here."

Both skits rely on hyperbolic class, race, ethnic, and sexual stereotypes to critique the Amy phenomenon. The absurdity of an upper-class British Amy having a highly refined (repressed) conversation with her parents about genital herpes and a black, jive-talking, oversexed Amy coming on to a black Italian, flirtatious Joey underscores the degree to which the "original" story is necessarily a story about white middle-class, heterosexual suburbia. The use of stereotypes of both the white upper class and the black underclass speaks in the multiple voice of parody, to the way in which upper-classness and blackness are already coded social narratives. For example, "race," or the social meaning of skin color, emerges out of a set of narratives. Stories, stereotypes, and other cultural texts shape our understandings and precede our experiences of race. This is true for whiteness as much as it is for blackness, though not to the same effect. Whiteness appears narrativeless, while blackness seems full of history, culture, stereotypes, parodies, anecdotes, and stories (Fanon 1967). The very textuality of race invites a narrative response, in Amy's case parodies of whiteness, middle-classness, and suburban girlhood. However, using parodies to critique is a risky business. For in parodying racist, classist, sexist, and ethnic stereotypes, the skits run the risk of reproducing that which they are supposedly undercutting. There is no correct or final interpretation of these skits; hence they clearly require that viewers actively sift through the layers, carefully considering their own positions with regard to these cultural stereotypes and the story they spoof. They ask that viewers responsibly examine their own interest or feigned disinterest in the tale and its many retellings.

Another skit, featuring an *SNL* cast member playing "Tori Spelling" playing "Amy Fisher," entitled "Amy Fisher 10516" (a reference to Long Island's area code, 516), toyed with her teenageness, with her Long Islandness, and with the degree to which the media have overproduced this suburban melodrama. The "real" Tori Spelling, the daughter of Aaron Spelling, a prominent Hollywood producer, plays "Donna" on the blockbuster teen television drama, *Beverly Hills 90210* (a Spelling Entertainment Production). *90210*, as its regular viewers affectionately call it, features an ensemble cast of overprivileged white teens living in Southern California. One reviewer described the show as a "teen-crisis series" with "whiter than white, as if they had been sprayed with peroxide" characters (Wolcott 1994, 74). For the most part, the show attempts to work through "real" (albeit "white-bread") teen concerns in a fairly straightforward manner, straightforward for TV that is. The plots typically revolve around such volatile issues as teen sex, alcoholism in parents and kids, and teen suicide, along with more mundane adolescent preoccupations with things like taking the SATs, applying to colleges, and generally being accepted by the right people. SWR kids watched this show religiously. Some even had a standing "date" to watch it together, and it was often a main topic of conversation on the morning after a new broadcast.

By mapping the Amy story onto the *90210* phenomenon, the skit locates Amy within this Hollywood teen generation of overconsuming, self-involved, naively political (unlovable) youths with whom the public seems to have a deeply ambivalent relationship. The early nineties saw an onslaught of nervous rumblings around "today's youth," including magazine cover stories on Generation X and films like *Trust* (1990, directed by Hal Hartley), *Slacker* (1991, directed by Richard Linklater), *Singles* (1992, directed by Cameron Crow), *Reality Bites* (1994, directed by Ben Stiller), and *Clerks* (1994, directed by Kevin Smith)—all portraits of aimless post-boomer MTV-saturated kids. The *SNL* skit ends with a voice-over snidely stating, "*Time* magazine says Tori Spelling makes Drew Barrymore look like Amy Fisher," a reference to Barrymore's starring role in ABC's *Beyond Control: The Amy Fisher Story*, and to Barrymore's own genealogy of bad-girl characters. "Amy Fisher 10516" effectively layers the Amy phenomenon into a thriving teen consumer-entertainment market, making it readily apparent just how much the widespread interest in this story taps into an already prominent cultural fascination (read anxiety) with white middle-class suburban teenagers and their imagined social, moral, and ethical decline.

In many respects, "The House of Buttafuoco," "Amy Fisher: One Messed-Up Bitch," and "Amy Fisher 10516" are more precisely media metaparodies in that they are parodies of parodies, or more specifically, the media parodying itself parodying itself: "*Time* magazine says Tori Spelling makes Drew Barrymore look like Amy Fisher." The Amy phenomenon is an interminable metaparody that cannot be finally interpreted so much as inhabited. To inhabit a text is to participate in this continual process of interpreting an interpretation of an interpretation. It is to position oneself in the text and to be continually faced with the possibility that this positioning will shift over time and context. To inhabit a text is to read responsibly, or at least to risk a responsible reading—love the unlovable—one in which readers may find themselves implicated in the act of reading. When I laugh at the racial stereotyping of lower-class, black sexuality, I come face to face with my own "whiteness." The fact that I know the stereotype and social implications bespeaks the degree to which I am already fully ensconced in a racialized and racist world and demonstrates further the way in which race is a textual phenomenon that positions its readers in a social hierarchy. I cannot react to this parody from outside of the racial order. I laugh as a white person caught in a hermeneutic conundrum: Am I laughing at the critique of the stereotypes, or am I laughing at the stereotypes themselves and thereby perpetuating them? The Amy Fisher story is a (meta)parody about whiteness, a whiteness inflected in the figures of suburbia, the teenage girl, and the married heterosexual couple. When we respond to the Amy Fisher story—whoever "we" are and whatever the response—we implicate ourselves in the process, the first step toward loving the unlovable.

Long Island, Suburbia: An Unlovable Land

This thing of darkness I acknowledge mine.
—William Shakespeare, *The Tempest*

In its time, the Amy Fisher story was a tabloid story to rival all tabloid stories.[8] As a form of "infotainment," the tabloids rely on the parodic and the metaparodic and on the ambiguous relationship between truth and fiction to capture an audience. Spoofing the more "legitimate" news media, the tabloid story magnifies social values and reveals what lurks beneath a community's desire to know itself and its neighbors. With its high-profile, low-class, crass sensationalism, a tabloid story like Amy's is only a story because it gives the lie to the otherwise quiet, supposedly more classy, private, and refined social order that keeps middle-class America running. As the *Saturday Night Live* (meta)parodies of this case suggest, this regionalized narrative of bad girls and victimized wives all too obviously and specifically speaks of contemporary white suburbia going awry. The Fisher-Buttafuoco affair is about heterosexuality and the transgression of marital and generational boundaries and codes of behavior and ethics. Moreover, it identifies female desire as the underside of white middle-class suburban familial culture. Amy and Mary Jo turn the most heads and occupy the narrative center of most accounts of this case. They are the anomalies, the characters that exceed expectations, not Joey, who in all his working-class, middle-aged, masculine bravado lives out the familiar cultural trope of the philandering, midlife-crisis husband. The ongoing cat fight between Amy and Mary Jo bears witness to the ways in which middle-class heterosexual-homocompetitive desire harbors within it—or one could even say is constituted through—anger, jealousy, greed, and uncontrollable rage. Amy Fisher is the conduit for the national press's feminization and demonization of suburbia, specifically in its Long Island incarnation.

In August of 1993, riding on the hype of the Amy phenomenon and other recent Long Island tabloid traumas, the *New York Times Magazine*'s cover story, "The Devil in Long Island," proffered some wry social commentary on what it hailed as "Long Island Babylon," a place of bizarre and sensational behavior, basically a suburban paradise gone to hell. In addition to musing over the Fisher-Buttafuoco affair, the piece literally maps out the numerous suburban atrocities that have taken place on Long Island in recent years, including the stories of a prostitute-stalking serial killer; a "homeroom hit man" hired by a teenage classmate to murder her incestuously abusive father (see chapter 3); a dungeon-building child kidnapper; a teenage-Satanist murder cult; an "Angel of Death" mercy-killing nurse; several wife murderers; a barge full of Long Island garbage, the Mobro 4000, that cruised up and down the eastern seaboard unsuccessfully looking for a dumping site—no one would have Long Island's trash; and a twelve-hundred-pound man who had indulged his appetite to such an extreme that he was physically incapable of leaving his bed until he died in early middle age and his casket had to be lowered into the ground by a crane (Rosenbaum 1993, 24–25).[9] These are the stories, with Amy arguably occupying center stage—tales of greed, calculated violence, sexual impropriety, and bureaucratic mismanagement—that have kept the national tabloid presses humming and have come to define Long Island as a site of social, moral, economic, and environmental decay.

Given these strange neighbors, it is perhaps no accident that "Lethal Lolita" arose out of the seemingly endless string of strip malls, multiplexes, housing developments, school districts, and expressways that gets called Long Island: the 200–mile-long, 15–mile-wide (at its widest point), whale-shaped land mass off the eastern edge of New York City.[10] Long Island is decidedly not Manhattan. The Hamptons, Fire Island, and the "Gold Coast" (Great Gatsby country) notwithstanding, Long Island has typically been understood to lack the urban sophistication of New York as well as the urban poverty and violence that supposedly constitute the street culture of Manhattan and New York's four other boroughs. Given the zeal with which the New York media powerhouses latched onto Amy's story, it is clear that the Fisher-Buttafuoco affair afforded Manhattan a chance if not to vindicate itself then at least to distract public attention away from its own bad-boy image, largely perpetuated by the media's portrayal of street violence as nonwhite, poor, and male. With Amy, the New York press could point a finger at the city's younger sibling, Long Island, the once beautiful, well-behaved, easily controlled good girl that lies to the east of Queens.

Long Island stands as an archetype of a U.S. suburb. Many histories of suburbia identify Levittown, Long Island, as the prototypical planned community that paved the way for a burgeoning suburban housing industry that reconfigured the nation's landscape following World War II (e.g., Fishman 1987; Jackson 1985;

Buhr 1990; Kelly 1993; *Newsday* 1994). As these records note, suburbia's history is also the history of automobiles, funding for interstate highways, the distribution of veterans' benefits, the management of the mortgage industry, and the determination of property taxes and zoning laws (Kelly 1989; Perin 1988; Lipsitz 1995). While on the face of it these practices sound relatively innocuous and certainly race neutral, they were not. Many were directly or indirectly deployed with racial differences and hierarchies in mind, including practices like "redlining," whereby the Federal Housing Authority (FHA, a New Deal program begun in 1934 to stimulate a building boom by helping [some] people obtain private loans to buy and construct homes) rated neighborhoods according to race. The FHA designated all-white, middle-class neighborhoods as "green" zones, meaning they had the highest property values and were good places for banks to invest in, while they marked nonwhite or working-class areas as "red," thereby warning banks not to lend money to would-be homeowners in these neighborhoods (Sacks 1994, 94–97; Lipsitz 1995). As a result of redlining and similar practices, the suburbs sprung up as largely white enclaves. The early history of Long Island's suburban development is littered with these and similar economic and structural decisions that enforced a culture of avoidance by keeping some people in and others out. (Chapter 1 looked at how this culture took root and burgeoned at Shoreham-Wading River; here I speak more generally of suburban Long Island.) For example, between 1920 and 1970, public-works developer Robert Moses intentionally authorized the building of low-hanging overpasses on many of Long Island's highways in order to keep metropolitan buses carrying the urban, non–car-owning, mostly nonwhite poor off certain roads, effectively restricting this population's access to many of Long Island's best beaches and their surrounding communities and limiting commuter traffic to the more affluent automobile-owning white populations of suburbia (Winner 1986, 23). This coupled with the racial distribution of jobs and the location of different types of industries—factories remained in places like Brooklyn and lower Manhattan when they weren't moved overseas—kept nonwhites off of Long Island.

Suburban sprawl—or more precisely "white flight" to Long Island—began wholeheartedly after World War II. With the help of GI benefits (including programs offering college tuition and living expenses as well as access to low-interest home loans to qualifying GIs) and FHA policies, white veterans settled in the communities of Nassau and Suffolk counties, leaving behind their immigrant parents' ethnic neighborhoods in Queens and Brooklyn and moving further away from the newly developed or developing public-housing projects that were being built to contain the growing population of the mostly nonwhite urban poor. In effect this migration de-ethnicized the population and reconfigured them as "white" suburbanites, ultimately demonstrating again that whiteness is not so much a state of body as a social, historical, economic, and geographic location. These social émigrés did not resettle in ethnic neighborhoods so much as "white" communities (see Sacks 1994; Lipsitz 1995). And they subsequently reared a generation of baby boomers on Long Island as white middle-class suburbanites. Many of these first-generation Long Islanders have remained there as adults. They've bought their own single-family homes and raised their children in the predominantly white, middle-class communities that continue to populate Long Island. Despite recent census reports that document a significant increase in the number of nonwhite populations living in the suburbs, many communities on Long Island persist as ostensibly white (De Witt 1994, A1, B6; Schemo 1994a, A1, B6, 1994b, A1, B5). As the *New York Times* reports,

> Lily-white communities tend not to become integrated but to remain largely lily-white, with the addition of well-defined minority precincts. On Long Island, 95 percent of black residents are concentrated in 5 percent of the census tracts. According to census data, the likelihood of a white resident of Nassau living in the same census tract as a black or Hispanic person is only 8 percent, and the chance that white children will find black youngsters in school with them is just 9 percent. (Schemo 1994a, A1, B6)

It is no surprise then that between 1982 and 1993, the school district in Amy and Joey's Massapequa stayed 97.6 percent white, a figure consistent with SWR's racial history and makeup (Brown 1994, A34–A35). Long Island is decidedly not made up of multiracial communities.

Amy Fisher is the progeny of white-flight suburban culture. She is, as the *Times* would call her, a Long Island (or make that *Lawn Guyland)* lifer (Rosenbaum 1993, 22, 26). For some, she is a baby boomer's worst nightmare; she personifies a generation of spoiled, aimless kids who lack moral and ethical foundations, whose lives are only about the conspicuous consumption of consumer culture. Amy Fisher is an "inevitable MTV byproduct" (Swinburne, Apice, and Cornbury 1993). She is a larger-than-life member of what some in the media have dubbed the "13th Gen" (the thirteenth generation after the founding of the country), or Generation X, a lost generation of unlovable kids without values or aspirations for the present or future. How "real" this generation is is up for discussion. While one might find kids or young adults who fit the bill, the media themselves have created the generation on a larger scale through naming it, describing it, analyzing it, and portraying it in movies (see partial list above), among other media productions. Generation X is good for the market; it makes a good story, identifies a core consumer group, and creates social and cultural anxieties, needs, and desires. The media both reflect and produce reality. Gen X is a perfect example of this practice and its effects. In a collection of essays, statistics, anecdotes, and quotes from popular culture representing and ultimately perpetuating this media-fabricated generation, *13th Gen: Abort, Retry, Ignore, Fail?*, Neil Howe and Bill Strauss define this group of teens and twentysomethings born between 1961 and 1981 as

> "the generation after. Born after 1960 . . . after it all happened." After Boomers. And before the Babies-on-Board of the 1980s, those cuddly tykes deemed too cute and fragile to be left *Home Alone*. Who does that leave stuck in the middle? Eighty million young men and women, ranging in age from 11 to 31. They make up the biggest generation in American history (yes, bigger than the Boom) . . . the only generation born since the Civil War to come of age unlikely to match their parents' economic fortunes; and the only one born this century to grow up personifying (to others) not the advance, but the decline of their society's greatness. (Howe and Strauss 1993, 7; see also Coupland 1991, 1992)

Amy Fisher and her less infamous Long Island cohort of teen girls constitute this "Gen," at least in some recesses of the popular imagination.

While suburbia's founding mythos rests on a white middle-class longing for a homogeneous haven from the racialized, ethnicized, and poverty-stricken urban centers of post–World War II America, at the turn of the millennium, this dreamland, as "The Devil on Long Island" makes clear, has (d)evolved into a place with too much present and not enough possibilities for a future. In a strange variation on this theme, the SWR community thought that it was building a future of privilege precisely by investing everything it had in the present when it embraced the Shoreham Nuclear Power Plant as its ticket to prosperity. The results, as the last chapter delineates, were less than satisfactory. Likewise, in a burgeoning multicultural world, Long Island's intended homogeneity is suffocating itself. How long will white English-speaking suburbanites be able to maintain that cultural differences are not their problem or rather that they themselves are not one among many different cultural groups? How will their children—the 13th Gen/Gen X—function in the global marketplace of ideas and commerce when they can't communicate beyond their communities and can't envision a world that doesn't look like their own? Amy Fisher and her generation of Long Island teens are trapped in the geographic and social narrowness of Long Island. Gen X may be a media fabrication, but it may also be a self-fulfilling prophecy and the outcome of a culture of avoidance that can no longer avoid itself.

In a recent Long Island murder trial involving a pulmonary specialist who confessed to murdering his wife, the doctor's lawyers attempted to convince the jury of what came to be called the "Long Island Defense": "that *living on Long Island itself* was enough to engender homicidal depression severe enough to be exculpatory" (Rosenbaum 1993, 26). The strategy didn't work; the court convicted the doctor, anyway. A character in CBS's version of the Amy Fisher story articulates a similar notion. Here an auto mechanic working in Joey's shop suggests that perhaps Amy suffers from "Mid-Island syndrome," a supposed brain-dementing environmental disease caused by the aboveground electrical wires that line the streets of this part of suburbia. "'It's the wires,' he explains to a TV reporter. . . . 'The wires aren't buried underground like in other parts of the country, so with all this electricity in the air, it fries some people's brains. Mid-Island syndrome—that's what Amy's got'" (Henneberger 1993, A16).

Despite the absurdity of these explanations, they point to a cultural understanding of Long Island as a contaminated and contaminating place that its inhabitants cannot escape.[11] As Rosenbaum points out, geographically Long Island is an isolated dead end; "the only link to the mainland of America from the 516 area code are [sic] the ferries to New London and Bridgeport. *Nothing goes through Long Island to get to somewhere else*" (Rosenbaum 1993, 26). And nothing gets off of Long Island too quickly either, to which the demise of the Shoreham Nuclear Power Plant and its administrator's inability to provide adequate evacuation plans attest. Long Island is literally and figuratively the end of the suburban line.

Given this restrictive geography, Rosenbaum identifies *longing* (word play intended no doubt) as the basis of Long Island's suburban culture. The longing of Amy, Joey, Mary Jo, and the rest of the notorious Long Island suburbanites who have recently called attention to themselves and their communities, including the SWR school board and its political allies, is not a nostalgia for a lost past but a longing for a missing or abandoned future. Rosenbaum concludes his assessment of the Island with a theatrical flourish, one that overdramatically turns this lost future into the nation's imminent future—as Long Island goes so goes the (white suburban) nation. He writes:

> Long Island, after all, was supposed to be the future *before* the future. We always had a head start on the life cycle of suburban baby-boom culture because we were the first-born burbs of the baby boom; a burbland created almost all at once, very fast and virtually ex nihilo, right after the war, a self-contained social organism. An organism whose sociobiological clock started ticking a little earlier than subsequent burbs, and whose shrill alarms now seem to signal that it has raced through its mature stage and is now rocketing headlong into the social-organism equivalent of senile dementia.
>
> And so the America that laughs at Long Island's nonstop Satanist Demolition Derby, the America that looks down on Long Island as something alien, some exotic, carnivalesque pageant separable from its mainstream because it's separate from the mainland, may have to think

> again. May have to learn to say of this unruly island what Prospero said of the unruly Caliban at the close of "The Tempest": "This thing of darkness I acknowledge mine."
>
> Because when America laughs at Long Island, it's laughing in the face of its own onrushing future. (Rosenbaum 1993, 44)

Though perhaps overwrought in its sense of impending social danger, the article's parodic style draws in the reader by calling for a kind of "responsible reading." The Long Island that Rosenbaum describes and its preeminent monster, white, Gen-X, teen-girl transgressor Amy, are the ultimate unlovable subjects, the things one cannot not acknowledge as mine or ours without dire consequences. If Long Island is *our* onrushing future, so is Amy. I use the universal term "our" intentionally; we may not all occupy the same position vis-à-vis Amy, but we all, nonetheless, occupy some position. Thanks to the media and to public interest, Amy and her suburban Long Island have an undeniable presence within the imbroglio of contemporary U.S. culture, whether we like it or not. What is this onrushing future we are so anxious about, enthralled with, and disgusted by? And how do the representations of Amy's story help us recognize who *we* are? Below I examine three different models for representing Amy. While each example purports to define Amy, they do so in the context of actively calling up a particular viewing public. The daughters below set up a house of cultural mirrors. Whose daughter is she? Where do you find yourself reflected in her story? And what is to be done with a problem like Amy, anyway?

Cultural Daughters

The responses surrounding and defining the Fisher-Buttafuoco imbroglio speak of Amy as either everybody's daughter, nobody's daughter, or somebody else's daughter. Respectively, she is someone to fear, someone to disavow, or someone to gawk at. And she is always somebody difficult to love.

EVERYBODY'S DAUGHTER

For those who take on Amy as an adopted daughter, she is an archetype, a prototype, a sign of the times, an artifact of suburbia gone awry, a "lonely '80s middle-class latchkey kid" (Gaines 1992, 39). She is our worst fear and our biggest failure; she is what we have come to; she is "but for the grace of God, there could go any of us."[12] Her story in these accounts stands as a morality tale and a parable with a message for Long Island in particular and white middle-class America in general.

This girl-next-door construction sustains the paperback version of the story, *Lethal Lolita*, by Eftimiades. The true-crime genre works by collapsing the distance between the potential buyers of these hastily produced "real-life" stories and their subjects. The market thrives on this perceived proximity. *Lethal Lolita* includes numerous striking examples of this approach. In the beginning it takes pains to introduce Amy, her family, and her neighborhood as "typical." In describing Amy's world before Joey, Eftimiades writes: "The neighborhood was quiet, tree-lined, an all-white, middle-class enclave near the beach"; she goes on to say that kids rode bicycles up and down the streets, parents cared deeply about their children, and neighbors were friendly but respectful of each other's privacy (Eftimiades 1992, 28). (The quote may sound familiar; the similarities are intentional. See the opening to chapter 1 and my description of Shoreham-Wading River.) Even after the narrative focuses on Amy and her crime, the book periodically reminds the reader that Amy is everybody's daughter (i.e., potentially *your* daughter). When a neighbor, Sally North, comes by to console the Fishers, the book presents the following exchange between Amy's father and Mrs. North:

> As she turned to go, Elliot Fisher stopped her with these chilling words.
> "You have three daughters; be careful," he said. "Keep a close eye on them, because somebody can just come one day and turn them completely around."
> Sally North nodded, her eyes filled with tears. She walked through the backyard to her door. She has played those words over in her head many times since. (145).

Presumably, the reader is also meant to replay these words over and over again in her head.

Like parody, the "true-crime" genre speaks to and evokes a particular audience, in this case, the white, middle-class, heterosexual suburbanite who can occupy this carefully constructed universalistic position without noticing that it is indeed a construction, one that serves a narrative as well as a social purpose. The Amy Fisher tale further defines this "universal" teenage girl, everybody's daughter, as an unlovable subject. In describing Amy, Eftimiades writes:

> By the time she met Joey Buttafuoco, however, Amy Fisher had developed into a young woman who clearly lacked a sense of self-worth and self-determination. Growing up with few limits and generally getting what she wanted made it hard for Amy to cope with rejection and disappointment. She expected things to go her way. "Her parents didn't set down a lot of rules," a close friend said.
> Although she liked to think of herself as much older than her years, in truth Amy Fisher was far more immature than her high-school classmates. Desperate for attention, even negative notice, Amy wanted little more than acceptance from her peers. She was a lonely child who

> grew up to be a lonely young woman, eager to be loved and admired. As the public would eventually learn, this wasn't just any insecure teenager. It was a young girl who acted and reacted on a thin tether of emotion, easily influenced and unable to foresee the consequences of her actions. (Eftimiades 1992, 43)

While proclaiming Amy's atypicalness, Eftimiades actually describes a well-rehearsed cultural stereotype of white middle-class female adolescence. As the story goes, girls lack self-worth (or self-esteem) and self-determination. Consequently, they can't cope with rejection or disappointment, and they are desperate for attention and love. But Amy is typical only insofar as she magnifies what supposedly lurks within the girl next door; she is a trompe l'oeil of teenage girlhood, or what I identify in chapter 6 as a false normal, an insider-Other, someone who can front for normal but ultimately cannot withstand the collective litmus test of normality. To be an effective "everybody's daughter" for the media, Amy must initially be rendered as close to normal as possible. As a white middle-class Long Island teen, Amy has what it takes to be just another suburban girl, but somehow the pieces refuse to cooperate. In rendering Amy's story by emphasizing all its perversions and lurid permutations, the media come to do the opposite: articulate and discipline the norm. If the norm, by its very definition, cannot be addressed directly, taking on the norm head to head calls attention to it, makes it strange, constitutes it as abnormal. Showing how a girl like Amy deviates from the norm ultimately defines what counts as normal. It is the difference between making an object visible by filling in the positive or negative space. A tree is still a tree whether it emerges as a white shape on a dark background or whether it appears as a dark shape on a white background. These two images are not exactly the same, but they are equivalent. In the case of Amy as everybody's daughter, she functions as the dark background defining the otherwise unrepresentable norm.

NOBODY'S DAUGHTER

From another perspective, Amy is totally outside of your familiar world. She is someone to ignore, someone who prompts you to announce that you are ignoring her just in case anyone mistakenly thinks you may be interested; she is mentally disturbed; she is a "borderline personality disorder with narcissistic features."[13] She is a tired stereotype, a cliché, a "willful child whose behavior was unique" (*Newsday* 1992, n.p.). This version of the story disavows its own interest and stake in the narrative. Here, Amy has nothing to say about our values[14] and her story is just "this tacky little affair in Long Island."[15] These accounts exemplify a classic "yes, I know, but" disavowal, and hence represent an irresponsible reading at its most flagrant. For example, ABC News media commentator Jeff Greenfield writes:

> As to why it [the Amy Fisher case] appeals, it's about sex and violence and "Peyton Place." There's no mystery to why people read stories like this. There is absolutely no socially redeeming message here at all and anyone who claims this is about how we live today is a total idiot. This is a scuzzy, get-down-in-the-mud story. It's the same reason people slow down to look at car wrecks, and it's not about what the American family is coming to, or the need for national health insurance or anything like that. . . . There ought to be a disclaimer issued by the media saying we are putting this on because it's smutty and steamy and you can't get enough of it. (*Newsday* 1993, 40)

Greenfield's call for a disclaimer divides up the world into those who know better and those who are void of any sense of propriety ("class"). One cannot disclaim, however, without implicating oneself in the story being told or in the analysis intentionally not being proffered. To suggest that Amy is not about how "we" live today is to demonstrate precisely the opposite. Greenfield doth protest too much. What is at stake in Greenfield's denial is a self-constituting idea of what counts as normal above and beyond the abnormal that Amy Fisher embodies so adeptly. But the norm is a relational category. And denying relationality will not insulate one from having to contend with conflict and the effects of social difference. Greenfield is holding onto a culture of avoidance even as the Amy imbroglio makes clear that this is not a culture worth salvaging.

SOMEBODY ELSE'S DAUGHTER

Amy as somebody else's daughter is the exoticized, ethnicized Amy. She is a member of a neo-"guido" suburban tribe of teenagers. She is an oversexed, lesbian-leaning Amy. She couldn't possibly be *your* daughter, but she may indeed be a daughter of that strange, trashy land known as Long Island. And if you happen to be a Long Islander, she's from that other county (Nassau) or the wrong housing development on the other side of the Island. This is the approach taken in full force in Amy's supposed autobiography, *Amy Fisher: My Story*.

In describing Amy and her friends, the book waxes sociological. *Amy Fisher: My Story* goes to great lengths to ethnicize Amy, and as a result calls attention to its own narrative strategy, inviting the reader to speculate about what's really going on here. Though in the following description there may be elements that bear some resemblance to Amy's social milieu, the framework is, to say the least, ethnically overdetermined. Like the *Saturday Night Live* parodies, this account relies on cultural stereotypes to situate the story and the reader.

> Guidos and guidettes had special ways of dressing their bodies, dressing their cars, and hanging out. It said something about the deep pull of Italian-American heritage (conveniently dovetailing with the popularity of high-bravado hip-hop and rap music) that girls like Lori, Jane, and

> Maria [Amy's "homegirls"] wanted to forsake the all-American image their parents had struggled to lead them to, and emulate instead the strutting Bensonhurst [a section of Brooklyn that is largely an Italian neighborhood] cugines (cousins) whose parents were fresh off the boat. . . .
>
> To cruise Bensonhurst effectively . . . you had to have a "guidomobile": a Cadillac Seville, Lincoln Sports Coupe (LSC), Ford Mustang, Pontiac Trans-Am, Pontiac Firebird or Chevrolet Camaro. The back should be jacked up, the windows tinted, and it had to be outfitted with a state-of-the-art sound system: tweeter, woofer, kicker box, 210 speakers. Sometimes guidos pinstriped their cars with sayings from songs, like "Can't touch this" or "For your eyes only." Guys hung "guido boxes"—big, cheap-looking, ready-made bouquets of plastic ribbons and streamers—on their rearview mirrors. Girls were given their boyfriends' guido bows. Those who didn't have guido bows made do with foam-rubber dice. The parade of ornamented cars, sociologists believe, dates back to the parades of painted wagons of Sicilian farmers; the car bows, to the chivalric practice of knights hanging their ladies' scarves over their battle swords. (Fisher and Weller 1993, 96–97)

The book alternates between sections told in this more distant, objective, analytical tone—the voice of academic authority, or what serves as academic in this popular genre—and sections written supposedly in Amy's voice. In the latter, Amy's lesbian/bisexual proclivities suggest themselves.

> I was seeing a lot of Jane. I'd go by her shop and she'd make me look beautiful. We'd rent video games. We'd drive in to Bensonhurst.
>
> Jane liked to show off how tough she was for me. When she did my hair and face, she touched me and hugged me a lot. Jane paid a lot of attention to me and it made me feel good.
>
> Jane is so pretty. Pretty people: I'm a sucker for them.
>
> I saw the movie everyone was talking about: *Basic Instinct*. Sharon Stone plays this sexy, gorgeous bisexual murderer, Michael Douglas plays this cop who falls in love with her. I was so taken by it, I saw it twice: once with friends; then at a drive-in theater, with Paul [another man with whom Amy was supposedly involved]. The sex scenes made me hot—like they were supposed to, I guess. The second time I saw it, I wasn't wearing underwear—like Sharon Stone wasn't, in the scene where the police take her in for questioning.
>
> She was very cocky and sure of herself in that scene. She made those cops look like jerks.
>
> She got away with everything.
>
> I think Jane saw the movie, too, also probably more than once. (134–135)

Still later Amy "writes":

> Jane always had the best hair—which isn't surprising, since she worked as a colorist and her mom was also a beauty operator. She dyed her hair eggplant and it looked great. I wanted that color for *my* hair. She would hug me and say, "Come by the shop and I'll make you so pretty." She was always hugging me, and she was always making me pretty: tweezing my eyebrows so they arched like hers; gelling my hair so it looked like hers; doing my eyes and my mouth. Jane was very protective of me. If somebody at Eighty-sixth Street said something snide to me—it didn't even have to be as strong as "fuck you"—Jane would give that person a narrow-eyed, deep, deep look and say very calmly, "Don't mess with my girl." I always felt safe after that.
>
> Jane called me her "girl" a lot. In late April she had also started calling me her "wife." At times it sounded like she was trying to talk me into having a really intimate relationship with her. I don't think Lori and Maria ever caught on to that part. (146)[16]

What could be masterful metaparody, however, turns out to be articulated in earnest. *Amy Fisher: My Story* is not performing a critical tour de force so much as absurdly enacting the set of cultural anxieties about the intersections between gender, race, and class that have surrounded and ultimately sustained the media's and public's interest in this case. What is most salient about this book is the way it investigates white middle-class femininity by emphasizing class differences. But class in the United States is tricky business. When asked to which class they belong, 80 percent of Americans will respond "middle" (Fussell 1983, 44). Even a superficial glance at statistics on poverty and wealth suggests otherwise. The fact that a majority of Americans self-identify as middle class indicates that the media, in addressing and largely representing the middle class, or at least an imagined idea of the middle class, effectively constitutes its audience regardless of incomes, job status, education levels, and lifestyles. This is not, in other words, a chicken-and-egg-problem, but a media-fabricated social imaginary. In her study of class in the United States, anthropologist Sherry B. Ortner observes, "class is central to American social life, but it is rarely spoken in its own right. Rather, it is represented through other categories of social difference: gender, ethnicity, race, and so forth" (Ortner 1991, 164). If it is difficult to speak directly of class in America, especially middle-classness, and if most people uncritically see themselves as part of a rather amorphous and hence universalistic and culturally neutral middle, how indeed are the media to articulate Amy's class position? In ethnicizing Amy, the media displace issues of class onto her Italian Americanness, a marker of lower-middle or working-class status as the stereotype goes, especially in its Queens and Brooklyn versions. Depicting

Amy as an ethnic white confuses her class positioning and makes it possible for the white middle class to feel protected from her flagrant class transgressions.

These representations of Amy also tend to bring up issues of parenting in what amount to admonishments against promiscuous middle-class disciplinary practices. Who, after all, if not her parents, is responsible for sixteen-year-old Amy's adventures in guido and guidette territory, beyond the supposedly safeguarded boundaries of Long Island? Barbara Ehrenreich observes that one of the major characteristics distinguishing the middle class is its ever-present anxiety about slipping below its accustomed standard of living. According to Ehrenreich, "What defines [the middle class] is its children, or rather the problem of its children. . . . In other classes, membership is transmitted by simple inheritance. . . . We may be born into the middle class, but we are expected to spend almost thirty years of our lives establishing ourselves as members of that class in good standing" (Ehrenreich 1989, 73, 75–76). Whether or not a person achieves this standing rests in part on middle-class parenting, on the transmission of middle-class values and cultural attributes to children born of the middle class. Therefore, discussions of class get displaced onto discussions of parenting, with permissiveness being a sign of everything that is wrong with the postwar middle class (Ehrenreich 1989, 68–74). Here, Eftimiades's characterization of Amy as a girl who grew up with few limits—"She expected things to go her way. 'Her parents didn't set down a lot of rules.'"—resonates, as do anecdotes that include examples of Amy's parents appeasing her with extravagant consumer items like a new Dodge Daytona on her sixteenth birthday.

Amy lives out the middle-class's fear of falling. But by ethnicizing her story, *Amy Fisher: My Story* ostensibly makes Amy someone for whom the de-ethnicized, fully white middle class does not have to take responsibility. She has, in a sense, been kidnapped (as the result of indulgent parenting) into this underworld of guidos, guidettes, car mechanics, and lesbians and is no longer in the purview of the middle class. She becomes somebody else's daughter in the popular imagination so that the suburban middle class does not have to claim her as their own, does not have to recognize her as their unlovable daughter. This approach sacrifices Amy in the name of protecting the middle class. It keeps under wraps the fact that the middle class does indeed have a cultural perspective, by which I mean a set of historically recognizable values that translate into social attitudes and aspirations. In order to raise Amy back into the middle class, the attitudes, aspirations, values, and everyday decorums of the middle class would have to be articulated clearly. Given the intentional ineffableness of middle-class life, it is no doubt easier and safer to let Amy fall by the suburban wayside by pawning her off as somebody else's daughter. But Amy's status as somebody else's daughter does not go unchallenged. The ways in which she transgresses middle-class femininity, in the end, more fully ensconce her and her story in a narrative about what it means to be middle class, what it means to occupy an anxiety-ridden cultural position where middle-class girls are made and not simply something to take for granted.

The Greenhouse Effect

How white middle-class girls are made is a concern that drives the narrative of this book in general. If middle-class parenting is about reproducing class attitudes, practices, and at times cultural misunderstandings in suburban daughters then one needs to consider the environment in which this reproduction occurs. In the first chapter, middle-class reproduction took place in the context of a community having to face the effects of its own culture of avoidance. Without the resources that the nuclear power plant provided, SWR will not so much be able to reproduce itself in its children as replicate the cultural practices that got it into this unenviable position in the first place: witness its daughters' moral confusions and awkward attempts to deflect and avoid difference. This culture and its contiguous media counterpart, the one Amy inhabits, resemble that of an overgrown greenhouse, an enclosed system that thrives on a certain insularity up to a point. The suburban greenhouse is a place of cultural replication as opposed to reproduction. In the reproductive model children come from but are also different from their parents; in a replicating system, children are their parents. Replication takes place in a culture in stasis and, hence, a culture in danger. Long Island is its own greenhouse. And Amy is a product of the replication process.

I borrow this notion of a cultural greenhouse from Marilyn Strathern's study of the making of the English middle class. She names the class that inhabits and consequently perpetuates the suburban greenhouse the "plasti-class . . . after its preferred mode of credit display" (Strathern 1992, 142). Strathern analyzes the ascent of this plasti-class (an apt moniker for Long Island's late-twentieth-century mall-going middle class as well) by tracing historical shifts in cultural understandings of the relationship between nature and society to show how the middle class came to see itself as a people without culture or perspective. Early in its history, the English middle class saw itself in a close reproductive relationship with nature. The middle-class kinship system, for example, found itself mirrored in nature, not culture. Hence the dominant heterosexual order of the middle class appeared natural and beyond reproach or interpretation. But by the late twentieth century, the period Strathern calls "After Nature," concepts of nature began to shift, as more and more of the so-called natural world found itself endangered by the so-called cultural world. Culture, in other words, began consuming nature and began replicating rather than reproducing itself. Strathern explains: "But what does one do with the idea of cultural replication?

Of self-consumption? If the question seems claustrophobic, this is greenhouse heat. Nature does not represent or model this new reproductive process; on the contrary, it is the substantive entity that is being eaten up without being regenerated. In some present visions of nature, consumption has become the very antithesis of reproduction" (171). Within this world of replication, the individual vanishes and the consumer takes his or her place. By designating this phenomenon as After Nature, Strathern underscores that nature, something that was once understood to exist as a fact outside of cultural relations, can no longer be taken for granted and can only be understood as a construct, something that can be made and unmade. Such a world has no Truths, no absolutes, no guarantees.

Amy Fisher and her Long Island, like Strathern's plasti-class, give the lie to the claim that the middle class is a naturally occurring phenomenon. Amy's story deftly demonstrates that suburbia is chock-full of perspective, that suburbia is overburdened by its own culture and drowning in its willful lack of critical self-awareness. Its self-knowledge is narcissistic, self-absorbed, and ultimately self-devouring. From the moment the media made Amy the headline-grabbing "Teen Fatal Attraction" and "Long Island's Lethal Lolita," they lifted the lid off the suburban hothouse known as Long Island, providing, perhaps unintentionally, a vantage point from which to name, and hence displace, the as yet and intentionally unspeakable perspective of this middle-class suburbia.

Looking in on this greenhouse, one sees not only suburbia consuming suburbia but the tabloids consuming suburbia consuming the tabloids. Amy replicated recent Hollywood blockbusters about white, middle-class, heterosexual, suburban angst, including films like *Fatal Attraction* (1980, directed by Adrian Lyne), *The Hand That Rocks the Cradle* (1992, directed by Chris Hanson), *Basic Instinct* (1992, directed by Paul Verhoeven), *Single White Female* (1992, directed by Barbet Schroeder), and real-life fatal attractions like the Carolyn Warmus murder-affair.[17] Not only did the media's obsession with Amy, Joey, and Mary Jo affect the actual course of events in the case as well as the legal strategies used in the various courtroom battles that ensued, it also insidiously created its own self-contained (greenhouse) industry. In November of 1994, the *Donahue* show featured a large panel of guests all of whom had gotten rich quick or had at least achieved a degree of notoriety and fame by exploiting Amy and Joey. These included tabloid author Maria Eftimiades, who sold her paperback version of the story for $100,000; the off-Broadway director Bill Weiler, who turned the story and hype into a traveling theatrical production, *Amy Fisher: The Musical*; the lawyer Joseph Moro, who produced the Amy and Joey comic book that helped make his First Amendment Publishing company a monetary success; several Joey and Amy look-alikes, who had been known to receive at least $1500 to appear at local social events in character; and Paula Fishman, who was "simply" in the audience when Joey and Mary Jo appeared on *Donahue* in January 1993. In the course of this earlier broadcast, Paula stood up and confronted Mary Jo, suggesting that "if it looks like a snake, talks like a snake, and walks like a snake . . . it is a snake" (the "it" in this case being Joey, or at least part of his anatomy). Not only did this comment turn into headline news, it also catapulted Paula into a career as a model and actress. As she stated on the 1994 program, "They [the agents] called me, I didn't call them." This later *Donahue* broadcast makes clear that the Amy and Joey story added fuel to the already sweltering, overgrown media greenhouse: a contained environment, which when left to its own devices cannibalistically feeds off itself feeding off itself creating a cultural imbroglio, an imbricated media extravaganza that knows no limits and, it seems, no shame. The show also underscores the degree to which this greenhouse fosters incestuous relations and vengeful lusts in defiance of responsible readings, ones that love rather than exploit the unlovable subject.

Writing and Reading in the Greenhouse

In many respects, this greenhouse is unavoidable. To write about Amy or teen girls more generally is to be part of the extravaganza, to add heat to the greenhouse effect. In writing from within this greenhouse, I cannot simply present a clever exegesis of the story, I cannot peel away cultural layers in search of a meaningful core. There is no core to the greenhouse, only an endless cycle of cultural processes and media representations. In foregrounding and in a sense embracing the excesses of Amy's story, I am searching for ways to acknowledge this thing of darkness as mine and to understand how I am implicated in this cultural analysis of Amy and her Long Island sisters.

While Strathern's imagery of the greenhouse and her history of the middle class offers ways of understanding what goes on inside suburban culture, I turn to another model to help me consider ways to configure myself in relation to this self-replicating social arena, namely Pandora's box. In an essay that attempts to map out strategies for feminist cultural analysis, film critic Laura Mulvey argues that once the lid is lifted off of Pandora's box, there is no clear inside or outside, there is only an in-between, an ambiguous space. Mulvey begins her essay with an epigraph from Gaston Bachelard's *The Poetics of Space*: "Chests, especially small caskets, over which we have more complete mastery, are objects that may be opened. When a casket is closed, it is returned to the general community of objects; it takes its place in exterior space. But it opens! . . . From the moment the casket is opened the dialectics of inside and outside no longer exist. The outside is effaced with one stroke" (Mulvey 1992, 53). Mulvey focuses on this notion of the "dialectics of inside and outside" to suggest ways of transforming feminist criticism into "feminist decipherment" or "curiosity." To decipher is to figure out the displacements and denials at stake in a cultural narrative rather than, once and for all, to peel away layers that conceal a core, an essence, "a long lost femininity," "a virgin state" (60). It is, in the manner described above in "Nobody's Daughter," to look at the negative as much as the positive space of a representation or narrative. To see the inside and outside as symbiotic. Given that Amy's story is built on displacements, denials, and ineffable longings, and that Amy's willful sexuality disallows any attempt to construct her simply as a victim, an innocent, a lost virgin, Amy's story lends itself to being deciphered rather than simply interpreted. However, I would caution against a notion of full disclosure and suggest instead that the act of deciphering, like love, is a never-ending process. There is no final decipherment to be attained. Instead, to decipher is to launch an ongoing critical investigation, to remain engaged with one's subject.

In the myth, Zeus forbids Pandora to open the box, warning her of the danger within. But Pandora—an unlovable subject herself, a consummate insider-Other, if you will—refuses to be controlled and contained by the rules designating inside and out. She opens the box. She gives way to curiosity. In this regard, Pandora stands for the feminist cultural critic, or more specifically in terms of this book, the feminist autoethnographer of the suburban teen girl, the one who ventures to inhabit an unlovable land and engage the unlovable subject to demonstrate that the transgressions of a girl like Amy were always contained within the every day, the normal, the supposedly safe, private, domestic, sanitized, and feminized space of the suburban white middle class.

Suburbia is not a gentle place. If suburbia is the domesticated, feminine, interior space, the space of presumed stability and security as opposed to the urban public arena of masculinity, capital, competition, and conflict (read violence), Amy, Joey, and Mary Jo, as well as Long Island itself make it all too clear that this notion of suburbia turns out to be the exterior to a kind of suburban Pandora's box, a place where the feminine conceals histories of exclusion, disavowal, betrayal, and domesticated violence. Amy's story, in all its unruliness, refuses to perpetuate the deceptions of suburbia. Here, the feminine appears vengeful and violent, conniving and complicit. In standing by her man, for example, Mary Jo personifies this complicity. Mary Jo is as much Joey's maker as she is Amy's victim. Likewise, in revealing the underside of suburbia, Amy's story begins to give the lie to Long Island's domesticated middle-class narrative. This is not a safe and conflict-free land, no matter what the myth about suburbia attempts to perpetuate.

Amy, as a modern-day Pandora, garners so much attention because the Fisher-Buttafuoco triangle is symptomatic of the instability of suburban conjugal heterosexuality, the bedrock of the suburban nuclear family. The institution of middle-class heterosexuality is what is at stake here and condensed into a figure like Amy. Like Strathern's late-twentieth-century nature, it is what needs protection; it is the natural thing that turns out to be so unnatural. Conjugal, domestic, suburban heterosexuality can no longer be understood as natural because as the Amy-Joey imbroglio demonstrates, it is in dire need of protection and policing. The next chapter explores this theme even further, again demonstrating the degree to which teen girls in suburbia are made to carry the cultural burden of normal heterosexuality. The popular lexicon surrounding white middle-class teen girls largely turns on questions of sexuality. If gender is the term that marks suburban teen girls as outside the norm, their sexualities become the lightning rod for reining them back into the status quo. Cheryl Pierson, one of the daughters in chapter 3, also lifts the lid off the suburban greenhouse, disrupting its ability to replicate itself and in the process, perhaps, like Amy, offering a way for me and by extension my readers to critically inhabit the space of the insider-Other. As an autoethnographer, I am already an insider-Other, but I need girls like Amy and Cheryl to help me see past the inside. From the perspective of the analyzed insider-Other, it is no longer possible to take suburban life, the norm, white middle-class America for granted, nor is it possible to position oneself as a disengaged outsider—the boundary between inside and out bears no relevance, Pandora's box is already open. This autoethnography of white middle-class suburban teen girlhood is not a self-fulfilling prophecy in the way that media discussions of the 13th Gen and Gen X are. It is closer to the *SNL* parodies in that it describes and renders the lives of teen girls and suburbia in the double voice of an insider and a concerned outsider. By loving the unlovable, by engaging the insider-Other, by acknowledging this thing of darkness as mine, I confront the culture of avoidance that has taken its toll on its suburban daughters. Though Pandora may have released the evils of the world when she defiantly opened her box, the myth does not end there, for Pandora's box is not left empty; in place of the unleashed evils, hope remains. In trying to name what lies in the wake of girls like Amy, Cheryl, Emily, and their SWR counterparts this book attempts to offer its own version of hope.

Chapter 3 Justify My Love

The Heterosexuality of Teenage Girlhood

Dora
In the first bloom of youth—a girl of intelligent and engaging looks. . . . [s]he was clearly satisfied neither with herself nor with her family. . . . One day her parents were thrown into a state of great alarm by finding . . . a letter in which she took leave of them because, as she said, she could no longer endure her life.
—Sigmund Freud, *Dora*

Cheryl Pierson was an old-fashioned girl . . . she did not drink or smoke or parade around in strange revealing clothes. She had never been in trouble or shown even the most remote signs of delinquency. Cheryl still slept with a teddy bear at night. She had never been to a discotheque. She believed in God. She still was unclear how babies were born. She had never tried marijuana. The most important thing in her life was her family. . . . This was the girl who paid a classmate $400 to murder her father—and whom society could judge only by breaking—
—Dena Kleiman, *A Deadly Silence*

THE ABOVE PASSAGES adorn the teaser pages of the paperback versions of the stories of two girls: one, Sigmund Freud's "Dora," a girl growing up among the bourgeoisie of Vienna at the turn of the twentieth century; [1] the other, Cheryl Pierson, a teenager living in a white middle-class neighborhood on suburban Long Island during the late 1980s.[2] Both girls are consummate unlovable subjects, whose stories are about what it means to be a daughter of privilege and denizens of cultures of avoidance.

Dora's story takes place in the context of a burgeoning modern middle-class order.[3] While Freud and his historical period had working understandings of childhood, puberty, and adulthood, in the telling of this case, Freud struggles to map out the distance between Dora's girlhood and her womanhood, or what has come to be known as the teenage years, marked largely by its "discovery" of sexuality. As rendered by Freud, Dora is the archetype of female adolescence, or more specifically white middle-class femininity in its nascent stages. As a modern science of the bourgeois self, psychoanalysis is one of the founding discourses of white middle-classness. And female adolescence is one of its by-products. Specifically, psychoanalysis came to define the (gendered) self in terms of the development of desire in the context of familial relations, or what Freud called the "Oedipus complex." At its most basic level, the Oedipus model describes the process whereby girls learn to identify with their mothers and (unconsciously) desire their fathers and boys learn to identify with their fathers and (unconsciously) desire their mothers. It is a model of how, when successful, the bourgeois self becomes the gendered heterosexual individual. When not successful, as the story goes, psychosis and hysteria—or the symptomatic expression of anxiety in physical illness or compulsive behavior—present themselves. Freud largely developed his theories by analyzing the stories of hysterical (white) girls or young women. Dora stands as one of the prime subjects of study in this theoretical enterprise. Indeed, Freud himself developed a kind of obsession with Dora, one that seems to have triggered a similar fascination in others, in what turns out to be a kind of academic version of the media blitz surrounding girls like Amy, and as we'll see below, Cheryl.[4]

I turn to Dora's case because it is a foundational text in the annals of white middle-class female adolescence. Through it teenage girlhood gets tied to the production of conjugal heterosexuality and white middle-class patriarchy. Indeed these institutions seem to rest on at least the appearance of a normative female adolescence. As we saw by the end of the last chapter, an undercurrent of this connection began to surface in Amy's story. Though Amy did not literally violate the terms of the Oedipus model, her sexual relationship with the older married man, Joey, certainly disregarded its main prohibitions—the girl is supposed to desire the father unconsciously; she is not supposed to act on any lustful urges; similarly, the father is not supposed to pursue the daughter, and the bourgeois couple (father and mother, Joey and Mary Jo) is to remain inviolate. In lifting the lid off of the suburban greenhouse, Amy's story revealed that the compulsory heterosexuality that undergirds white middle-class America is a kind of self-consuming institution that has reached its limits.[5] Amy's is a case of excess and parody; Dora's is a case of excess and hysteria (in the normal teen girl, parody and hysteria are ultimately almost interchangeable modes of self-presentation and -preservation; see chapter 4); and both girls expose the unnaturalness of the extant white middle-class heterosexual order. Below, I look at the way Dora's case defines female adolescence in relation to questions of heterosexuality and patriarchy and then turn to a more contemporary story of Long Island teen girlhood, where a latter-day crisis of the Oedipal model again surfaces in relation to a teenage girl, namely Cheryl Pierson. Cheryl's story bridges the gap between Dora's hysteria and Amy's parody and shows how much rests on white middle-class girlhood.

Though neither Dora's nor Cheryl's story explicitly raises questions of race and whiteness (they are clear-cut about class and gender), considered in relation to the history of suburbia and Long Island presented in the previous two chapters and to the connection between (hetero)sexuality and race developed in chapter 6, the latent racial positioning of both girls becomes a salient feature.[6] I am arguing throughout this book that middle-classness is a racialized category. This is not to propose, however, that everyone who is middle class is white and vice versa, but that there is an historical and discursive link between the two concepts, especially in the context of the rise of the bourgeoisie in Europe at the turn of the twentieth century and in relation to post–World War II suburbia and its aftermath—Dora's and Cheryl's social landscapes, respectively. In analyzing white middle-class femininity it is difficult, if not impossible, to keep all the salient identity categories in the foreground at all times, especially when those positions function through a kind of anonymity or disappearing act (i.e., white middle-classness, the norm, thrives on not being recognized or named). The various parodies in Amy's case enunciated and elaborated on different aspects of her identity, with class sometimes taking precedence over race or ethnicity over gender, and so forth. The model gives us pieces of the puzzle, but one piece does not tell the whole story. It is through the analysis of several parodies and numerous stories that one can begin to draw the necessary connections as well as give substance to each social fragment. It is in this spirit that I use Dora's and Cheryl's cases to highlight and analyze the relationship among questions of *class*, *heterosexuality*, and *female adolescence*. Though (middle-class) whiteness itself is merely implied here, it is not insignificant and should be read as the silent partner in the above triumvirate.

In a similar vein, there is a shadow character in both Dora's and Cheryl's stories, namely the figure of the father or in its less-personalized form that of white middle-class patriarchy. In the case of Dora, the role of the father is played by Dora's actual father, who lurks in the background of the text; Herr K., an older man, with whom Dora has had apparently some sexual contact; and Freud himself, with Freud taking on the primary position, though not necessarily consciously, of the patriarch. In Cheryl's story her real father is played by a corpse, and the figurative father, the voice of society, the patriarch is played by a judge at Cheryl's sentencing hearing. In both cases, the girls' mothers are virtually absent, rendering them socially insignificant in their teenage daughters' lives and making this a father-daughter world. Each narrative attempts to protect the figure of the father, deflecting any critique Dora's or Cheryl's stories could successfully launch against a heterosexual patriarchal order. This chapter analyzes how the representations of these cases accomplish this, demonstrating how these are not just stories about two hysterical girls so much as they are the stories of white middle-class patriarchy's dependency on its daughters.

Daddy's Little Girls

Dora's story begins with her father. He brings Dora to Freud for analysis when she is eighteen years old, after he has discovered a suicide note she had written, and after she has experienced her first attack of loss of consciousness. Three months later, Dora ends the analysis of her own volition. In the course of the treatment, Dora tells Freud that her father is having an affair with Frau K. and that Frau K.'s husband, Herr K., kissed her when she was fourteen and made similar sexual advances toward her when she was sixteen. As noted above, Dora's mother appears largely absent from Dora's life, indeed from the family's life in general. Based on Dora's and her father's separate accounts of Dora's mother, Freud concludes that the mother suffers from "housewife's psychosis": she obsessively cleans her house at the cost of estranging herself from her husband and children. Dora and subsequently Freud in the course of the case history negotiate this complex web of love and sexuality within Dora's family and their bourgeois social circle. Dora presents numerous somatic (hysterical) symptoms, including aphonia, nervous asthma, coughing, migraines, bed-wetting, and an imaginary pregnancy. Freud attempts to fully grasp the origin of these abnormalities by interpreting two of Dora's dreams: in the first, Dora dreams that her house catches on fire while she is asleep in bed and that her father wakes up and saves her; in the second, she dreams that her father dies and she must travel home to attend his funeral (an unconscious patricide to Cheryl's conscious staging of the same act; see below).

In the media, Cheryl's story begins on the corpse of her father's murdered body. In the early morning of 5 February 1986, James Pierson—widower of Cathleen and father of nineteen-year-old James Jr., sixteen-year-old Cheryl, and eight-year-old JoAnn—was shot dead in his driveway on his way to work. Eight days later, exactly one year after Cathleen had died from a six-year battle with a kidney disease, the local police charged Cheryl with second-degree murder for hiring a high-school classmate, Sean Pica, to kill her father in exchange for $1,000. (Before their arrests Cheryl had paid Sean only $400 of what she owed him.) In police custody, Cheryl confessed to arranging the murder, explaining that her father had sexually abused her since she was eleven and that she had recently become fearful that he was going to start abusing her younger sister.

For the next four years, Cheryl's story received much local and national media attention, a display only to be surpassed later by the coverage of the Amy Fisher imbroglio. In this sense, Cheryl is Amy's media big sister, but the little sister here eventually outdoes her older sibling. Why? I can only speculate that Cheryl's story with its incest and patricide may be too hot even for this suburban greenhouse. In other words, Cheryl's story may actually be more threatening to the status quo (compulsory white middle-class heterosexuality) than Amy's tale of attempted murder and statutory rape. Headline versions of Cheryl's story in Long Island's *Newsday* and the *New York Times* ranged from "Homeroom Hit Man" to "Cheryl Pierson: Haven't I Been Punished Enough?" to "The Last Taboo: Case on L.I. Pierces the Silence on Incest." The *New York Times Magazine* ran a feature on the case, "Murder on Long Island," and the ABC TV-news magazine *20/20* and the CNN talk show *Larry King Live* aired segments on the story. A mass market paperback called *A Deadly Silence: The Ordeal of Cheryl Pierson: A Case of Incest and Murder*, by Dena Kleiman (the reporter who covered the story for the *New York Times*), later became the basis of an ABC TV movie-of-the-week, *A Deadly Silence* (1989, directed by John Patterson for Robert Greenwald Productions, Inc.). In professional legal journals, Cheryl figured in articles arguing that a history of incest serves as justifiable grounds for homicide (Chambers 1986; Blodgett 1987; Moreno 1989). And eventually, Cheryl's story won a prominent place within the archives of Long Island's social history. On 14 October 1990, *Newsday* featured a reprint of a 9 March 1986 article on Cheryl in its commemorative issue, *Celebrating Fifty Years of Newsday and Long Island*, which announced, "of the several murders that shocked Long Island in the '80s, perhaps the most provocative was the incest-triggered slaying of James Pierson Sr. by a classmate of his 16–year-old daughter, Cheryl" (Perlman and Durkin 1990, 69). Still later, Cheryl played second fiddle only to Amy Fisher's notorious bad-girl act in the *New York Times Magazine*'s "The Devil in Long Island" (Rosenbaum 1993; see chapter 2 for a detailed discussion of this essay). By including Cheryl's story in its popular record of the region, the local press acknowledged Cheryl as one of the homegrown "things of darkness" constituting the culture of Long Island. Cheryl, like Amy, is part of Long Island lore, where the white middle-class teen girl in all her feminized, unruly glory stands for everything that is wrong with this suburban greenhouse.[7]

When She Was Good, She Was Very, Very Good, but When She Was Bad, She Was Horrid

Both Cheryl and Dora function as ambiguous unlovable daughters. They are "bad girls" because they take matters into their own hands and thereby reveal the inadequacies of the adult worlds through which they travel. They refuse to perform as their respective social settings expect young girls to behave. Cheryl will not play the dependent, young, female victim who turns to sanctioned (adult) familial, educational, and social-service institutions for protection and help. Dora repeatedly refutes Freud's analyses and eventually leaves him with just a fragment of a case history. Similarly, in both stories the authorities (Freud in Dora's case and lawyers and a judge in Cheryl's) and the girls' families and friends suspect that the girls know more than young girls are supposed to know about matters of sexuality. How and why Dora and Cheryl have lost their sexual naiveté becomes the ground upon which both cases articulate relative norms of female adolescence. But they are also "good girls": Cheryl is the sweet, popular high-school cheerleader, the attentive older sister, and the dutifully helpful daughter around everyday household chores; and Dora is the appealing, intelligent companion to her father, her father's friends, and their children. This ambiguity and the familial dramas upon which it is embedded catapult Dora's and Cheryl's stories into the public imagination. As unlovable icons, not unlike Amy Fisher, Cheryl and Dora evoke horror, disbelief, and sympathy as well as pleasure, as they transgress the boundaries of femininity, youth, the nuclear family, and conjugal, consensual heterosexuality. They are the enemy within, the insider-Other, the girls we cannot not love without consequences.

Numerous accounts of their stories, wittingly or not, demonstrate how the unlovable subject is precisely a trickster good-girl, bad-girl figure, someone who draws us in while at the same time making us recoil in, at best, discomfort, a feeling that comes from recognizing the Self within the unlovable insider-Other. Such a relationship between the good-girl Self and the bad-girl Other is not always easy to admit to oneself or reconcile to one's politics or social conscience. But it is also not easy to turn your back on. For example, in a feminist dramatization of Dora's case, Hélène Cixous presents Dora as a volatile and contradictory figure by turns shrill and demure. She is both the defiant feminist voice standing up to her father, Herr K., and Freud, and she is also the voice of deceit and defeat, betraying her mother for her father's mistress, Frau K. (Cixous 1983). It is this ambiguity and the duality of Freud's own position as the insightful and yet at times foiled analyst/patriarch in the case that seems to attract Dora's feminist audience. She is both an icon and an iconoclast for the feminist and the patriarchal cultures she simultaneously inhabits. Likewise, her story demonstrates that feminism and patriarchy, like the inside and outside of Pandora's box, like the Self and the Other of identity politics, exist in a symbiotic and dialectical relationship.

Cheryl also garners attention because she is neither all good nor all bad. In an interview with Larry King, on CNN's *Larry King Live*, reporter Kleiman explains: "You know, I wanted to like Cheryl Pierson. When I heard about this story, my heart went out to her, and my heart still goes out to her, but she is a hard person to like. She has no remorse, she's very cold, she's very manipulative. Cheryl Pierson is a liar and a sneak" (*Larry King Live*, aired 20 April 1990). But unlike the feminist critic who seems to delight in Dora's ambiguities and unlovableness, the popular media desire a more lovable subject. It is difficult for Kleiman to accept that Cheryl is perhaps both a bad girl and a good girl—a complex unlovable suburban daughter. Though the two positions are not mutually exclusive, numerous reactions to Cheryl's case manifest a desire to keep both goodness and badness categorically separate and hence to reproduce an untainted vision of the suburban greenhouse, to keep Long Island's Pandora's box shut. For Marilyn Adams, Cheryl's paternal aunt, Cheryl's integrity rests on one lie. If Cheryl lied about one thing, then she fabricated everything else. The following exchange took place between Kleiman, Adams, and King during the April television segment:

> MS. KLEIMAN: At the time that Cheryl was arrested and she told police why she had had her father killed, she told them also that she was pregnant with her father's baby. She was pregnant.
>
> MS. ADAMS: She made a very important statement that—
>
> KING: That was a lie.
>
> MS. ADAMS: Yes, it was her father's child, and that's how she was going to prove the sexual abuse. Well, it just turned out to be that it wasn't her father's child, it was her boyfriend's child, so, I guess the sexual abuse was a lie.(King 1990, 4)

In the end, Kleiman reconciles the contradictions or, at the very least, ignores them, becoming one of Cheryl's most consistent advocates in the media. Perhaps she figured out a way to love the unlovable subject. On the other hand, all accounts show Adams abandoning Cheryl. Initially, Cheryl and her sister, JoAnn, moved in with Adams and the Pierson's paternal grandmother. This living arrangement quickly became intolerable for all involved. Subsequently, Cheryl moved in with former neighbors of her parents, the Kossers, who various accounts present as first and foremost loyal friends to Cheryl's mother, Cathleen. Aside from the Kossers, the relatives and family friends appearing in Cheryl's story are all paternal connections. Cathleen and her family are portrayed, at best, as ineffective and, at worst, as responsible for James's abusive behavior. In the latter version, if Cathleen had not fallen terminally ill, James would not have turned to his daughter for sexual comfort, and the Piersons would have remained a happy, hard-working, nuclear family. By casting Cheryl's story as a mother-daughter drama, this approach leaves James Pierson's agency in the matter and his role as the powerful patriarch unscathed. But given the terms of the case, this is a rather implausible plot. Instead, the father-daughter drama more typically gets written as the story of an unlovable teenage girl and not of a criminally negligent, sexually predatory father. The results of either narration—mother-daughter plot or bad-daughter scenario—are unfortunately the same, and the transgressor (the unlovable teen daughter) once again is thwarted in her attempts to disrupt the underlying normative suburban order because the role of the patriarch remains intact.

Sex and the Teenage Girl

This narrative move to "blame the victim" is the oldest trick in the book of gender and gender construction even in texts that purport to be more critical than productive of the status quo. In *The History of Sexuality*, for example, Michel Foucault investigates the proliferation of discourses on the emerging sexualities of children and adolescents in the eighteenth and nineteenth centuries, drawing a relationship between the act of talking about sex, monitoring sexualities, and the production of a normative sexual order. By articulating prohibitions against the expression of sexuality (like masturbation, for example) and disciplining children accordingly, Foucault argues that modern culture finds a way to actively define, produce, and talk excessively about the very thing that is supposed to remain unspoken: sex. However, in the process, Foucault—not unlike the media, the courts, the family, and the medical, psychiatric, and social-service agencies in Cheryl's case and Freud in Dora's—ignores the specific uses and abuses of power that operate when heterosexuality emerges in relation to teenage girls and adult males.[8]

In elaborating his position, Foucault tells the story of a farmhand in the late nineteenth century who apparently molested a girl at the border of a field. Foucault's description of the incident oddly conflates the farmhand with "the village urchins" and makes the girl responsible for the farmhand's actions. These parallel moves erase the age difference as well as the probable social and class differences (her parents, as will become clear below, have access to the existing power structure) between the girl and the itinerant farmworker, while minimizing his agency in the encounter. The text states: "At the border of a field, he had obtained a few caresses from a little girl, just as he had done before and seen done by the village urchins round about him" (Foucault 1980, 31). The story concludes when the girl's parents turn in the farmhand to the mayor, the gendarmes, a judge, a doctor, and two other "experts," who indict him for his crime, study him for signs of degeneracy, acquit him, and yet sentence him to a life under medical surveillance in a hospital. What interests Foucault in this matter is the

> pettiness of it all; the fact that this everyday occurrence in the life of village sexuality, these inconsequential bucolic pleasures, could become from a certain time, the object not only of collective intolerance but of a judicial action, a medical intervention, a careful clinical examination, and an entire theoretical elaboration. . . . So it was that our society—

> and it was doubtless the first in history to take such measures—assembled around these timeless gestures, these barely furtive pleasures between simple-minded adults and alert children, a whole machinery for speechifying, analyzing, and investigating. (31–32)

Here, Foucault bespeaks his disinterest in the young girl's well-being in this heterosexual encounter across genders, generations, and social-economic positions.[9] The move reverberates through Dora's and Cheryl's stories, where Dora's father and Freud and later Cheryl's mother, her neighbors, extended family, and teachers avert their attentions away from the improprieties being perpetrated against their "daughters" by trusted male authority figures—Herr K. in Dora's case, James Pierson in Cheryl's—choosing instead to hold the girls responsible for the socially disruptive situations that result. However, it is important to note that in the farmhand story, the male perpetrator does not walk away from the imbroglio scot free as most of the other male figures in this chapter appear to accomplish. As a "simple-minded," itinerant farmworker, this male is an Other in the girl's bourgeois social milieu. Consequently, unlike Dora's or Cheryl's, this young girl's sexuality needs to be protected from a socially contaminating (lower-class) presence. What is of utmost concern here is the successful reproduction of the bourgeois order and not the protection of the girl's libidinous desires; these need to be disciplined as much as the farmhand's social transgressions.

What Foucault does not account for in this story is the technology of (bourgeois female) adolescence:[10] the way stories, social rules, and common knowledge define, naturalize, and institutionalize adolescence as a liminal period in the human life cycle between childhood and adulthood, where girls in particular are caught between being and not being sexual beings. The situation for boys is less severe, or at least figured differently; boys are encouraged culturally to be (hetero)sexually active; if they are not they draw suspicion and attract ridicule. Cheryl's and Dora's cases portray girls caught in the double bind of adolescent girlhood. Adolescence is the time when girls are supposed to know and not supposed to know about sex. Adolescence teaches girls to be heterosexual women while enjoining them to remain innocent. Teen love, heterosexual dating, and sexual fantasy function as reassuring, nonthreatening markers of female heterosexuality. Girls need to stage a kind of heterosexual public performance (parody), but they better not be practicing sexual subjects. In the farmhand story, it is supposedly the "little girl" who caresses the interloper. The fact that he, rather than she, is punished suggests that class, age, and gender differences do indeed play a salient role in the making of bourgeois girls. The lower-class, adult male is subject to a life of surveillance; the text is silent about the little girl's future; her surveillance is perhaps more internal. Unlike the little girl's advances toward the farmhand, Cheryl's sexual agency with regard to her boyfriend—who is of the same age and class—gets her into trouble. Cheryl's pregnancy by her boyfriend undeniably violates the rule that white middle-class girls should be heterosexual, but not really sexually active. Therefore, the narrators of Cheryl's story and the arbiters of her case, depending on whose side they are on, are forced to either work overtime to portray her sexual naiveté (desexualize her) or present her as blatantly violating the acceptable rules of conduct and desire for teenage girls. Ultimately, the court, her family, and her suburban community are more disturbed by her precocious sexuality than by her father's abuse.

Given Foucault's insistence on the relationship between speaking about sex and the making of sexual subjects, it seems necessary to consider: Who gets to be a qualified speaker? Who is silenced? And what can be heard in those silences? Both Cheryl's and Dora's stories rest on these questions. Cheryl's status as either a victim or a cold-blooded, unremorseful father-killer pivots on the fact that prior to the police investigation, Cheryl did not tell anyone about the sexual abuse, except for her boyfriend Rob Cuccio, and then only after he confronted her directly. Ironically, when seen in the context of the culture of avoidance and moral minimalism that bred a girl like Cheryl and made her father's sexual violations possible, Cheryl's silence is perhaps her greatest crime, but only after the fact. The courts and media, and by extension the public, seem profoundly troubled, indeed offended by her refusal to seek or even consider seeking outside help. In this respect her silence—her lack of trust and belief in authority and her refusal to be a dependent, nonsexual girl—became her most direct attack against the social and legal institutions and community culture entrusted with her well-being. Her story clearly shows the downside of a culture of avoidance. In the end, this revelation is precisely what must be covered up and for which Cheryl must be punished. The defensive reactions toward Cheryl's silence demonstrate the degree to which legal, educational, social-service, and community structures in the suburban greenhouse are not designed with girls like Cheryl in mind. Such institutions do not fully comprehend what it means to be young, female, sexual, and in trouble at the hands of one's father or comparable authority figure.

Freud also does not adequately account for the relationship between the sexuality, gender, and youth of his female subject. Though he never quite articulates his problem with Dora's case study in these terms, his own working and reworking of the text suggests such an analysis. Freud bases his understanding of Dora's experience of her sexuality largely on conjecture. In considering Dora's first sexual encounter with Herr K., which took place on the staircase of his office, where he "clasped the girl to him and pressed a kiss upon her lips," Freud concludes: "This was surely just the situation to call up a distinct feeling of sexual excitement in a girl of fourteen who had never before been approached. But Dora had at that moment a violent feeling of disgust, tore herself free from the man, and hurried past him to the staircase and from there to the street door"

(Freud 1963, 43). Freud goes on to imagine that when Herr K. kissed Dora she probably felt his erect penis against her body, which led her to feel "an analogous change in the corresponding female organ, the clitoris" (46).

It turns out, however, that Dora abhorred Herr K.'s sexual advances. Freud's unsympathetic reading of Dora's disgust at Herr K.'s kiss points to his inability to step outside of an Oedipal heterosexual framework and to recognize Herr K.'s culpability in this matter (arguably two sides of the same coin). Why doesn't Freud consider that Dora's reaction may legitimately indicate her lack of attraction to Herr K.? Instead he insists "I happen to know Herr K. . . . and he was still quite young and of prepossessing appearance" (44), as if by this admission Dora—and any woman, young or old—should follow suit and swoon at Herr K.'s every advance. It would seem just as plausible that Dora is disgusted because Herr K. is old enough to be her father, and she is socialized (through the successful completion of the Oedipal scenario) not to want to kiss her father (or his equivalent) as she would a lover. Though my reading also situates Dora's response within an Oedipal model, it shifts the burden of guilt onto Herr K., rather than on Dora's supposed (hetero)sexual dysfunction. Herr K. is breaking the rules, not Dora. Similarly, Freud could understand Dora's reaction as her response to the way in which this experience with Herr K. underscores the general lack of agency she has within her cultural context to determine the character of her own sexuality and subjectivity. Soon after discussing this incident, Freud acknowledges Dora's assessment of the relationship between herself and Herr K. vis-à-vis her father and Frau K. According to Freud, Dora believes "that she had been handed over to Herr K. as the price of his tolerating the relations between her father and his wife; and her rage at her father's making such a use of her was visible behind her affection for him." However, Freud quickly dismisses this reading, suggesting that Dora herself "was quite well aware that she had been guilty of exaggeration in talking like this" (50). By choosing to privilege Dora's quick aside here—something he refuses to do at other points in the analysis when they don't suit his theories—Freud once again finds the means to shelter Dora's father.

In refusing Herr K.'s advances, is Dora being a good girl or a bad girl? Freud attempts to determine this by cautiously questioning her about her sexual knowledge. Does she know anything about male sexual response, and if so, how? Notably, he does not even begin to consider whether she knows anything about female sexual response. Instead, throughout this passage he ostensibly reduces normal female sexuality to a biological response and thereby concludes that "I should without question consider a person [a woman] hysterical in whom an occasion for sexual excitement elicited feelings that were preponderantly or exclusively unpleasurable" (44). In the end, Freud's presentation of Dora's sexual knowledge tells the reader more about what Freud wants to know than what

Dora herself actually knows or has experienced. Throughout the text Freud periodically steps back from the analysis to cover his tracks and justify his practice of speaking frankly with Dora about sexual matters. He has a clear investment in convincing the reader that Dora is not "innocent of mind." In fact, he asserts that sexual knowledge is a precondition for hysteria. In this regard, he writes: "There is never any danger of corrupting an inexperienced girl. For where there is no knowledge of sexual processes even in the unconscious, no hysterical symptom will arise; and where hysteria is found there can no longer be any question of 'innocence of mind' in the sense in which parents and educators use the phrase" (66).

The source of Dora's knowledge remains an enigma for Freud. Though he goes to great lengths to trace the connections between Dora and Herr K., Frau K., her mother, her father, her cousin, her aunt, and two governesses, he leaves one possibility unturned, the one that would find an incestuous relationship between Dora and her father. When Freud searches out the origin of Dora's sexual knowledge, he finds Frau K. responsible for imparting the "facts of life" to Dora. Following this discovery, Freud concludes in a footnote to the postscript that

> I failed to discover in time and to inform the patient that her homosexual (gynaecophilic) love for Frau K. was the strongest unconscious current in her mental life. I ought to have guessed that the main source of her knowledge of sexual matters could have been no one but Frau K.—the very person who later on charged her with being interested in those same subjects. Her knowing all about such things and, at the same time her always pretending not to know where her knowledge came from was really too remarkable. I ought to have attacked this riddle and looked for the motive of such an extraordinary piece of repression. (142)

Is Dora's "gynaecophilic love" the only possible motive, the only secret that Dora needs to repress? For that matter, who is doing the repressing, Freud or Dora? And to what end? Throughout the text Freud's descriptions of the relationship between Dora and her father contain numerous references that should have, at the very least, raised the specter of the possibility that things are not always what they seem between father and daughter, and that Dora could have conceivably garnered some sexual knowledge out of her relationship with her father—either through direct sexual contact, observation of his affair with Frau K., or through intimacies he divulged to her in their more collegial moments. Freud does, after all, acknowledge that Dora's father had "made her his confidante while she was still a child" (74). Freud is either blind to these possibilities, or willfully looks away, leaving Dora's father, for the most part, unaccountable to his daughter, even when his actions directly bear on her state of body and mind.

At one point, Freud quickly dismisses Dora's reproaches against her father for passing on to her what she perceives to be a venereal disease. Instead, following what he then believed to be the cause of a vaginal discharge in young girls, Freud tries to convince Dora that her condition resulted from masturbation (an explanation he assesses as "extreme" in a footnote he added over twenty years after writing the initial version of the case).[11] He then attempts to manipulate Dora (or as he calls it, to meet her halfway) into confessing that she had masturbated in childhood. Dora refuses to go along with his diagnoses. According to Freud, "Dora denied flatly that she could remember any such thing" (94). Unwilling to accept defeat, Freud waits for Dora to slip up and admit to her childhood autoerotic practices. Within days, Dora unwittingly provides Freud with her "confession" when she arrives in his office wearing "a small reticule of a shape" around her waist, which she "kept playing with—opening it, putting a finger into it, shutting it again, and so on" (94). In a moment of sheer desperation, it would seem, Freud reads this gesture as Dora's way of metaphorically letting him know that yes, indeed, she had masturbated as a child, which in Freud's logic explains the origins of her current vaginal discharge. Confronted with this reading, Dora once again dismisses Freud by tossing up to fashion her donning of the reticule, which Freud takes as a denial on Dora's part. At the hands of Freud, it is difficult for Dora to get the last word.

At crucial moments in the case, Dora places herself in a parallel relationship with her mother in regard to her father, though Freud chooses not to make too much of this identification. For example, according to Freud, Dora knew that

> her mother was suffering from abdominal pains and from a discharge (a catarrh) which necessitated a cure at Franzensbad. It was Dora's view—and here again she was probably right—that this illness was due to her father, who had thus handed on his venereal disease to her mother. . . . The persistence with which she held to this identification with her mother forced me almost to ask her whether she too was suffering from a venereal disease; and I then learnt that she was afflicted with a catarrh (leucorrhoea) whose beginning, she said, she could not remember. (93–94)

The conviction with which Dora identifies with her mother and the fact that she has some inkling as to how her mother contracted a venereal disease suggest that she also believed that she became infected through similar means—whether she "remembers" it or not, or whether she is willing to tell Freud what she knows and break the codes of silence in this bourgeois familial circle. Within this somewhat convoluted and lengthy exchange between Freud and Dora regarding the state of health of her vagina, Freud presents Dora as, at best, the confused, and at worst, the deceitful, obstinate girl, incapable of deciding what is best for her own mental and physical well-being. She remains in need of care and discipline even if she is unwilling or unable to recognize her own dependency and thereby submit to his authority. In leaving the struggle for meaning unresolved between Dora and himself, Freud structurally maintains his own position as grand narrator of Dora's story, while he simultaneously and deftly writes Dora's father out of the scenario. Freud becomes the patriarch to Dora's daughterly position, a narrative maneuver that ostensibly obscures Dora's father's role in his daughter's affairs.

Freud's predilection for shielding Dora's father from suspicion of wrongdoing results in part from his inability to recognize the way in which transference and countertransference operate within Dora's treatment. In the postscript, Freud claims that the case's merit is also its greatest defect. Namely, he failed to account for the role of transference in Dora's reaction to the analytic relationship. Consequently, though the analysis failed Dora, the case allowed Freud to refine his understanding of transference and countertransference, or at least begin to recognize the merits of what I have called in chapter 2 a "responsible reading," or learning to love the unlovable. In particular, I am interested in Freud's countertransference, or the way in which the analyst projects his or her own desires and identifications onto the analysand. If learning to love the unlovable is in turn recognizing this thing of darkness as mine, then it also entails a kind of countertransference. Analysis here, be it psychoanalytic or cultural critique, is always to a degree an inside job, or at least one that demands an active and engaged relationship between the analyst and the patient, between the cultural critic and the subject, between the Self and the Other. Within his discussion of transference and countertransference, Freud suggests that he replaces Dora's father in the girl's imagination. This identification between Freud and Dora's father coupled with the degree to which Freud protects Dora's father suggests that Freud did not want to see the father's culpability because he wanted to maintain at least the appearance of a father-daughter relationship that would not disrupt his Oedipal model. By protecting Dora's father, he is also protecting himself, or at the very least, his theories. From Freud's perspective, Dora's ties to her father are about her love and desire for him rather than his wanton violation of any psychosocial injunctions. Freud reads Dora's empathies for her mother and Frau K. as indicative of her unconscious desire for her father, effectively underplaying her father's agency in the matter. Freud contends that

> her behavior obviously went far beyond what would have been appropriate to filial concern. She felt and acted more like a jealous wife—in a way which would have been comprehensible in her mother. By her ultimatum to her father ("either her or me"), by the scenes she used to make, by the suicidal intentions she allowed to transpire,—by all this

> she was clearly putting herself in her mother's place. If we have rightly guessed the nature of the imaginary sexual situation which underlay her cough, in that phantasy she must have been putting herself in Frau K.'s place. She was therefore identifying herself both with the woman her father had once loved and with the woman he loved now. The inference is obvious that her affection for her father was a much stronger one than she knew or than she would have cared to admit: in fact, that she was in love with him. (73)

From here Freud launches into a general discussion of the Oedipus complex, relegating Dora's father to the backseat and moving Herr K. and Frau K. into the fray as the object choices of Dora's Oedipal drama and the key players in the successful completion of her move from childhood to womanhood. In so doing, Freud places the Oedipus complex at the cornerstone of this period of Dora's psychosocial and sexual development, making it one of the primary technologies constituting female adolescence.

I'll Give You Something to Cry About, Young Lady

While Dora lived in a world that was in the process of articulating a relationship between female adolescence and Oedipal heterosexuality, Cheryl's middle-class community actively presumes this connection and hence cannot even imagine, let alone intervene in, the violence it generates. For Cheryl, the very sanctity of the relationship between normative heterosexuality and female adolescence in the context of a suburban culture of avoidance renders her experience unspeakable. Incest is not supposed to happen, and moreover, neighbors are supposed to mind their own businesses. Cheryl's TV movie, *A Deadly Silence*, depicts the result of this moral minimalism with the following exchanges:

> GIANELLI: I believe she was sexually abused, the Kossers believe it, even the cop who arrested her believes it, but we don't have any proof. And the thing that is going to hurt us the worst is Cheryl herself.
>
> PSYCHIATRIST: How so?
>
> GIANELLI: She is so cold, totally unremorseful.
>
> PSYCHIATRIST: That coldness you're seeing is how she coped, Paul. She learned to push her feelings down so that she could handle the two lives she was leading. She was a schoolgirl by day and she was literally her father's wife at night. She had to separate those two in her mind. That's how she survived.
>
> I don't have to tell you about incest. It's the best-kept secret in America. These kids live in silence inside. They can't talk about it because there is a part of them that refuses to believe it's true.

Later on Cheryl concurs, testifying through tears: "I just lie there. He breathed in my face. He'd just stare at me. I'd put a pillow over my face until it was over. I blocked it out" (see also Kleiman 1987, sec. II, 1). Though these scenes do not shy away from acknowledging the horror of Cheryl's existence in her father's home, they do not indict Cheryl's father or the culture of avoidance that facilitated the continuation of the abuse. Instead, Cheryl is held fully accountable for her silence. Even the voice of psychiatric authority states: "They [victims of incest] can't talk about it because there is a part of them that refuses to believe it's true." No one ventures to put Cheryl's plight in the context of her family and community. I contend, however, that the deadly silence here is not Cheryl's so much as white middle-class suburban Long Island's refusal to critically examine its own normative order, to challenge the authority of suburban fatherhood, to question the link between the teen girl and compulsory heterosexuality. To do so would have been to recognize that something was terribly, Oedipally wrong in the neighborhood.

As with Amy, the media exhibit a near obsession with Cheryl's "teenageness" and her femininity, suggesting that it is precisely female adolescence and its responsibility for forming—as in body type, desire, and social and sexual practices—white middle-class heterosexual women who fit into a culture of silence and avoidance that Cheryl's story potentially threatens. Representations of Cheryl's story relentlessly describe her as the paradigmatic teenage girl—to the point of parody—and in so doing clearly demarcate the cultural definition of female adolescence that operates in this case, namely one that is tied expressly to suburbia and middle-class consumption.

> With her red and white kick skirt and matching saddle shoes, Cheryl Pierson could have been a poster girl for the all-American high school cheerleader. Attractive, popular, with an easy sense of humor, she was the kind of girl everyone at Newfield [High School] seemed to know, the kind that could have been Homecoming Queen if she set her mind to it; a teenager who seemed destined to have everything she wanted. The boys all wanted to go out with her. The girls envied her clothing, appearance, and seemingly effortless charm. . . .
>
> If anything, Cheryl Pierson was an old-fashioned girl; somewhat naive for her age; more gigglish and childlike than hardened and sophisticated in the ways of the world. Sweet was one word people often used to describe Cheryl Pierson. Thoughtful and sensible were others. (Kleiman 1988, 36–37)

Kleiman also tells the reader that Cheryl's room included a cache of stuffed animals, a sound system, color-coordinated sheets, and a VCR, a veritable "showroom for everything a [middle-class] teenage girl would want" (26). Likewise, her book emphasizes that Cheryl was not interested in "current events"; she didn't read newspapers or listen to the news. "Her interests ran more to the humanly dramatic television shows like 'Divorce Court' and 'General Hospital'—dilemmas and situations about illness and romance with which she could identify" (35).[12] And just in case the nuances of this portrait remain unclear, Kleiman drives home the stereotype by evoking the connection between romantic love and teen girlhood.

> Cheryl was one of those teenagers who from a very young age are in love with the idea of love. Even as a youngster, she would spend unparalleled amounts of time dreaming, scheming, planning to bump into Joey, Glenn, Steven, someone. She would write them letters. She would write her girlfriends letters about them. Wherever she went Cheryl studied young couples to decide whether they were truly "meant to be." She could tell by their tone of voice, how tightly they wrapped their arms around one another, how openly affectionate they were with their kisses, whether they were "in love." To Cheryl, "true love" was the ultimate. (37)

Kleiman presents all of this in the first two chapters of her book and continues to reiterate and expand this representation throughout the story. The TV movie and the newspaper accounts also expend a great deal of effort portraying Cheryl as the typical, girl-next-door teenager, the good girl. For example, the TV movie often shows Cheryl dressed in her cheerleading outfit or in some version thereof—complete with red and white miniskirt, tight letter sweater, varsity jacket, and saddle shoes—even when the rest of her classmates don the more typical, middle-class, suburban wear of the late eighties, jeans and T-shirts. Consequently, Cheryl looks like she dropped out of a 1950s time capsule, out of the bygone postwar era that historically introduced the very idea of the all-American teenager in response to and in the service of a burgeoning U.S. consumer culture. In the hands of the media, Cheryl becomes a parodic version of this teenager; she is an anachronism, a paradigm, and therefore it is this ideal that seems most at risk in this suburban saga, but the analysis goes no deeper. Cheryl the icon floats in a cultural void. Her normalcy is without context. It is a mechanism for catching the attentions of a white middle-class reading public, for making her "everyone's daughter." It is not a means for critically examining this normalcy. The conclusion of the *New York Times Magazine* article "Murder on Long Island" shamelessly manipulates the lure of the normal when it cites Karenanne Pica, Sean-the-homeroom-hit-man's stepmother, as stating "'What's so frightening is that we are all so *normal*'" (emphasis added, Kleiman 1986, 66). In an effort to seize the public's and the judge's sympathies and facilitate their identification with the characters in this drama of incest and murder, the media and her attorney, respectively, portray Cheryl as normal and typical with a vengeance. This excess, however, is not in the service of critique; it is not a double-voiced parody so much as a self-replicating drama. Insisting on Cheryl's typicalness here deflects attention away from her father and the suburban greenhouse, and gives the authorities an escape valve.

But casting Cheryl as a typical American teen girl sets her up to fall and makes her more vulnerable than she already was: while she will not be believed unless she appears innocent and remorseful, if she presents herself too effectively as a good girl, the courts will feel obliged to make an example of her. She fits what Anna Tsing, in her discussion of cases of young women who are charged with harming their newborns, has identified as a new criminal profile: "the girl next door." Tsing writes, "The women are depicted by both the horrified and the sympathetic in imagery that evokes 'any young American woman.' . . . Indeed, from the perspective of those eager to punish them, this is why these girls are threatening, and why an example must be made of their cases to instruct the others" (Tsing 1990, 290–291). By making Cheryl's case about her "girl-next-doorness" and not about her father or his milieu, the courts and the media can discipline a façade of normalcy without having to really face the root of the problem: the limits of a culture of avoidance. Cheryl's attorney's closing argument and Judge Sherman's decision, as dramatically portrayed in the conclusion of the TV movie, vividly delineate the public stakes in this case.

JUDGE SHERMAN: The toughest thing for this court to accept is that there was help available. It would have taken so little for her to tell someone.

GIANELLI: Like Mr. Jablonski [prosecuting attorney], your honor? He wouldn't have believed her. He would have demanded proof.

Sir, we've heard police testimony that in 1987 there were 356 reported cases of incest in single-parent homes in this county. Not one report was made by a victim. In asking you to not send Cheryl Pierson to jail, I would also ask that you consider the kind of girl she is. She's not a streetwise kid [a euphemism for poor and nonwhite]. She's an immature, sheltered girl of the suburbs [again, she's white, middle class, and normal]. At some point she is going to have to put all this behind her and get on with her life. She did live through the hell of Magnolia Drive [her family's home]; I suppose she could learn to live through the hell of prison, but I am asking the court to be merciful.

Two scenes later, at the conclusion of her hearing, Cheryl faces Judge Sherman to make a final statement. She is crying and too weak to stand up. Through broken speech she states:

CHERYL: I realize that what I did was wrong, I'm sorry.

JUDGE SHERMAN: Is that all?

[Cheryl nods]

JUDGE SHERMAN: There are some things that I want to say. During the course of these proceedings, I have received over a hundred letters from people urging me to be lenient with you; most were victims or survivors of domestic violence including sexual abuse and incest. Many of them exhibited great sympathy and interest for what you suffered and your need to escape, although none of them condoned the method you used to end your plight, and nor do I.

The publicity and interest engendered by your misfortune may produce some benefit for other victims who seek a way out of their unhappiness. They must be made aware of the many agencies that exist to help the innocent. Perhaps victims such as yourself, and friends of victims who are aware of their condition, will be encouraged to report to these agencies and thus avoid the consequences of the actions you took.

Cheryl Pierson, I hereby sentence you to five years' probation and as part of that sentence you are to serve six months in jail.[13]

Though the judge makes an example of Cheryl, his touch is light. The girl-next-door image is both a curse and a blessing, insuring that she will be punished, but also sparing her from harsh treatment. She is still, after all, a daughter of suburbia, and as such she is a redeemable prodigal daughter (see also Tsing 1990, 291). However, if the media and courts had put Cheryl's father on trial and thereby scrutinized the patriarchal foundations of the suburban greenhouse, would he and what he represented have been redeemable? Sean, the kid who actually pulled the trigger on Cheryl's father, clearly was not. He garnered a minimal amount of attention in the media and received the stiffest sentence. He was tried as an adult while Cheryl and her boyfriend, Rob, both received youthful offender status. In the end, the judge sentenced Sean to twenty-four years in prison with no eligibility for parole before eight years. And with that Sean fades further into the background of the story. The media do not analyze Sean's lack of importance in this story. They dutifully report on his fate, accepting its terms. Clearly, one could speculate that Sean's lack of motivation (other than money, which was clearly minimal given the enormity of the task) for committing the crime makes him a more heinous character, and thus he deserves a stiffer sentence. But there is a resounding silence on this topic. There is no TV movie or paperback bestseller on Sean, the homeroom hitman. Would focusing on Sean's motivation be too threatening to the suburban order, as it would have been to put the murdered James Pierson on trial? What would make a boy of relative privilege, the son of normality, do such a terrible thing? How is his act symptomatic of a widespread suburban disorder? Is Sean's act a more symbolic and hence more socially threatening patricide? These are the questions that lie behind the silence in Sean's case. Consequently, Sean is not as redeemable a figure as Cheryl clearly was.

In sentencing Cheryl essentially back into a middle-class life, Judge Sherman sets aside larger sociopolitical questions, leaving unscathed the institutions that in some way contributed to or ignored Cheryl's condition as an abused daughter of suburbia. Instead, the judge simultaneously inscribes Cheryl as victim and criminal, and as recalcitrant and redeemable subject. Like Freud with Dora, Judge Sherman does not seem able to step outside of his own adult, male, and in his case, legal framework in order to comprehend the logic behind Cheryl's inactions and actions and her silences and lies. To a great extent the incommensurability of the court's and Cheryl's positions provides the drama and passion in the representations of the case. Aside from Cheryl's aunt, her paternal grandmother, and her younger sister, everyone in her familial, social, and legal circle (including the prosecuting attorney and judge) believe that Cheryl was sexually abused. Nevertheless, they disagree on the extent to which her actions are justifiable and punishable. Like Freud's account of Dora and his manipulation of his and her father's positions within the text, the judge's inscription of Cheryl's story within an overly generalized moral framework occludes the bad patriarch's (Cheryl's father's) role in this crime and shifts the spotlight onto the judge himself, as the good father teaching Cheryl and other girls like her a much-needed lesson. Cheryl's own refusals both to seek help from the proper authorities and later to stage an appropriate amount of remorse before the eyes of the court and the media, make Cheryl the bad daughter in need of disciplining. But because she is also a good (white middle-class normal) girl, she is an ideal subject for the court. She needs to be punished gently. She needs to be made into a cultural example and then welcomed back into the fold. The battle is ostensibly played out over Cheryl's character; setting the terms as such masks what is truly at stake: the authority and ability of social, familial, and legal institutions to, in part, protect young girls from the sexual advances of their own fathers and to thereby facilitate a normative heterosexuality. But no matter how effectively Judge Sherman positions himself as the good father, the evidence in the case underscores the degree to which Cheryl's suburbia failed her across the board.

However, the judge's verdict also leaves Cheryl hanging, and with her the hegemony of heterosexuality. Will Cheryl eventually leave jail as a remorseful, good girl, who has learned her lesson, and who can ultimately find it in her heart to let her father rest in peace, transferring her desire onto a more socially sanctioned male figure? Throughout their accounts, the newspapers, the true-crime paperback, the docu-drama, and the talk shows lay the groundwork for this outcome by consistently attending to Cheryl's ongoing committed relationship with her boyfriend, Rob. The media present Rob as a magnanimous guy, one who agrees to testify against Cheryl in exchange for a lesser charge, all in the name of helping Cheryl out of her predicament. In the TV movie, Rob asks Cheryl, "What good would I be to you in jail?" Similarly, after Cheryl starts serving her sentence, *Newsday* runs a photograph of Rob tying a yellow ribbon around an oak tree in his front yard with the promise that he will tie a new ribbon on the tree each day until she is set free. The media follow this potentially socially disruptive tale until it is possible to tack on to it a happy, heterosexual ending. Cheryl's public narrative ends with the news that after serving three and a half months of her sentence, Cheryl leaves jail and marries Rob.

Both Cheryl's and Dora's stories demonstrate that learning to be a teenage girl requires negotiating potentially treacherous familial, social, legal, medical, and political terrains. Girls are asked to know too much and too little at the same time. They need to know when and how to behave or misbehave as good or bad girls or to speak or remain silent within a specific set of sexual practices and moral values. By refusing to act accordingly, girls like Cheryl and Dora invite irresponsible readings by the very institutions and authorities that the girls' rebellions challenge. These irresponsible readings are self-protecting. The courts, nuclear families, and media in Cheryl's case, for example, are not up to risking themselves for the sake of their daughters. That would mean acknowledging this thing (incest, patricide) of darkness as their own. They choose instead to perpetuate Cheryl's deadly silences in the service of protecting the specious foundations of their normal lives. In part, they do this by finding ways to blame, punish, and redeem their wayward daughters, leaving the critical interpretation to the wiles of the public. In Dora's case, Freud begins to offer a model for enacting a responsible reading when he realizes his own mistake: his inability to account for the role of transference and countertransference, or what amounts to his stakes and culpabilities in Dora's story. But in the context of Dora's case history this responsible reading remains a footnote, an afterthought to the main body of the text. Learning to observe how transference and especially countertransference operate in our own understandings of girls like Dora, Cheryl, and Amy (the main daughters we've met thus far) is key toward recognizing them for what they are: unlovable teen girls whose so-called hysterias and parodies are social narratives that potentially can disrupt the status quo. As unlovable teen girls, they are not easily silenced or redeemed, even when their narrators work overtime to do just that. The subjects of these narratives are not so much the girls themselves as the institutions that try so hard to redeem them. In the end, unlovable daughters' stories still rattle the foundations of the culture of avoidance, calling into question the normalizing logics of female adolescence and making it clear that there is nothing particularly innocent or natural about the heterosexuality of nuclear families or the teenage girls they produce and depend on to make themselves whole.

The next chapter wallows in SWR teen girls' hysterias or, after Dora, what can be understood as parodies of teen girlhood. Moreover, it looks at how girls' excesses make a normal life possible. Through Dora's hysteria, Freud defined normality but did not grant Dora much agency in the process. For him, her hysteria remained a symptom of something wrong with Dora and not wrong with the world she inhabited. SWR girls taught me that not all hysteria is the same and that hysteria can be a symptom not so much of the normal not working as the normal working all too well to self-replicate.

Chapter 4 Among Friends

Stories That Make a Normal Life Possible

Can We Talk?

THE SOCIAL WORLD OF SWR girls moves fast and furiously; it is dynamic, situational, ephemeral, and narrative. Stories are for telling your friends and not telling your enemies. SWR girls' story-talk is endless and, to the unaccustomed listener, frantic and disjointed. It took me weeks to be able to follow some girls' talk. The velocity of their speech, coupled with their "New Yawk-Lawn Guyland" accents, their popular and invented vocabularies, and the subjects of their attentions—this girl's fight with that girl over this or that boy, et cetera—left me flailing for comprehension. After a concerted effort and with some practice, I could keep up with the best of them; but this was definitely an acquired social skill.[1]

Following their talk, however, does not mean analyzing in print what they say and do. In this sense, the act of writing an ethnography about SWR girls' talk necessarily deviates from their commonly upheld rules of everyday exchange. Though the girls write, some on their own, all for classroom assignments, their written stories are, for the most part, about "big" events in their lives and not about the continual narrativization of their everyday interactions. Their word-of-mouth stories do not have beginnings and endings; they are serial and not necessarily linear; and they thrive on exaggerated retellings. Though mostly not as glamorous or dangerous as the serial stories told on their favorite nighttime soap operas, *Melrose Place* and *Beverly Hills 90210*, the poetics of SWR girls' everyday lives bear some resemblance to the complex narrative patterns of these shows. This is a he-said/she-said and she-said/she-said kind of world that moves with conviction from "crisis" to "crisis," no matter how big or small.

Spurred on by their talk, their friendship circles ebb and flow, turning on stories circulated, stories embellished, stories disclosed to the wrong person or clique of friends, stories told as acts of revenge, and stories relayed in the drama of compassion. This is not a social world that stands still for long. In my first day of field notes, I wrote: "I am struck by the amount of energy in this building [the middle school]. They [the students] are in constant motion."[2] I would learn fairly quickly that this motion was both physical and social. As a result, one can say nothing definitive about who is friends with whom or why one girl is liked or disliked over another. While the girls often preface their talk about someone with statements that acknowledge past relationships—"I used to be best friends with her, but then she'd talk about you behind your back." "Chrissy and Becky used to be friends in sixth grade before . . . "—this social memory counts for less than what may happen or what one may hear about someone in the next class or by the end of lunch activity. This is not to suggest that the SWR girls do not form alliances or loyalties, but that their relationships are either deepened or tested by the perpetual exchange of talk.

What remains constant is how friendship groups and girls' identities are continually made and broken through the brokering of stories, or what amounts to girl power/knowledge. To know something about someone that others don't is to possess a highly valued social commodity and hence social power. The process literally turns what counts as knowledge among SWR girls into what counts as power. In addition, as stories move from speaker to speaker the stakes tend to get higher. This became apparent when a rumor about me made the rounds. Once the final version came back to me, I was taken aback by how something fairly innocuous had turned into something more extreme. After two months of me playing surrogate advisor to the five eighth graders in the vice principal's advisory, she was ready to return to work, and I was to relinquish my responsibilities as an advisor. This did not mean that I would stop hanging out with girls both in and out of school. The girls, however, had turned my stepping down as an advisor into a rumor about me abandoning them and my whole project. I learned this when Lisa B. came running up to me and said, "I heard you're leaving!?" There was a sense of urgency and even thrill in her voice. I had become fairly close to Lisa, so I was pretty certain she would not want me to leave. At the same time, I sensed that she liked "knowing" something other girls probably didn't know. I assured her that I wasn't leaving. With the drama of her tale cut short, in an easy-come, easy-go manner, she moved on to more mundane matters. Without missing a beat, she told me she was going to Connecticut that weekend to visit her dad and asked if we could maybe go to the movies the following weekend. I said sure, and we got on with our day.

This chapter tries to make sense of SWR girls' drama-rousing talk. It follows their storytelling practices and watches how the girls make and break their social world and their own identities through things said and things left unsaid and through stories exaggerated, passed on, and vied for. Moreover, it is about how this seemingly chaotic process fits into a larger framework and produces participating girls as normal. It shows how the girls' collective staging of the abnormal—the out-of-control talk among peers, the kind of group hysteria that continually erupts among them—ultimately maintains the larger community's social equilibrium and identity status as part of the normal white middle class. Girls' wild stories make being normal possible. They fill in the perceived cultural void of being normal, while also performing a key normalizing process. By way of contrast, this chapter also considers seemingly normal, or what I alternately call hypernormal (as in excessively normal) or false normal (a cognate of false positive) girls—girls who on the surface appear above the fray of all this collective dramatizing, but whose normalness turns out to be a trompe l'oeil. The social aspect of most girls' story making is what makes this otherwise hysterical process normal. Likewise, it is the seeming lack of control that makes a normal life bearable and ultimately possible. In attempting to make sense of the whirlwind of girls' story making, this chapter critically looks at the cultural dynamics of being normal, a process that directly informs and reflects back onto the culture of the white middle class.

In the Realm of the Hypersocial and Hypersymbolic

I have positioned this chapter after "Justify My Love" because Cheryl's and Dora's stories are also about making the normal possible. Like the SWR girls, they do this by turning on things said and things unsaid, or things heard and things unheard, consciously or not. Cheryl's mistake was not telling anyone but her boyfriend her story. Dora's was talking to someone who was not listening to her story very astutely. At points, both girls were talking to people who weren't listening, weren't able to listen, or weren't listening correctly. For example, by encouraging Cheryl to take matters into her own hands, Cheryl's boyfriend broke what I witnessed as the rules of engagement among suburban Long Island teens: sometimes kids tell other kids "secrets" because they want those kids to get them help. In a study of the storytelling practices of urban adolescents, Amy Shuman makes a similar observation. She writes: "Listeners can be held accountable for withholding information, and the corollary to entitlement to tell narratives is the expectation that an ally who hears relevant information has an obligation to pass it on to others" (Shuman 1986, 25). Listening, in other words, means knowing when and how to act responsibly. It means knowing who and when to tell what you know about someone. It involves a system of entitlement and obligation.

One day, Caitlin made the relationship between the entitlement to tell and be told and the obligation to repeat a story to the right people explicit when she told me: "Rachel doesn't like to bring things up, but once people know, she wants to talk about them. That's why Rachel told me that her parents weren't getting along. She wanted me to tell Mr. Richards [a middle-school teacher]." Caitlin then explained that Rachel's father goes away for periods of time and that Rachel's parents fight. "But Rachel's mom would never get a divorce unless she absolutely had to." This was not the first time I had heard about this marital unrest. Weeks earlier, as I was preparing to spend the day shadowing Rachel, Mr. Richards had told me that Caitlin had told him that Rachel's parents were probably *getting a divorce* (notice the escalation of the story). For Rachel's sake, he thought I should be apprised of the situation before I found myself in the middle of rocky familial ground. Rachel never did broach the subject with me, either that day or in the weeks that followed, and I never let on that I knew. On the morning I met Rachel at her home so that I could take the bus with her to school and follow her throughout the day, my interaction with her parents was a bit awkward. Her father joked about me missing "the beating Rachel gets every morning." Given that I never saw even a hint of evidence that any kind of domestic violence existed in this household, I understood his remark and the clumsy attempts at small talk that her mother and I engaged in as defensive reactions against my intrusion into the private sphere of the suburban family. With their typical half- to one-acre plots landscaped and fenced-in with discretion in mind, SWR single-family, suburban homes are bastions of familial privacy. The white middle class here is not used to being the object of ethnographic scrutiny, and anomalous adults like the prodigal-daughter ethnographer do not often make it past the thresholds of the faux colonial front doors. Nevertheless, here I was, and Rachel's parents were struggling to graciously, or not, incorporate my presence into their morning routine.

I surmised that Caitlin had told me that Rachel's parents were having difficulties out of concern for Rachel, as a way of marking her own relationship with Rachel as close, and because I had gained a place of entitlement and obligation in this community. By being told things, I was also being entrusted with information for which I have responsibility. As an ethnographer in the field, I wrote everything down. SWR eighth graders were very conscious of and self-conscious about this. They would often look over my shoulder while I wrote, ask to read my notes, ask me what I was writing about them, and sometimes write notes on my notes. Other times, if something "outrageous" happened, or a girl said something she shouldn't have (e.g., a curse word or negative comment about a teacher), the offending party would look to see if I was writing it down. And if I was, she would often squeal, "Oh my gawd, she's writing that in her book." Taking field notes in this sense was awkward, it didn't follow the girls' everyday talk and storytelling patterns. My note writing was more about preserving their stories for later analysis rather than passing them on in the here and now. However, in rereading my notes about Rachel's parents' "divorce," I discovered that I too escalated stories. I kept at least two levels of field notes while at SWR. The first I wrote on legal pads while I was with the girls, often writing down verbatim what students or teachers said. I then went home and wrote more proselike reflections on the day. The subject of Rachel's parents came up on several occasions. The only version of my notes that does not say that they are getting divorced is the one I wrote immediately following my conversation with Caitlin. I guess my note taking was more a part of the girls' talk than I initially realized. In sharing their talk with me, in making me an entitled listener and hence reteller, SWR girls obliged me to pass their stories on responsibly, to know which ones to tell and which ones not to tell to whom and under which circumstances. While I was in the field, I needed to learn how to do this effectively on a day-to-day, conversation-by-conversation basis. As a writer of this autoethnography, I need to do this on a broader scale. I need to retell stories in ways that first and foremost take girl talk seriously, and I need to help my listeners (readers) appreciate that girls' collective dramatizing is a socially productive process and not just frivolous adolescent patter.

Like Cheryl's and Dora's worlds, the SWR girls' lives are multiply storied. In fact, all the daughters of suburbia in this book know how to create semblances of high drama out of their day-to-day lives. Unlike SWR girls' stories, Cheryl's drama came too late and crossed the lines of productive social fiction. In the end, sexually abused and dead bodies are beyond the symbolic; they are *hypo*symbolic (devoid of symbolism, too absolute). On some level, they are uninterpretable, or at least interpretation is beside the point. If making sense of things means finding frameworks and logics that offer contexts for understanding and even empathizing with other people's perspectives, incest and patricide defy comprehension. Though the representations of Cheryl's case endeavor to portray her as hypernormal—the everyteen—in the end, her life is tragically anything but normal. By contrast, Dora's hysterics—her suicide note, her somatic symptoms, her overt displays of affection and repulsion—can be read within the realm of a normalizing drama. By acting out, by being *hyper*symbolic or hysterical, Dora presents her life as a ready-made case history to be interpreted, analyzed, and eventually contained within the parameters of what stood in her world as a normal life. In their storytelling and community making, the SWR girls are not unlike Dora. They too rely on excessive discourse to react to and make attempts at controlling and tolerating the terms of their lives. If a normal (read white middle-class suburban) life is supposed to be uneventful, unspeakable, cultureless, and without stories worth telling, being hypersymbolic affects a kind of abnormality that imbues a normal life with meaning, adding layers of excitement to an otherwise mundane existence. It is the very excesses and the communal aspect of this process that make the normal possible. In the case of SWR girls, the hypersymbolic turns out to be deceptively abnormal. While Freud scrambled to protect the hegemony that Dora's case history threatened to topple—the normalizing narrative of the Oedipus complex—my reading of SWR girls' story making does just the opposite. It attempts to unseat the normal by explicating its very production. To say the unsayable is to undercut its power to be the last word. In writing this chapter, I am closer to Dora the iconoclastic analysand than I am to Freud the normalizing foundational-analyst of the bourgeoisie.

While SWR boys also had their stories to tell, and some even participated in the girls' narrative exploits as will become clear below, the storytelling I'm describing in this chapter is, in the end, a girl thing. In part, white middle-class girls have to work harder or at least in a distinctly gendered fashion—precisely as a result of their marked gender status—at normalizing themselves than their male counterparts. Since, culturally, they are given more leeway when it comes to displays of emotion and collective expressions of anxiety, it makes sense that this would be the mode they perfect in their efforts to construct their identities. Moreover, their lives appear more accelerated than their male classmates', if for no other reason than the fact that their bodies are developmentally rushing toward adulthood, while the boys' bodies (and social interests) seem stuck in boyhood.

Defining the Normally Undefinable

In a critical history of medical theories of health and disease and, to a lesser degree, of the social normal and abnormal, Georges Canguilhem notes by way of analogy that "the laws of acoustics are not broken in cacophony" ([1966]1991, 55).[3] Here, like the hypersymbolic of teen girls, cacophony is the fodder for disciplinary action. And in disciplining excess and chaos, we articulate, pass on, and reaffirm the laws of acoustics or, in the case of SWR girls, the rules of being normal.

By normal, I do not mean something that is absolute or a fait accompli. As Canguilhem writes, "strictly speaking a norm does not exist" (77). Like the socio-racial identity of whiteness, the normal is the thing that cannot be named; its effects are great, its presence ominous, but its properties elude direct analysis. To name the normal is to call attention to it and thereby make it abnormal and strange. Like whiteness it depends and thrives on anonymity. One can never actually be normal; one can only constantly strive for or ward off normalcy, which in many instances amounts to the same thing. Teens are often grandly abnormal, dressing and behaving against the grain of their peers and their parents. However, in the end, there is nothing so unremarkable as a suburban white teen dressing in a black leather jacket, walking around sullen faced, and hanging tightly with other kids who do the same.[4] Nor is there anything particularly strange, as I witnessed, about a teenage girl with a pacifier in her mouth literally sucking her way through the school day. While I was in the field, pacifiers were a media-generated trend that caught on ever so slightly at SWR. The sight of one girl dabbling in this activity suggested only that she was an avid MTV watcher, and that she may have been looking for a little bit of garden-variety attention. These and like-minded abnormalities follow normal patterns and meet normal expectations. Within reason, white middle-class kids are supposed to test the limits of their world. If the adult world they're surrounded by or their peer group balks at or in some fashion disallows, rejects, or puts down a social performance of the abnormal, they are merely doing their job: disciplining the transgressors to be normal. In other words, staging or reacting to abnormalities sets the parameters for what will pass as normal.

The impulse to fashion oneself as not normal points to a conundrum. SWR girls would often ask, "Why do you want to write about us, we are *sooo* normal?" which in their estimations meant that they were "*sooo* boring." I would tell them that that was exactly why I wanted to study them to look at what's "interesting about being normal." Some obviously got what I was after. Others just moved on to asking me if they were going to be in the book, and if so, could I use their real names and could Winona Ryder play them in the movie.

Here, to be normal is to lack. On the one hand, it is to desire a way out of the perceived boredom and nothingness that couches the normal, and on the other, it is to take on all the trappings of living a visibly invisible life. Not being noticed accords its privileges, or what turns out to be for some a dubious privilege (see below, "False Normal" and chapter 5). Telling "big" stories, knowing more about another girl's story than your classmate does, and rallying around someone else's problems temporarily fills the lack that is normal without truly altering the norm. Living a hypersymbolic and a hypernormal life is not a radical move. It is a productive coping mechanism. It socializes girls into a normal life and makes that life bearable.

The Tragedy of Being Normal

Being normal was something most girls strived for and felt a certain discomfort with. Most did not want to stand out from the norm, even if being normal was "sooo boring." But most also felt a certain lack in their normalness. In an intentionally self-reflexive piece about writing, Christine D. underscores the degree to which being normal in a teen-girl world that thrives on the hypersymbolic leaves a girl floundering.

What should I write about?
by Christine D.

> God, what should I write about? I hate when I get writer's block. Maybe I could write about something I like to do, like gymnastics or listening to music. . . . No, those are boring [i.e., normal] topics. This is so annoying, I have nothing to write about. Why do we even have to write an interior monologue, anyway? It's like my teacher is writing crazy or something!? Must be because we've only had two weeks of school and we've written a couple [of] poems already. But he's cool. Oh, back to the poem, what should I write about?

This essay appears at the end of an anthology that a teacher put together of his students' writings. It reflects a common sentiment among the SWR eighth graders. To be normal is to not have a story to tell. As an autoethnographer of the normal, I empathize with their plight.

In their writing, girls tend to fill this felt lack of culture with stories of accidents, suicides, alcoholism, diseases like cancer, deaths of loved ones, stories of divorce, and stories of friends torn apart as families move to new states and new school districts. The girls who have these stories to tell are the lucky ones. For example, in this same anthology, Christine eventually does find a story to tell. She titles it "A Tragedy with My Father."

> It all started one day when I came home from school. It was the end of 6th grade, and I had just turned 12 a couple of months earlier. My mother told me that my father had either passed out or fainted. He was brought to the hospital to have tests done. Within a couple of days, the tests came back negative. The doctors didn't know what caused my father to faint. Within about 2 months, my dad fainted about 5–6 times.
>
> Two weeks later, my mom, my dad, and I were gardening. It was extremely hot outside. We just got back from buying flowers, and now we were planting them.
>
> I looked over at my father as he sat down on the front steps. In a period of about 5 seconds his eyes rolled back into his head, he started to slightly shake, and he fell backward. It was the scariest moment of my life. Right away my mom took my dad's pulse. She said that it was very faint, and she could hardly feel it.
>
> In about 1 1/2 minutes he woke up. He later told us that he knows when he's going to pass out because he gets dizzy right before it happens (that's how he knew to sit down).
>
> My dad went to the hospital for a series of tests including an EKG, an EEG, Halter Monitor, a MRI, an Echo Cardiogram, and some blood work. After all the tests, the doctors didn't find out what was wrong. And to this day, nobody knows.

Girls without "tragedies" write more abstract pieces on friendship and love, like Kelly K.'s "Friends." Here, Kelly defines friendship in terms of a system of entitlement and obligation and, at times, overidentification. She also underscores just how social a girl's life is. These are recurring themes in girls' stories that this chapter explores at length below. For now, I am interested in how Kelly's lack of a dramatic story to tell leads her to emotional generalizations. She writes:

Friends are supportive
and comfort you when you're upset
when you have a problem
so does your friend.

I need my friends
they help me,
they keep me out of trouble
and keep me laughing.

When I'm upset
my friends cheer me up
I'm glad I have my friends
without them
that would be the end

Friends forever
Trusting each other
Including each other
Never ending
Fun to be with
Understanding
Keeping secrets.

Still other eighth graders without good stories to tell will write fantasies located in outer space or in the heart of their suburban lives.

Things in my room
by Paul J.

In my room
I have grass as carpet
And walls like silk
And a bed like a magic carpet
Taking me to faraway lands
I have lamps that look like cat eyes glowing in the night
I have mirrors that I look into to see my future
I have a radio that turns me into a dreamer
And I have windows that I look out of to bring me back to reality

Here, Paul contrasts his fantasy world, which is full of cultural and sensuous objects, with the presumably less colorful, less inhabited "reality" of his suburban neighborhood. What story would or could he tell of the reality outside his window? This is the one left for this autoethnography to articulate.

Whether tragedy, abstract reflection, or fantasy, the students' written stories infuse an all-too-normal life with content. This rush to fill up an otherwise storyless life is an interminable and necessary condition for maintaining and enduring normality. Without it, their lives are just too boring, or so they think. This is never more apparent than when girls' stories become part of their everyday social lives.

Stories of Middle-Class Life

In an ethnographic account of coal camps and hollers in West Virginia, Kathleen Stewart writes of a world in which people's stories and "re-membrances" "in-fill" the historical, physical, and social landscape of a place Stewart refers to as "the space on the side of the road": a space of communal memories and a space where the present and past collide, the places where accidents happened, goats were slaughtered, families perished in fires, the roadsides where old women wander hurling invectives at strangers and greetings to "old-timey" friends, and the places where neighbors post "No Trespassing" signs and then call up everyone to let them know that it doesn't mean them. In the larger scheme of things, this space represents the cultural realm of poor white America, so far off from the mainstream that it barely registers in white middle-class America's (SWR's) cultural imagination. Yet, like this autoethnography, Stewart's is an ethnography of "the thickets of a storied sociality." One of the differences, and there are obviously many of varying degrees and consequences, between the space on the side of the road and SWR teen-girl culture—the space just beyond the mall—is that Stewart's subjects endlessly remember and retell stories as a way to wade through and one might even say survive a harsh "cultural [and material] real" (Stewart 1996, 9).

In the space just beyond the mall, the space of my study—white middle-class suburbia, Long Island, Shoreham-Wading River, eighth-grade-girl life—my subjects tell stories to get by not in the face of material harshness or lack, but in the face of cultural starkness. They in-fill their sooo boring lives with a plethora of spoken and written stories and kid-created ephemera. They accumulate mass-produced objects, consume popular culture with a vengeance—clothes borrowed and newly purchased, backpacks filled with makeup and CDs, magazines read aloud or passed around, rooms full of entertainment equipment, and whole libraries of home-videotaped episodes of *The Real World* or *Regis and Kathie Lee*—and they participate in or actively refuse to join structured activities like band, chorus, interscholastic sports, theater, professional ballet lessons, and church music groups, to name a few. What hovers in the space beyond the mall is an excessively normal life that the girls, their families, and in some cases their teachers clutter with consumer items, organized activities, and stories of personal tragedies, petty jealousies, and locally minded disputes.

SWR eighth graders are not alone in their efforts to maintain a life of drama and conflict. I read in their in-filling and cacophony not just a teenage thing, but a larger cultural phenomenon, a white middle-class suburban thing that the girls both indulge in themselves and observe in the adult community raising and educating them. In chapter 1, I wrote of an adult world trapped in a predicament and sometimes a battle of its own making. With the closing of the Shoreham Nuclear Power Plant, the community became economically strapped and parents began to bicker with parents, taxpayers with taxpayers, teachers with teachers, administrators with administrators, neighbors with neighbors, and all the possible permutations herewith. Though not explicit, questions about middle-class life linger in the editorial comments and letters to the editor printed in the community papers, in the chat of neighbors as they stand in line at the local bagel shop or meet up in the parking lots of the nearby Catholic and Protestant churches, or in the public talk of the weekly school-board meetings and in the rhetoric of the yearly school-board elections. What does the community value more, its pocketbooks or its children's educations? What counts as a good education? What and who can be sacrificed? How will they maintain the life of the upper middle class, especially when doing so means having to face conflict or trouble directly? Will they pass their lifestyle on or will it wither away as they spend down their nest eggs or 401Ks (if they indeed have them and aren't just living off of credit)? Rumors and stories proliferate in this crisis of values and ultimately of class—if class is defined not just by how much equity people enjoy but by how much cultural capital they wield and which moral and ethical principles they uphold. This is the stuff of serial drama. Stories travel through the community at lightning speed. Lines of friendships, loyalties, and antipathies cross. People talk behind each others' backs. The weekly board meetings are public spectacles, where suburban powermongers try to consolidate their positions, and various community groups come to monitor or gawk at this unseemly (unmiddle-class) activity. Here, alliances are made or broken on a turn of phrase or in the wake of a condescending or inflammatory remark. At moments, the battle over the school budget is better than TV, and the sometimes capacity attendance at these meetings suggests that I am not alone in this assessment.

This public imbroglio over the school budget and property taxes is not an isolated struggle so much as the latest magnet for this community's nervous middle-class attentions. (See Ehrenreich 1989 for a discussion of middle-class insecurities.) The storied dissonance was always already alive and well in the interstices of the housing developments that make up this suburbia. The deepseatedness of this culture of serial, in-filling talk became all too apparent to me one sleepless night in a Boston hotel room I was sharing with a woman who was a resident of one of Shoreham's more affluent developments, a parent of school-age children, and a teacher in the district. Lest one thinks that the excessive filling up of a normal life is just a passing adolescent phase, I offer the following account as evidence to the contrary. Girls are inventive, but they do not operate in a hormonally charged, pubescent vacuum.

Four eighth-grade girls, two eighth-grade boys, two teachers, and myself had left for Boston on a minibus on a Friday morning in April to attend an education conference. On the drive up, kids listened to show tunes from Broadway musicals—*Joseph and the Technicolor Dream Coat*, *Cats*, and *Les Miserables*—while they covered the windows with signs that said things like "Boston or Bust"; "Honk if you love the Rangers" (the New York Rangers had recently made it into the NHL playoffs, an event that took the eighth-grade boy community—along with some girls and adults—by storm); "Visualize World Peas"; "Stop the Violins"; "Follow the Directions," a favorite expression of one of their teachers; and "'Some days people expect me to walk on water. SO I DO! Except it's not exactly water and I am not exactly WALKING.'—Nancy Karrigen" (their spelling). As we stopped to pay tolls, the kids amused themselves by paying for the car behind us, a gesture that they called "a random and senseless act of kindness." All this took place in between eating and rummaging through their copious pieces of luggage. One girl had actually brought a whole extra suitcase packed with "food." (I put this in quotes because the nutritional value of most of these rations left something to be desired.) The trip was only a weekend excursion, leaving on Friday, returning on Sunday evening, yet the students packed as if they would not return to civilization for at least a month. Despite all this kid excess, to my surprise and at moments dismay, the thicket of stories I found myself ensnared in on this trip had less to do with the girls' social reality and more to do with the adult community's.

As the demographics of our trip would have it, I got paired to share a room with Ann, one of the teachers and the only other adult woman in our little entourage. Ann proceeded to spend a great deal of the trip relating to me the details of her life, basically lamenting her past, present, and future. Being a wife, a mother, and a professional woman in white middle-class suburbia had apparently, by her own account, rendered her insecure, anxious, and overwhelmed. In the parlance of 1990s popular psychology—a discourse to which she subscribed wholeheartedly—Ann lacked "self-esteem," a common plight, as the story goes, of white middle-class women and girls (Orenstein 1994; Pipher 1994; AAUW 1992; Brown and Gilligan 1992).[5] Ann rarely asked me questions about myself and when she did, decidedly did not listen to my responses. Though she continually punctuated her talk with the refrain, "Do you know what I'm saying?"

the question was rhetorical, meant to give her a chance to catch her breath or switch narrative threads rather than to solicit a comment from me. As the attentive autoethnographer, I had no choice but to function as her confidant for the weekend. As a result, I found out more about what goes on among neighbors across the carefully and often professionally landscaped lawns of Shoreham than I had originally thought possible. Ann gave me a way past the small talk and sarcasm that Rachel's parents had put up between me and their private nuclear-family world. In Ann, I also came to recognize a pattern of storytelling that would later help me make sense of SWR girl talk, whether it was collectively fabricated or the result, like Ann's, of an internal and self-consuming narrative process.

By the second night of the trip, Ann's monologue took on a possessed quality. The evening began with a group outing to dinner at Pizzeria Uno and a movie, Spike Lee's *Crooklyn*. The kids ate with some gusto. This was familiar food, something they could have eaten not as far from home. The movie, on the other hand, left them a bit bored and baffled. They couldn't understand why some people in the audience thought it was really funny. Tellingly, they didn't mention (or notice?) that these same people were mostly African American, while their group was completely white. One girl mused that "it would have been better if you grew up in Brooklyn." "Perhaps, or at least certain sections of Brooklyn," I mused to myself. Once back at the hotel, with the students tucked away in their respective rooms, Ann and I were left alone. Lying in bed, Ann embarked on a stream-of-consciousness monologue that lasted until about three-thirty in the morning. She barely paused for a breath or a response from me as she told what amounted to tales from the dark side of suburban neighborliness.

She spoke mainly of the relationships between her family and two others: the Dorfmans, one of the few Jewish families in the community, consisting of professional parents who commute to New York City, an eighth-grade girl, her two younger siblings, and their Latina nanny (not a common arrangement in Shoreham-Wading River, despite the growing population of Latinos in nearby Nassau County, many of whom work as (female) domestics and (male) gardeners in other Long Island towns [Mahler 1995]); and the Hutchinsons, consisting of a stay-at-home mother, a professional father, an eighth-grade son, and his younger sister. Ann had both eighth graders in her classes. For the most part, Ann's narrative fragments centered on the mothers and their children.

"Can you believe, Lorraine, one day Beth Hutchinson had the gall to hand out invitations to her daughter's birthday party to all the kids in her class except Sonia [Ann's oldest daughter]. I just told Sonia not to pay any attention. I think Beth is just jealous. Do you know what I'm saying?" Then she talked about how after Mr. Hutchinson had spoken to her at a party, "Beth came up to me and told me that her husband just 'likes a pretty face.' And can you believe that in a parent-teacher meeting about putting kids in interage classes at Briarcliff [one of the local elementary schools], Beth went on about how teachers were *her* civil servants," an attitude that Ann, the public-school teacher, clearly found offensive. Beth elected to keep her daughter out of the interage program, but then, according to Ann, made sure that Ann's daughter who was in the group wasn't learning more than her daughter. Ann also said she had had to put an end to her daughter's relationship with the Dorfman's youngest girl. She indicated that she thought the Dorfman's home life "strange" because the mother is "never" home, and they have a (nonwhite) nanny. "They were always calling to invite Sonia over. It was really too much. I felt like they were trying to take over my daughter. You know what I'm saying?"

Ann's level of intolerance became even more pronounced when she started talking about two eighth-grade boys, David and Brad. In a rare moment, she asked me what I thought of them and then waited for my reply. I hesitated, but decided to be candid. "I suspect that they are both probably gay." Though I had a good rapport with both boys, we had never discussed their sexualities directly. Both made gestures toward having girlfriends. David said he had one in Switzerland. Brad had a girlfriend in the eighth grade for about two days; the match was set up and dissolved through a third party. David had his eye on a modeling career, walked around with a baseball cap with "CK" on it for Calvin Klein, and asked that I refer to him as "Calvin" in my book. Brad was obsessed with *Melrose Place*, *Beverly Hills 90210*, and the Academy Awards. Both surrounded themselves with female friends, while they limited their male contacts to each other and one other eighth-grade boy. None of this, of course, makes either of them gay, though I was sensitive to the possibility and ready to listen supportively if the topic ever came up. Growing up anything but heterosexual at SWR would be difficult. (See chapter 6 for a discussion of the place of gayness among SWR eighth graders.) At the very least, Brad and David bent the normal laws of gender in this community. Once I had acknowledged my suspicions about David and Brad, Ann latched onto the idea (obviously, the thought had crossed her mind as well), stating that "according to the latest research, gay men have overbearing mothers and Brad and David certainly do. You know what I'm saying?" Since I didn't know either boy's mother and neither of them spoke of their mothers in any unusual way, I didn't know what she was saying, but that didn't matter to Ann anyway. It turns out that she especially disliked David and his mother because they had called her teaching into question earlier in the year. As a result, she said, she thought David was vicious and not to be trusted. I suspected that her disdain for David and his mother went beyond this earlier incident. After all, they did live in the wealthiest, old-money section of Shoreham, while Ann *merely* lived in one of the posher new-money areas. In an attempt to dredge up some compassion in Ann, I eventually said that I really liked Brad, thought he seemed depressed lately, and commented on how I thought it would be pretty tough being a gay kid in Shoreham-Wading River. My plea fell on deaf ears.

Soon after this exchange, Ann put her monologue to rest for a few hours and allowed us to sleep. The reprieve was brief; the next morning upon waking up, she immediately picked up her story where she had left off. This time I escaped to the lobby and waited for the girls to come down for breakfast.

Normal Hysteria: Making Something Out of Nothing

Ann's talk departs from girl talk in that normal girls don't talk in isolation. Their rantings, their escalations, their sometimes less-than-kind words for each other take place in a hypersocial context. They care about what other girls think. And like an ethnographer, girls listen to each other with an intent to retell and pass stories on in order to have an impact on their social world. In leaving me mostly out of her monologue and in knowing that I have no role (or at best, a remote role through the writing of this book) in her immediate social world, Ann acknowledged that she is locked in her own private suburban greenhouse. While Ann's life had all the external trappings of a successful, normal, white middle-class life, her profound isolation pointed to a normalness that had gone too far. In this sense, Ann is hypernormal, or false normal. Ultimately, her normalness is barely skin deep.

Below, I explore girls' story making that is about establishing connections among themselves and about becoming and enduring being normal together. I look at three modes: "Stories of Entitlement and Obligation," "Infectious Stories," and "Stories That Make Perfect Sense." While these are not the only modes that girls engage to dramatize their lives, all three point to the ways that normal storytelling is collective. All these narratives are hypersymbolic and hypersocial. In this sense, they are collectively hysterical. And in the end, they are all normalizing tales.

"Stories of Entitlement and Obligation" is about how girls take care of each other and position themselves within their circle of friends by dramatically tending to one another's stories. These stories are as selfless as they are self-interested and self-making, setting girls within a social hierarchy of who is most entitled to social knowledge. Caitlin telling me about Rachel's parents is one example of this kind of story making, one that was fairly self-contained. The narrative I explore below is on a much grander scale. It is a public tale in which many more girls jockey for a position of entitlement. Hence it shows the social stakes involved in stories of entitlement and obligation and tracks the process that determines these stakes.

"Infectious Stories" demonstrates that social narratives are sometimes more powerful than words alone. This is especially true when the stories entail some form of resistance to institutional authority. Exchanging these kinds of stories can literally mean catching (in the bodily sense) somebody else's tale. While stories of entitlement and obligation position girls in a collective, each girl manages to maintain a semblance of herself as an autonomous actor. With infectious stories, the line between Self and Other, between one girl and another, constantly fluctuates as girls move between asserting their "individuality" and overidentifying with another girl's plight. Moreover, infectious stories can be particularly effective at slowing down, at least temporarily, the onslaught of adult culture in girls' lives. They are a means of resistance, though one that is ultimately stuck within the confines of what it means to be normal. In somatizing their narratives of resistance, girls work within the given parameters of white middle-class femininity. "Infectious Stories" articulates the link between SWR girls' storytelling and the concerns of race, class, and gender that delimit their lives. Specifically, it shows how infectious stories are uniquely a "girl thing."

"Stories That Make Perfect Sense" is about hearing girls' stories in the context of teen-girl culture and not simply in relation to the adult world's expectations for what counts as acceptable (normal) behavior. Using adult frameworks to analyze why the girls do what they do makes the girls look out of control rather than wholly socially logical (normal). Taking a girl's eye view reveals the limitations of the common adult perspective. And thereby suggests ways for teachers and parents to refashion their understanding of their daughters' lives and to adjust their own responses accordingly. Which adult expectations are worth fighting for and which are beyond reason? Indeed, which girls are truly in need of adult supervision and which are well on their way to "becoming normal" despite outward appearances? Moreover, "Stories That Make Perfect Sense" explores the connection between disciplinary practices and social class. What disciplinary methods socialize girls into middle- and upper-middle-class lives? And what kind of lives are these?

By way of contrast, the penultimate section of this chapter, "False Normal," looks at what happens when, like Ann, girls put up a good normal front but remain caught in their own private, self-devouring dramas. In juxtaposing these story-making practices—the normal hypersocial with the asocial hypernormal—I hope to underscore just how important teen-girl collective hysteria is in facilitating their life as part of the privileged white middle class.

STORIES OF ENTITLEMENT AND OBLIGATION

At SWR, entitlement was serious business. I would learn this both by watching the girls and by having my own entitlement and obligation tested.

I walked in a little later than usual one day. Second period was already in progress.[6] Students in the front wing's English-social studies class were scattered about, working on a research project. Their regular English-social studies teacher was away and a substitute was wandering around checking on their progress. As soon as I walked through the double-glass doors, excessively fast-talking Lisa "I♥MikethereforeIam" B. and Jessica "MysecondcousinisMariahCarey" T.[7] accosted me. Jessica blurted out, "OhmygawdLorraineIhavetotawktoyou." The two of them proceeded to tell me that their classmate and Lisa B.'s neighbor, Lisa G., had tried to kill herself twice in the past two days. Lisa G. was not in school that day. Lisa B. told me that Lisa G. had bought a "huge" bottle of aspirin and that she "had to tickle her to death" to wrestle the bottle away from her the other night. Jessica read me a letter exchange between herself and Lisa G. In the first note, Lisa G. said she wants to kill herself because she's not getting along with her family. Jessica wrote back and told Lisa that she had a lot to live for, all her friends and her boyfriend, Tom. Lisa responded by assuring Jessica that if she kills herself it won't be because of all of them.

This incident took place late in my stay at SWR. From the beginning, I had always told the girls that I wouldn't tell anyone—neither a teacher nor a parent—anything about them that they didn't want told, unless they were doing something that was seriously harmful to themselves or someone else, like threatening suicide. But I also assured them that I wouldn't tell without consulting them first. This was the first time I found myself having to make good on this promise. Like Caitlin telling Mr. R. that Rachel told her that her parents were not getting along so that Mr. R. would talk to Rachel about the situation, I was quite certain that Jessica and Lisa B. were telling me about Lisa G. because they wanted me to do something about it. I tried to ascertain if an adult knew about the situation. The girls told me they would have told Mr. R. but he was away. They didn't want to tell the vice principal or Mrs. R. (Mr. R.'s wife, who taught eighth grade in the other wing) because "they would tell everyone in the whole school." On that note, Sue and Rachel showed up. Jessica suggested that we go get Mary out of Mrs. M.'s class because Mary had been with Lisa B. the night before. They seemed to want me around so that I could legitimize their somewhat transgressive behavior. Students weren't really allowed to roam the halls and pull other kids out of classes as they pleased. But since it happened so infrequently, it was not a regularly policed activity. I told them I didn't have the authority to take Mary out of class but accompanied them on their mission anyway. Once we got to Mrs. M.'s classroom, Rachel took over and managed to abscond with Mary. Mary didn't seem to know much more than anyone else. I kept trying to find out if Lisa G.'s mother knew what was going on. In the midst of all this concerned confusion, someone blurted out that Lisa G. had taken forty aspirins (I would later find out from a teacher that it was only four or five). On that note, I strongly suggested that they call Lisa G.'s mother. Lisa B. thought that would be okay because Lisa G. was their friend and they didn't want her to get hurt. We all trudged down to the vice principal's office to use the phone.

Of course, the sight of this gaggle of known busybody girls did not go over big with the administrative staff in the office. The adults started swarming around us as Jessica and Lisa B. tried to convince them that they needed to use the phone because it was a "life or death matter." I backed them up, explaining that they needed to use the phone because they wanted to call someone's mother about something serious and that they didn't want to tell any teachers or counselors. Since my arrival in the school, I had noticed that the vice principal's secretary eyed me with a lot of suspicion and what seemed like some resentment; this was a woman who definitely liked to play by bureaucratic rules, which she took upon herself to enforce at every turn. Students asking to use the vice principal's telephone offered just such an opportunity. Luckily Mrs. R., the teacher Lisa B. and Jessica had not wanted to talk to earlier, was in the office. She saw that I knew what was going on, and she pulled rank over the secretary and arranged to let me accompany Jessica—and Jessica only—while she made this "life or death" phone call.

In the privacy of the vice principal's office, Jessica called Lisa G.'s mom, who said she knew what was going on, though she appreciated the phone call and asked to see the notes Lisa had written. While we got what we wanted—access to the phone—the breaking up of the group set off another girl drama. Lisa B. called Mrs. R. a "bitch" and said it was unfair that Jessica got to call because, having been with Lisa two nights earlier, "I know more than Jessica"; what she really meant was, "I'm more entitled." After the phone call, Jessica and I learned that Lisa B. had burst into tears and gone to the nurse's office to call her mother. Over the course of my field research, I noticed that the nurse's office prominently figured in eighth-grade-girl in-school dramas. It was the hub of hysteria, the place to which girls escaped to act out or somatize their reactions to the world's demands on their psyches, emotions, and egos. The nurse's office served as a way station between the public life of the school and the private life of the girls' homes. This will become even more apparent in the section on infectious stories below, where girls literally medicalize their social dramas.

By the time Jessica and I got back to class, the wing was abuzz with questions about what had happened to Lisa G. and why was Lisa B. so upset. I went to find Lisa B. in the nurse's office to assure her that everything was okay. The nurse had let Lisa B. call her mother. When Jessica found out that Lisa B.'s mother might pick her up and take her home (that was the circulating rumor), Jessica was "pissed" because she thought that meant that Lisa B. would go see Lisa G. Such a face-to-face meeting between the two Lisas would have supplanted Jessica's recently attained narrative hold on the whole affair, moving Lisa B. into the reigning position. As it turned out, Lisa B. stayed in school and went out to the local pizza place for lunch with Sue and me. I had invited Jessica, but she said, "It would depend." On what, I never found out.

When word got out that I was taking Lisa B. and a friend to lunch, Karen, a girl Lisa hung out with at her convenience, came running up to me in the front hall. Karen was worried because all of her friends were going to be gone during lunch. In the course of about a minute, she told me that she liked a particular boy, and Lisa had asked him if he liked her (Karen), and he had said yes, and now she (Karen) was "sooo nervous." On that note, Lisa came up to us, blew off Karen, and went to lunch with Sue and me. At lunch Lisa talked about a friend she had in Connecticut (where she had lived before moving to Wading River the previous summer) who had tried to commit suicide "'cause her stepbrother was sexually abusing her. She stayed over at our house for like two weeks. My mom knew, but like Debbie didn't like want anyone in her family to know. So like my mom didn't tell anyone." I don't know the intricacies of the system of entitlement and obligation that operated among Lisa, her mom, and Debbie, so I have no way of knowing how responsibly Lisa's mother acted in this situation. I do know that at the time Lisa told this story, Debbie had neither killed herself nor told her family about the abuse.

Like many SWR stories, Lisa G.'s suicide attempt moved carefully but quickly through the eighth-grade-girl ranks, dodging adult supervision and nosy outsiders (girls who had never been and would most likely never be part of the entitled clique). The primary tellers, Lisa B. and Jessica, clearly had personal investments in the unraveling of the episode and could only maintain their displays of compassion for Lisa G. up to a point. Once the height of the drama had passed, the empathy broke down and Lisa B. and Jessica began to vie openly for the social property rights to Lisa G.'s drama. On the surface, the girls' reaction appears selfish and even callous. However, a more generous reading recognizes that the boundaries that differentiate one girl's life from another's in this excessively social narrative space—the space of collective normalizing hysteria—are fluid and lines of identity and identification permeable at best. While Lisa B. and Jessica took Lisa G.'s threats seriously, they did not or could not fully empathize. Suicide was not entirely real to them, nor was it to most SWR eighth graders.[8] Suicide was something media figures did, as had Kurt Cobain, the lead singer of the grunge group Nirvana, earlier that year. Cobain's death resonated with SWR students, as did the overdose death of the young movie actor River Phoenix that same year. Boys and girls alike responded to these deaths with some incredulity and a sense of loss; in ending—intentionally or not—their own lives, Cobain and Phoenix had undermined SWR kids' ability to idolize and live vicariously beyond suburbia through these popular bad-boy figures. What may have once looked like a life worth desiring could no longer in-fill the tedium of their normal lives. Tommy, who was a loyal fan of Nirvana, eventually turned Cobain's death into a joke. One day he leaned over and wrote on my field notes: "What was the last thing going through Kurt Cobain's head??? His teeth!!!" and he drew a schematic picture of a gun with bullets flying out of it grazing the top of a head. In addition, he would quip periodically that he was "gonna do a Kurt Cobain." His threat was intentionally never meant to be credible. Current events and popular culture often figured in Tommy's humor. This mode of joking fit a much larger pattern that pointed to Tommy's connection to, rather than suicidal isolation from, the world. In the case of Lisa G., the girls' immediate social reality was more tangible and long-lived than Lisa G.'s threat. Consequently, once the proper adults had Lisa G.'s well-being in mind (i.e., the girls had fulfilled their social obligations), both Lisa B. and Jessica turned their attentions toward other things that mattered: Who knew what when? And who would tell what to whom?

Lisa G.'s story had given her and her friends the opportunity to refigure their ties of entitlement and obligation to each other. As the girls tended to the "problem" at hand, they stirred up an emotional frenzy within their immediate circle and a curiosity frenzy among girls on the periphery. The participating girls decided when to put up boundaries between themselves and particular authorities, who among them to draw into the drama, and when. That the incident peaked in an emotional breakdown by one girl over the fact that outside authorities had let another girl take care of the situation once and for all demonstrates the degree to which the girls' collective handling of the Lisa G. story was as much about the girls' social hierarchies and systems of entitlement and obligation to each other as it was about Lisa G. and her threatened suicide.

INFECTIOUS STORIES

Many kinds of stories of varying consequence traveled with force among SWR girls, affecting them both individually and collectively. When it came to infectious stories the emphasis was definitely on the collective. Infectious stories flared up when the girls as a group were, or one among them was, subject to unreasonable adult authority and control. When pushed too far, they consolidated their community. Here, one girl's story could become a group's story in the blink of an eye. But unlike the Lisa G. incident in which girls mainly tended to their friend's story as third parties, orchestrating from the sidelines with half a mind turned to their own social positioning, in the case of infectious stories girls took their empathy and identification to new heights. They literally embodied one girl's story as their own and in the process abandoned, to one degree or another, their own places in the social hierarchy for the benefit of the whole. Here, girl culture prevails—if only for a few brief moments—above individual self-interest or adult authority.

After I had been in the school for about three months, I decided to ask specific girls if I could shadow them for entire days. As I had suspected, this afforded me different perspectives on what it was like to be an eighth-grade girl at SWR. The technique also altered my relationships with girls by allowing me to mesh, for a day, my own identity boundaries with theirs. For the most part, girls moved, especially during lunch activity or at "teen rec" or at a school dance, in what I came to call "clumps," after their dominant mode of physical display: groups of girls huddled together often with their backs turned to unimportant outsiders. The primary clumps were almost always homogeneously made up of either girls or boys, though heterosexual clumps existed or came together as secondary clumps on a regular basis. For example, the same girl group would interact with the same boy group, forming a larger identity group. These clumps were fairly impenetrable. Clumps would address other clumps more or less collectively. When they weren't turned inward, keeping a tight rein on the social knowledge that flowed within the confines of the group, they maintained a defensive stance, eyeing outsiders suspiciously or all-too-obviously not at all. As I wandered among the eighth graders, especially in the beginning of my fieldwork, I mostly got the suspicious treatment. Girls I knew particularly well would say hi to me and maybe strike up a conversation, drawing me into the inner circle, but since not everyone in a clump knew or trusted me equally, these moments were always a little awkward and short lived. One such instance happened at the spring dance when Lisa B. called me over to join a group of girls sitting on the floor in the hall. At one point one girl said something I couldn't quite hear. Karen admonished the speaker, "Don't say that, Lorraine's here," and then turned to me and said apologetically, "No offense." Lisa broke in, "It doesn't matter, Lorraine said 'shit' once when she was mad." I surmised that this was Lisa's way of assuring her friends that I was not there to discipline them directly or to tell on them, and that I was entitled, at least from her perspective, to hear what they had to say to each other. Unfortunately, the exchange called too much attention to my nebulous nonkid-nonadult status, so I moved on, making my way among the clumps as the "wallflower" ethnographer of the dance.

Though I was not alone in this outsider status that night at the dance, I avoided, somewhat guiltily, associating with the girl-loners. Like the moment early on in my fieldwork when I simultaneously encountered Elizabeth (a loner) and Kerri (a clump ringleader) in the hall and realized my own vulnerabilities to the vagaries of eighth-grade-girl culture (see the introduction), I feared that associating with girl-loners at the dance would jeopardize my chances of breaking into the established and popular clumps at a later date. Shadowing specific girls for a day liberated me from having to choose among clumps, sheltered me from the humiliation of not being accepted into any clump or the "right" clump, and absolved me of all adult responsibility for those girls who were perpetually stigmatized as outsiders. As the shadowing ethnographer I was Kathy or Rachel and as such privy to the interiors of clump culture, or at least to whichever clump the shadowed girl belonged.

On the day I shadowed Kathy, the gym teacher decided to hold class indoors since it had rained the night before and the ground was still fairly wet. So instead of playing a team sport that required an open field, the teacher divided the class into two teams, lined them up along opposite stretches of the perimeter of the gym, and instructed them to run a two-team relay race for the rest of the period, about thirty minutes. Each eighth grader ended up running as fast as she or he could for about five laps around the gym. The exercise seemed pretty innocuous and even socially beneficial for some kids; the fastest runners in the class were not, by and large, the most popular eighth graders. The relay races gave these students a chance to be in their peers' spotlight at least for the duration of the class. The only glitch in the exercise took place when Lisa B. walked into class. Mr. K., the gym teacher, and Lisa had a running (no pun intended) battle going between them. Mr. K. had a very short fuse when it came to Lisa. In a booming, accusatory tone he would often belt out "Beirut," which was how he (mis)pronounced her last name, and then quickly admonish or attempt to humiliate Lisa for one indiscretion or another. It was never clear to me if in his slip of the tongue he intended any reference to world terrorism. The suggestion was not lost on Lisa, who one day in social studies giggled knowingly when the topic of conflict in the Middle East and Beirut came up. She clearly made the connection. On this particular day, Beirut's/Lisa's offense was coming to class dressed in street clothes. Mr. K. told her that she had to participate in gym or she couldn't be on the track team, a passion of Lisa's, one of the few, as far as I could tell, that wouldn't get her in trouble with the adults in her life. In the fall semester, Lisa's first in the school, she had failed gym. In a diary entry that Lisa wrote for an English elective, she comments: "I'll admit I'm not doing good in school. I heard that I'm the only one in this whole school to fail gym! I hate gym. But Mr. K. my gym teacher is also the track coach. So I have to show him I can do something. Because track is my life I ♥ it." On this particular day, Lisa avoided Mr. K.'s wrath and retribution by acquiescing. Not surprisingly, she outran most of her classmates.

After gym, which ended in the locker room with Lisa G. randomly spraying deodorant around as she complained of the body odor that she perceived to be permeating the atmosphere, girls hurried off to English class. Not long after Kathy and I had settled down to work—the kids were writing articles for the school newspaper, and Kathy was reporting on the upcoming dance—word started traveling that several eighth graders were holed up in the nurse's office either getting sick or complaining about not feeling well. Reportedly, Brad had thrown up six times, David four; Jennifer was having an asthma attack; Brianna felt faint. As the period went on, girls started dropping like flies and making their way to the nurse, either because they didn't feel well or because they "needed" to check on a friend. Kathy seemed to feel fine, though she decided she had to talk to the music teacher about missing her clarinet lesson the following period. She wanted to go to math class instead because they were having a test the next day, and she was concerned that she didn't know the material. As it turned out, Kathy stayed home from school the next day because she suffered from "exhaustion." Regardless, her music-versus-math predicament gave us a chance to drop by the nurse's office and scope out the scene.

By the time we got there, Lisa B. had joined the ranks of the infirm. Brad was lying on a cot with cold, damp paper towels on his forehead, and Lisa was gently teasing him, "Brad, you are such a girl." Brad blushed slightly and smiled. Lisa's observation was on some level astute, and Brad took no offense. In fact, the only eighth graders who had fallen ill were indeed girls, except for Brad and David, the two boys in the class whose gender identification seemed more fluid than that of most of their male peers. This "illness" did indeed seem like a girl thing, though no one other than Lisa acknowledged this directly.

By lunch, Lisa had gone home with her mother. She had sustained other social injuries. Not long after the gym-class humiliation, a boy from another wing had come up to Lisa's locker and maliciously popped her birthday balloon, which was left over from the day before. Lisa, who was prone to fighting with her mother and her teachers, had been fairly even tempered the preceding few days. At her birthday lunch at Taco Bell with Mr. R., myself, and about five other eighth graders, Mr. R. had acknowledged Lisa for being "so sweet lately," and asked her, "Wazup?"[9] To which Lisa replied, "My mother is letting me have friends." Lisa and her mother continually struggled over who Lisa chose as her friends. Expressly, her mother didn't want her hanging out with kids from nearby Riverhead, a lower-middle-class, mixed-race community. In one conversation I had with Lisa, she explained that her mother thought Riverhead kids were "white trash." When I asked her what she meant by "white trash," she said, "White people who try to act black. My mother isn't prejudice [common SWR kid diction omits the "d" in prejudiced], she just doesn't like white people acting and dressing black." Despite the newly found truce with her mother (one that would not last for long), on this particular day, the gym and birthday-balloon incidents proved too much for Lisa to handle. As a result, she hauled herself over to the nurse's office and got herself excused from what remained of the school day. Meanwhile, the rest of her infirm gym-class partners were back on their feet going to classes, hanging out in clumps, doing what SWR girls do. I, on the other hand, was left wondering what the etiology of this collective outbreak of "illness" was. And why was this physical breakdown a girl thing? The array of prone bodies in the nurse's office had had a surreal quality to it; this was more than a medical emergency.

In an ethnographic account of young Malay women making the transition from a peasant society to one based in global-capitalist labor practices in recently introduced factories of transnational corporations, Aihwa Ong observes her subjects engaging in direct and indirect forms of resistance that bear some resemblance to SWR "girls'" gym-class breakdown. Factory women would cry, deliberately slow down their work pace, become careless in assembling components, lose their tempers, leave the shop floor to attend to "female problems" in the locker room, and experience debilitating spirit attacks all in the course of the work day. Ong contrasts such collective performative displays with anonymous "microprotests" or "deliberate but surreptitious attacks on factory equipment" (Ong 1987, 213, 210). For Ong, such individual and anonymous acts of sabotage lack focus in that they don't make specific demands on management. Though Ong finds the collective "ritualized rebellions" equally diffuse, she also notes that the visibility and social character of such irruptions force shop managers to confront and even make concessions to the women's physical and cultural needs.

In analyzing the women's protests, Ong writes, "At issue [was] not a conscious attack on commodity relations but rather the self-constitution of a new identity rooted in human dignity" (196). The demands and disciplines of this new factory work did not respect Malay women's conceptions of themselves as workers or women. And because this new identity interrupted Malay cultural understandings of gender—young women working in transnational corporations no longer met *kampung* (village) expectations for how women should behave in public and private—these women had become anomalies within their own community. Questions of gender and personhood were at stake both on the shop floor and in their personal lives. To a large extent, these women somatized these conflicts. On the shop floor, women became physically ill or possessed by spirits. On the streets and at home, they began to act, in the context of traditional village life, in a more sexually promiscuous manner by publicly dating and dressing seductively. These behaviors demonstrate that while their cultural and economic lives were in transition, these women used their bodies to resist the unreasonable demands placed on them (and their working or sexual bodies) by both the newly introduced capitalist culture and the traditional village culture under which they grew up.

How much of what took place on the gym floor and in the nurse's office at SWR Middle School represents a similar gendered and collective response to disciplinary control and the girls' ambiguous status—as not quite women, not quite children—in their homes and in the school? Numerous texts, ranging from Paul Willis's *Learning to Labor* (1977) to Douglas Foley's *Learning Capitalist Culture* (1990) to Penelope Eckert's *Jocks and Burnouts* (1990) to Philip Wiseman's documentary film *High School* (1966), have demonstrated the degree to which schools discipline their students into specific ways of occupying the world. [10]

For the most part, these texts focus on class and do not offer an explicit analysis of gender. In the case of SWR girls, their social, familial, and educational world revolves around facilitating (disciplining) their emergence as white middle-class women. On the microlevel, this entails following rules in gym class, going from one class to another in a reasonably orderly fashion, and getting busy with work when adults expect you to do just that, that is unless you put the brakes on and feel sick, have a music lesson, or have to attend to some crisis, yours or your best friend's. Such girl-fabricated measures, however, are largely stopgap; they interrupt the flow of events, but in the larger scheme of things, they continue to produce girls as normal subjects. Middle-class life expects a certain amount of rebellion out of its youth. Not following the rules can sometimes help middle-class adults advance professionally, economically, and socially. Therefore, part of being a successful middle-class subject is knowing when to break which rules and knowing how to get away with it. SWR girls were in the process of figuring out these boundaries for themselves and they were doing it in the context of being girls.

Like the Malay women, SWR girls primarily have control over their bodies and stories, while their bodies and stories are also a concentrated site of cultural, educational, religious, and parental anxiety. The culture at large envisions middle-class white girls as physically and sexually vulnerable. The media abounds with stories of teen-girl anorexics; bulimics; runaways turned prostitutes; incest or gang-rape survivors; cigarette, alcohol, and even Ridilin or Ecstasy abusers; to name a few prominent scenarios. Though these stories are not often explicitly about white middle-class girls, a cursory analysis shows just how raced and classed these gendered stories are. The media are horrified if a white suburban girl runs away and turns into an urban call girl and barely takes note if an African American or Latina teen resorts to similar measures. The latter don't make for as good a story.

Any delusion I may have had that these national news stories were not about "my girls" was quickly set to rest one night when I attended religious instruction with three SWR girls at a nearby Catholic church. Unbeknownst to my hosts, the night they invited me to their class a guest speaker, Mary Ann D'Angelo, a gray-haired, portly woman with a Barbara Bush look, was slated to present a program on abstinence. Mrs. D'Angelo—for she let us know under no uncertain terms that she was a *Mrs.*, happily so for over thirty years, and a mother of two beautiful grown-up and married children—stood in front of the altar before a group of about one hundred middle-schoolaged girls and boys, their religion-instruction teachers, and myself. She led us in a collective reciting of the Our Father and a Hail Mary and then proceeded to barrage us with (mis)information about sex, AIDS, abortion, love, lust, and teen pregnancy for the good part of an hour. The white middle-class teenage girl's body stood at the center of her diatribe.

Mrs. D'Angelo encouraged those in the audience who had already "fallen prey to their hormones" to take stock and claim their "secondary virginities." To those who hadn't succumbed yet, she said: "Sex is a decision that will affect your life forever. You will look back and regret it. You won't be able to look back and do things differently. When you have sex you degrade yourself and usurp your power by giving yourself up to someone else." Here the "you" was clearly directed toward the girls in the audience. She told horror story after horror story. In one such legendary tale, when the parents of a pregnant twelve-year-old girl took her to have an abortion, the girl ended up bleeding to death because the "abortionists" had punctured her uterus. Lest we miss the main point, Mrs. D'Angelo quickly added, "As Catholics we don't even consider abortion." Then she explained that "abortion was ripping apart babies. We have the photographs of babies' body parts to prove it." She told us that condoms don't work—"They may be able to keep out sperm some of the time, but not the AIDS virus." Moreover, she said that then–Surgeon General Jocelyn Elders had knowingly handed out defective condoms while she was Bill Clinton's state health director when he was governor of Arkansas, and asked, "Are you going to trust someone who gives you a condom?" She concluded by claiming that sex causes cancer, that girls can become sterile from using birth control (which means that when they're adults, "after they're married, [formerly sexually active girls] will be denied family life"), and that "girls think tenderness is love while boys think release of sexual tension is love."

The underlying message to her homogeneously white middle-class audience was that these girls' bodies were to be protected from the boys, doctors, and politicians who were poised to take advantage of them. After the talk, one SWR girl, recognizing that Mrs. D'Angelo's narrative was about policing girls' bodies, said, "She just talked at us and wants us to wear frumpy clothes and just go out on group dates. It's stupid." Though the girls had strong negative reactions to Mrs. D'Angelo's talk, I couldn't help but wonder if they would internalize some of what she said, if only in the form of a generalized discomfort with and mistrust of their bodies and sexualities.

While Mrs. D'Angelo may represent an extreme, in their day-to-day lives SWR girls knew that their bodies were a site of control and hence potential resistance. The recurring presence of the nurse's office in their social dramas was more than a coincidence. Given the dominant culture's anxiety about and oftentimes medicalization of white middle-class girls' bodies, school authorities, for example, don't tend to challenge girls who express their social discomforts through their bodies. Being "sick" is an acceptable middle-class mode of retreat or method of procuring positive adult attention. SWR girls' big and small rebellions often manifest themselves physically and narratively and emerge in relation to familial, educational, or social pressures. Caught in a transitional moment, teen girls must learn to accommodate the values and expectations of their parents as well as those of their teachers and peer group. At times these worlds are in conflict, forcing girls to devise ways to move in and out of these different contexts while simultaneously holding onto or adjusting their sense of who they are accordingly. Sometimes the transitions are smoother than others. Lisa G. threatens suicide because she is unhappy at home, turning her emotional distress into a physical crisis. Likewise, she writes notes to her friends, drawing one of her worlds into the other and attempting to take control of her own narrative. Lisa B. adds another hole to one of her ears every time she has a "big" fight with her mother over who she can and can't go out with. A personal ritual that literally brands her social conflicts and frustrations on her body. By the end of eighth grade, she had about eight holes in each ear. On almost a daily basis, thin LeeAnn makes pronouncements about being "fat" while she distributes the contents of her lunch to her friends who tell her how skinny she is in an effort to encourage her to eat. In SWR girls' bodies and words, in their sartorial displays, their eating habits, their sexual activity or nonactivity, and their storied collective dramas, they resist, react, and manipulate the world around them. When Lisa B. exclaimed that the sick-out was indeed a "girl" thing she was offering a succinct cultural analysis whether she could articulate it as such or not.

But just who benefited from the gym class sick-out? And how effective can girls' rebellions be? Do they work against the grain of normalization or do they function as prime disciplinary moments? Suicide and anorexia clearly do not alter the tyranny of bodily control in white middle-class girls' lives. These acts turn in on the self, replicating, however perversely, rather than rupturing norms. Like the Malay women's spirit possessions, SWR girls' bodily and narrative (hypersymbolic) actions often appear diffuse and unconscious. In true middle-class form, they do not confront their oppressors—be they teachers or the school or the gender system itself—directly. However, when they protest in a hypersocial manner, using their bodies as the primary mode of expression, SWR girls begin to act out a critique of normalizing disciplinary practices that is beyond adult reproach. What can you say to a roomful of nauseous girls? Likewise, I can't help but wonder how much of the mini-epidemic following the gym class relays was brought on by Mr. K.'s attack on Lisa B. at the beginning of the period rather than on the strenuous activity of the race itself. Instead of leaving Lisa to her microprotests, SWR "girls" rallied around her and staged a collective (albeit somewhat unfocused) rebellion. Lisa B. resisting Mr. K.'s disciplinary actions alone makes Lisa B. the problem; ten or more girls leaving class sick to seek comfort and solace in the nurse's office turns an accusatory finger toward institutional disciplinary practices. Moreover, the sick-out offered a hypersocial, hypersymbolic (an infectious and hysterical) drama the girl community could use to liven up their sooo boring suburban lives. Though no school authorities took specific actions to alleviate future sick-outs, the girls had managed to stop the institution, for the time being anyway, from running smoothly. Unfortunately, the rebellion and its effects were short lived. It did not take long for things to fall back into their normalizing routine. The girls would eventually complete their English assignments and once again attend gym class with Mr. K. The underlying structure of white middle-class normality remained.

STORIES THAT MAKE PERFECT SENSE

Lisa B. figures prominently in this and other chapters of this autoethnography because she struggled most visibly with the normalizing forces she confronted on a daily basis. In being an extreme case, Lisa B. was an anomaly. She constantly had a good story to tell because she spent much of her time making sure that her sooo normal life was not going to be too unbearably boring (cultureless). But Lisa was not an anomaly in the sense that she almost always did what she did in a hypersocial context, and she often knew how to make sense of her white middle-class life even if she couldn't translate that understanding into a peaceful existence. Lisa was so busy being "bad," and the people around her (other girls as well as adults, though her peers were much more forgiving than her teachers or parents as far as I could tell) were so busy identifying her as such, no one—except the constitutionally interested autoethnographer—seemed to recognize that Lisa often rapidly articulated uncanny observations and useful everyday analyses about SWR life. In part, Lisa could do this because she was somewhat of an outsider. As a recent émigré—I use the word advisedly; Lisa's family's move to middle-class Long Island had something to do with a divorce and a remarriage—from a more urban neighborhood in Connecticut, the suburban homogeneity of SWR was new and somewhat strange to her. Hence she could name it, or at least sensed that there was something there to name. As an outsider struggling to locate herself within her new culture and seeming to fail at almost every turn, Lisa made the process of becoming normal visible. In the end, Lisa's stories narrated and justified her existence and located her firmly within the social cosmology of SWR girl culture. In this sense, her seemingly wild stories were perfectly normal and certainly worth considering on their own merit. Seeing the world through Lisa's logic reveals complex details about the middle-class life she was being socialized to lead at SWR.

One day after school, I wandered off to the SWR athletic fields. As I approached the track, I could see that Lisa was "having words" with the coach, this time not Mr. K., but his colleague, Mr. D. I hung back. She stormed off the field and when she caught sight of me came up to tell me her story. The altercation again revolved around whether or not Lisa was going to get dressed to run. She said that she wanted to go home at three-thirty instead of four-thirty when the track team usually stopped practice. She wanted to go home with Karen. "Karen is in gymnastics, and she's leaving at three-thirty today. I'm afraid that Fran is gonna try to beat me up again." Earlier that afternoon, Lisa and Karen had run up to me in the hall to tell me that Fran had just "beat up" Lisa. There were no visible signs that Lisa had been in a fight, but I knew that Lisa was in an ongoing feud with Fran and her friend Amber. They explained that they had already talked to the vice principal about the situation. "At first she told us she would take care of it; now she says it's our fault." Then, as quickly as the conversation had convened, Lisa and Karen were on their way. By the time I caught up with Lisa on the field, she started complaining that "Mr. D. is not being very understanding. I'm having a bad day. Other people come out and just watch sometimes." In Lisa's eyes, she was being a good team member and taking care of herself and her friend. She had gone out to the field to see if Mr. D. and Mr. K. were teaching them anything new. She kept telling me that she told Mr. D. that "it wasn't his team; it was our team," and her teammates didn't care if she practiced today or not. He reportedly kept telling her that she couldn't be on the team unless she made a commitment like everyone else.

The conversation went on along this vein with Lisa telling me other details about how her mother just bought her sixty-dollar sneakers and new shorts, and how SWR's track team "sucked" compared to the team she used to run on at her school in Connecticut. "In Connecticut there were black kids on the team and I was faster than all of them except one. All we do on this team is run. In Connecticut, we did relays around the block, and I always won." She explained to me that she liked track meets because "you get to meet new people, like this one time this short black girl was standing next to me in the starting line, and she said, 'You're gonna beat me,' and then she went and beat me."[11] In the course of Lisa's talk, her then-boyfriend, Mark, came up to us and teasingly said, "You two sure have a lot to talk about." Then Lisa's friend Becky came up and told Lisa she couldn't quit the team. To which Lisa replied, "If they don't want me, I'm not gonna be on the team." Eventually Mr. K. passed us on his way out to practice, "Hey Beirut, where were you today in class?" "I didn't cut," Lisa responded, "Jessica didn't feel well, and Sue and I went into the locker room to sit with Jessica. And then the period was over." By this time, Mr. D. had come up to see if Lisa was "ready to talk." She resisted a little but decided to make an attempt at resolving the situation. I left them to work things out.

The next morning, Lisa told me she was still on the team. I'm not exactly sure what transpired between Mr. D. and Lisa, or, for that matter, Mr. K. and Lisa, but I do know that Lisa's story made perfect sense. In suggesting how the track team should be governed—"It's not your team; it's ours"—and in explaining why she didn't participate in gym—she was helping a friend in the locker room—yet still wasn't technically cutting class, Lisa spoke firmly from within the parameters of everyday girl culture at SWR. Tending to a friend's needs is top priority. Moreover, Lisa's version of acting as a "team" extended the official school logic that structured the overall educational program. At that time, the middle school was divided into four academic teams. Each team included about fifty students from each grade level. Two instructors, an English/social studies and a math/science teacher, served as the core faculty of each team. Teachers who taught subjects like art, physical education, Spanish, and French, for example, were assigned to one of the four teams as advisors. Depending on the mix of adults and kids, the teams had decidedly different characters. Lisa's team was particularly group oriented. From the beginning of the year, they had gone on team-focused trips and participated in numerous team meetings and team-building activities. Lisa's idea that the track team should be run by the players made pedagogical sense within this context. What would interscholastic sports look like if the athletes set the rules, if their commitment was to each other and not to a coach? Such a move could turn school athletic fields into exercises in community building and governance. Girls like Lisa would have an immediate stake—their relationships with their peers—in whether or not they followed through on their commitments, and they would have the opportunity to develop civic consciousness and responsibility. Such a nonhierarchical, collective approach, however, would go against the grain of a key white middle-class normalizing institution, the interscholastic athletic team. While competitive team sports are not just a white middle-class phenomenon in the immediate sense—clearly nonwhite, nonmiddle-class kids, and adults for that matter, play team sports—in their current configuration, interscholastic sports function as a key site for transmitting dominant values of class, gender, and race (Foley 1990). Learning to be a competitive team player—keeping commitments, working together, getting along while striving to develop individual skills and talents, and following the appropriate authorities—will take SWR kids far (at least to management status) in corporate America. This would be the basic class analysis operating here. But what of gender and more complex notions of class?

In part because of Title IX, the 1972 law that required federally funded schools to provide equal athletic opportunities to students regardless of gender, the presence of girls' interscholastic teams had grown by leaps and bounds in the twenty years since I had run on the same track on which Lisa now excelled. I remember enthusiastically playing soccer in seventh grade only to find out that there would be no girls' team the following year because we were not allowed to play "contact sports." In the intervening decades, white middle-class women have increasingly entered into professional careers and are now expected to thrive in the capitalist marketplace. Directly and indirectly, team sports facilitate this process. It is no accident that affirmative action supporters advocate for a "level playing field"; the metaphor is apt. Though the school's more student-centered pedagogy would seem counterintuitive—as it clearly did to Lisa—to the kind of discipline enforced in the realm of interscholastic sports, in the end the contradictions underscore the privileges of this community. SWR girls are not merely being taught to be middle managers (good team players); they are expected to be strong leaders who can withstand the disciplines of capitalist culture while also succeeding as compassionate professionals and cultural innovators. They are being socialized to be upstanding members of the upper-middle class. Lisa was caught between the two worlds. By disciplining Lisa, her coaches were effectively attempting to perpetuate one side of the equation. By resisting, Lisa was playing out the other side, extending the values of SWR girl culture, which were in some ways closer to SWR pedagogical practices than not, to larger concerns of gender and upper-middle-class privilege.

False Normal

What happens when girls don't participate in their peers' collective hysterias? When they don't drop everything to help a friend? When they don't participate in the system of entitlement and obligation that constitutes SWR girl culture? When they don't "catch" each other's narratives and stage indirect collective protests against unreasonable disciplinary control, or when their stories don't make collective girl sense?

Some girls make a conscious choice to strike out on their own. They have better things to do or other ways and places to belong. Others make attempts at being included, but they can't quite find a place for themselves or can't sustain a connection. Though not all girls fit with the "popular" crowd, most have a place within less visible clumps and are busy filling their own lives with narrative trouble while keeping tabs on the popular girls. In these ways, most eighth graders are not completely isolated or cut off from collective normalizing activities. A few, however, seem profoundly disconnected. Oddly enough, these outsiders can be extremely elusive. They don't stand out from the crowd unless you really start paying attention. On the surface, they appear terribly normal. However, seen in the context of the larger girl culture and even in the context of their own life narratives, the seamlessness of these girls' lives begins to break down.

Tracey was what I am calling a false normal. On the day-to-day level, she didn't call attention to herself. She did her schoolwork, participated in some after school activities, and basically acted and looked fairly average. Initially, her appearance was the only thing setting her apart, ever so slightly, from most, but certainly not all, of her peers. She was physically younger than the majority of the other eighth-grade girls and dressed in a less fashion-conscious style. In addition, I started to notice that Tracey remained quiet in a classroom unless a teacher called on her directly, and she didn't interact with many other girls or get involved in their everyday dramas. At first I thought this made her a model middle-class girl. Despite her young appearance perhaps she was more mature than her peers, more able to follow the institutional rules, more focused on succeeding than on being popular. But something did not seem quite right with this initial assessment. And I began to pay closer attention.

In putting together her final project for the diary elective, Tracey worked with Dana on an album they called "A Look at Our Lives." In general, Dana was more social than Tracey, though she was not as conscientious a student. In the end, Dana didn't complete her half of the project. Tracey put together a collection of family photos she captioned and surrounded with keywords, like "family," "house," "love," et cetera. On the final page, she incorporated these words into a crossword puzzle. "A Look at Our Lives" was tidy and literal. The sentences "This is my family's house. It is red" accompanied a snapshot of the outside of her red house. Such a juxtaposition was as far as Tracey could or would take the concept of her family album. When I asked her questions like "What kinds of things do you think of when you think of your house? What childhood stories do you remember when you look at that picture?" she just insisted that she didn't think of anything other than the fact that the house was red. After several attempts at trying to get her to think more creatively, I gave up. As an autoethnographer-teacher, I felt like I had slammed into a brick wall. There was no room for abstract thinking in Tracey's suburbia. Life to her was utterly literal or hyposymbolic, devoid of narrative and seemingly beyond interpretation.

As I continued to interact with and observe Tracey, I began to figure out what Canguilhem meant when he noted that there is an "ambiguity of meaning in the term normal" ([1966] 1991, 126). In the end, I surmised that like Ann, Tracey exemplifies a "false normal" life. She is someone who is in some sense sooo normal she is hypernormal, isolated in a seemingly impenetrable façade of normalcy. She is a good little girl who writes in pink diaries, does all her homework, and doesn't get involved in the trouble her peers stir up around her. She fills her life not with stories that beg retellings and exaggerations, or entail entitlements and obligations, or are based on girl rather than adult logic, but with stories that she is caught repeating endlessly and unproductively to herself.

Being normal is being able to adjust to new environments. Normative behavior is flexibly situational and collectively understood. In other words, normal girls can tolerate infractions of the habitual norm and institute new norms in new situations (Canguilhem [1966] 1991, 196–197). Tracey could do no such things. Away from her home and school—her habitual surroundings—Tracey's (hyper)normalness began to unravel. On a trip down to Washington, D.C., where a group of students, two teachers—Mr. R. and Mrs. T.—and I went to attend a National Middle School Association conference—the teacher driving the minibus, Mr. R., was making an excessive number of bathroom stops. On other trips of comparable distance that I had made with eighth graders and this same teacher, we had pulled off the highway for, at most, one combined lunch-bathroom break. This time we seemed to be stopping once an hour. When I inquired into this aberrant pattern, Mr. R. responded, "Tracey supposedly has a kidney problem." Mrs. T. jumped in and asked me if I had noticed how Tracey is always late for class. "She goes to the bathroom in between every class," she explained. Neither teacher seemed convinced of the physical origin of Tracey's "illness." Regardless, they accommodated her idiosyncrasies as best they could.

Throughout the trip, Tracey refused to drink anything but water and cranberry juice, and these if and only if they met her standards of purity. At dinner one night, when the waitress brought Tracey some ice water with a lemon slice on the lip of the glass, Tracey immediately grabbed the lemon and without uttering a word dumped it into her "friend" Jane's glass of Sprite. Jane ignored or simply tolerated this and other of Tracey's trespasses. After wiping the lip of her glass with a napkin, Tracey called the waitress over and asked her if she had put any of the lemon in her water. Tracey would take a sip only after the waitress had assured her that she hadn't polluted the water with lemon. I had never witnessed even remotely similar behavior from Tracey back at SWR, where, presumably, she had more control over her environment. Away from home, her habitual norm could not adjust.

This would not be the last time I observed Tracey holding up the group, eating in a bizarre and controlling manner, or speaking harshly or acting badly toward her one companion on the trip, Jane. Since I had not seen Jane and Tracey hang out together at school, I surmised that this was a friendship of convenience. None of Jane's regular friends were on the trip, and Jane didn't seem to fit in with the other "popular" girls who were. Consequently, Jane seemed resigned to putting up with Tracey and what turned out to be her outrageous and somewhat contradictory (ambiguous) behavior. For example, one morning at breakfast Tracey would eat only a plateful of bacon. When she was done she announced that she and Jane were done, and they were going to the hotel gift shop. Jane, still in the middle of eating, sheepishly said she had left her money in the room. "Stupid," Tracey snapped. "I told you to bring your money so we could shop." Jane recoiled under Tracey's recriminations.

When she wasn't bossing Jane around or making demands about what she consumed or when she expelled substances from her body, Tracey appeared shy and little-girl-like. When her peers stood up to make presentations before an audience of teachers at the conference, Tracey was visibly uncomfortable and audibly almost imperceptible. Her voice became small and childish. This behavior stood in stark contrast to that of the rest of the SWR eighth graders on the trip. One by one they stood before the roomful of teachers, competently said what they had to say, and even added a personal flourish or two. Some, like Justine and Tommy, completely charmed the audience. Teachers flocked to them at the end of the session wanting to hear more about their lives as SWR eighth graders. Tracey faded into the background.

I only saw Tracey join in with her peers when I found them watching a porn channel in the boys' hotel room. Here, the two boys on the trip and Tracey were nearly enraptured; Jane was watching out of the corner of her eye in the back of the room; and Rebecca was squealing and begging me not to ask them to show me what they were watching. It was late afternoon. The kids were without supervision because both teachers were attending to the needs of another student on the trip. We had all recently returned from an afternoon on the Mall in downtown D.C. On the Metro ride back to the hotel, a man had grabbed one of the girl's breasts while saying, "Nice tits." The incident left everyone a bit stunned and the girl and her best friend on the trip, Rebecca, rather distraught. Tracey showed only fleeting concern for her classmate, and she saw to it that Jane followed suit. It was as if she didn't want to entertain the closeness and tangibleness of this real-life sexual assault and instead retreated into the excesses of representation, the porn channel on the hotel cable—a highly antisocial response in the context of the existing girl culture.

While Tracey filled her life with dramas, unlike the crises of the other SWR girls, which were collective and socially performative, hers were private, individualized, and static. Not surprisingly, Tracey had run in the gym relay races that had driven many of her "girl" classmates to the nurse's office. Tracey was not among them. In general, Tracey's hypernormalness consigned her to a life beyond becoming normal. To be normal among the SWR girls was to participate in turning your everyday life into a kind of dramatic, ongoing miniseries. It was to use stories to make connections with your peers; to make trouble with, bypass, or communicate with adults; to give an intentionally unnamable life substance; to in-fill the boredom of a life where things are always already supposed to be taken care of. Tracey already knew how to name her life: This is my family. This is my house. But a normal life cannot be named directly. Instead it must be expressed in wild stories and identified through consumer acquisitions and media fabrications. Tracey's "This is my house" way of naming was more hypo- than hypersymbolic. It did not lead to deeper understanding or stronger social connections. It existed in a symbolic void. Moreover, Tracey's (hyper)normalness was already filled, chock-full, with trouble, leaving her little room to tend to other people's problems or partake in the very effervescence of middle-school girl life, the pleasures of being caught in the throes of a collective normalizing hysteria.

Recycling Memories

Gym class and the track team aside, the official school culture often tolerated and at times humored the girls' hysterical story making. The most effective teachers among the SWR faculty worked around or with the girls' everyday traumas, incorporating their storied realities into the curriculum and the culture of the school. Girls' serial dramas were background music (or cacophony) to the "work" of the classroom, a labor that included teaching students to be better readers and writers as much as helping them to make their way in the world as members of a community and identity group—white middle-class America. In a session at the D.C. conference, Mr. R. declared, "Recycling memories and experiences is important to kids." Doing this recycling as part of a community was fundamental to the teachings of this school. Toward the end of the school year, eighth-grade teachers had their students write "Letters to Self." Once the letters were composed and sealed in an envelope, the kids handed them in. They would receive them back when they graduated from high school in 1998. Each year, before high-school graduation, the twelfth graders get together for a "Senior Brunch." There, in a ritualized collective act of remembering, each student rereads his or her "Letter to Self." The Self here, while clearly individuated, is also part of a community, a culture, and a way of life. The eighth graders' letters will be reread with a social purpose, one that gives their sooo normal lives a memory of their own making, or so it will seem. They will have a storied past to take with them or to leave behind, though not far behind, as they leave high school to move on to college or a middle-class life of work and family on or off Long Island.

Not long after they had written their "Letters to Self," Lisa B. asked me if my project was like a "Letter to Self." I hesitated, again, a bit unnerved by how perceptive Lisa could be, but then quickly acknowledged her insight, "Yeah, a long 'Letter to Self.'" Like the girls' storied reality, my "Letter to Self" is filled with larger-than-life stories—Amy, Cheryl, Dora, and Emily—and with everyday serial dramas—Lisa G.'s suicide episode, the girls' collective sick-out, Lisa B.'s track team saga, as well as the school board's infighting and the unneighborly neighborhood of Ann's late-night monologue. In returning to the site and personification of my past (SWR and its current fleet of eighth-grade girls) and in setting down and interpreting the stories of this place and subject, I am also looking to in-fill normal, white middle-class girlhood, this black hole of culture that is actually filled with a thicket of storied sociality. My "Letter to Self" is a serial, hypersymbolic, hypersocial narrative about becoming normal. What makes it different from the girls' narratives is that my story is not so much normalizing as potentially antinormal. I am not reproducing the norm, for in describing it directly, I am analyzing a process of production that struggles not to call attention to itself and disguises itself in teen-girl mayhem. In the end, chaos is made up of a set of normalizing and discernible patterns that are neither beyond interpretation nor implacably determined. When understood in the larger context of collective white middle-class teen-girl culture the normal is chaotic and the chaotic normal.

Chapter 5 I Was a Teenage White Supremacist

There's all kinds of madness in the world, that's what I tell Johnson. Some of it gets you locked up. Some of it puts you on pills so you don't have to think, just remember to breathe and eat. Most of it leaves you in the here and now, not quite broken, not quite whole.

—Paula K. Gover, "Chances with Johnson," in *White Boys and River Girls*

Living with a Past

WHEN I MET Emily it seemed that no one wanted to tell her story as she wanted it told. Numerous media outlets—ranging from the *New York Times* to the *Montel Williams Show*—had already featured Emily's story in articles or television segments. However, none had told the story to Emily's satisfaction. Some had even deliberately distorted the facts. Others didn't talk about things that were important to Emily. I was called in by her aunt, an eighth-grade teacher at Shoreham-Wading River who knew of my interest in the racialization of white teen girls and, because of our own long-standing friendship (she had been my eighth-grade teacher), she trusted my narrative and analytical instincts, as well as my motivations. As it turns out, however, this chapter is not so much Emily's story as it is about what I learned about whiteness and about the link between normative whiteness and teen girlhood from interviewing Emily and from paying close attention to how the media have portrayed her story. Like all the other representations, this version of Emily's story is not the true or last word on her life. Instead, it is about the impossibility of final narrative solutions to questions of racial identity. It is about how whiteness—which in some guises could be understood as this thing of darkness I acknowledge mine—needs to be continually critically engaged by girls like Emily and by autoethnographers like myself.

In writing about Emily, I give her story context and thereby try to understand it largely by analyzing popular representations of her case and by tracking related discursive constructs, like the historical and political manipulation of the figure of the (racialized) teen mother. Like Amy's and Cheryl's stories, Emily's *is* her media portraits and their making. However, this chapter differs from the previous accounts of wayward daughters because both Emily and I get to talk back to the media here. For Emily, talking back to the media is, in part, about setting the record straight and, I suspect, also about learning to live with her past. In this vein, this chapter foregrounds the making of Emily's story and her reactions to it.

By joining and then later leaving a supremacist group, Emily constituted herself as a white girl with a big, public story to tell. Unlike the SWR girls in the previous chapter who search for ways to fill the void of their sooo normal, sooo boring lives, Emily has already accomplished this and now looks for a way to reconcile this past with the normality she covets for herself and her daughter. By cluttering her initially normal life with a media-sized personal history she must learn to live with, Emily—like the unlovable daughters who have come before her in this book and in the media—has broken a golden rule of privilege: to be a white middle-class suburban girl is to be seen and not heard, to not rock the boat, to grow up without a past, or at least without a past worth examining or publicly representing. In telling and retelling her story, Emily's personal project is not unlike my own in this autoethnography. Both Emily and I are in search of a way to articulate and live with what it means to have a past as a white middle-class suburban girl. This chapter is one installment in that journey for both Emily and myself.

In making her own past larger than life and taking the process of being white to an extreme—becoming a white supremacist—Emily has not only given herself a namable (racial) past; her story also points to a relationship between mainstream (normal, suburban) whiteness and white supremacy. This is why Emily's story is part of my own story on white middle-class America and part of the lives of current SWR girls. Both suburbia and white supremacist groups historically define themselves in opposition to nonwhite Others, including in this context Jews and Catholics (with regard to suburbia's anti-Semitism and anti-Catholicism, see Jackson 1985, 241; and Blee 1991). The difference between the norm and the extreme here is clearly one of degree, directness, and single-mindedness, with the supremacists practicing not so much a culture of avoidance as a culture of confrontation between themselves and everybody else, including mainstream whites as Emily herself will make clear. Nevertheless, though I did not encounter any self-identifying white supremacists at Shoreham-Wading River, I did witness certain underlying ideological affinities between the practices of these mainstream whites and the version of white supremacy that Emily espoused. Moreover, Emily's quest for a white identity, which was in part what led her to join the racial hate group in the first place, tells us more about normative whiteness and its relationship to its Others, both insiders and outsiders, than it does about white supremacy. White supremacy in Emily's case becomes a foil for normative whiteness as well as a window into its production.

Though the local SWR culture of avoidance kept girls from actively discussing racial differences (see the next chapter for a detailed analysis of the ways in which girls and the community as a whole assiduously avoided talking about race, theirs or anybody else's, too directly), the territory of Jewishness and anti-Semitism—a favorite target, among others, for white supremacists—was less clear cut and hence the silences less strictly honored; anti-Semitism would at times slip through the social cracks. Hence, I turn to a couple of instances where Jewishness became part of the conversation at SWR to show that the extremities of white supremacy may not be as far outside of the mainstream as normative whites would like to believe. Jewishness at SWR was by no means as invisible as other social differences ostensibly were—there were known Jewish teachers and students, though they were definitely in the minority, and, for the most part, they were considered white, with the exception of a girl like Amy (see chapter 1) who was Korean-American and adopted by a Jewish family. Regardless, the community neither fully acknowledged nor comfortably incorporated the differences Jewishness posed into the middle-school curriculum or their everyday life. For instance, in response to one unusually pronounced anti-Semitic incident, the middle-school principal, Dr. Williams, suspended two eighth graders—a girl and a boy—from school for a week and from teen recreation (or "rec" as it was colloquially known) for the rest of the year. The offending students had thrown pennies at one of the few Jewish eighth-grade boys one night at rec. The attack precipitated a debate among middle-school teachers. At a weekly Monday morning faculty breakfast, a non-Jewish teacher took offense when his Jewish colleagues interpreted the penny throwing as an anti-Semitic inference about Jews being cheap. Dr. Williams indicated that he had asked the students to explain their actions and that they had dodged his inquiry. His tone suggested that the girl and boy knew what they should not say or admit in this community and context; in other words, he intimated that they fully understood the anti-Semitic origin of their actions.

Though the school's administration would not tolerate blatant expressions of anti-Semitism, the attitude lurked in the silences, denials, misperceptions, and ignorances of the community at large. Their children knew the stereotype about Jews being cheap from somewhere. Jewishness apparently still posed enough of a social problem in this community that they deliberately considered it an irrelevant difference (a kind of denial), or they only acknowledged it under their breaths or in jokes. This became more apparent to me during a small-group discussion between a teacher and some of her students, following a class field trip to view the newly released *Schindler's List* (1993, directed by Steven Spielberg). In this context, several students disclosed that they "didn't know that Jews were still discriminated against in the United States." The teacher and the one Jewish classmate in the room, Ben, offered anecdotes that suggested otherwise, though neither used the terms anti-Semitism, anti-Semite, or anti-Semitic. Ben, for instance, talked about his synagogue being vandalized and the neo-Nazi propaganda that had been distributed clandestinely in the nearby town of Commack the year before. Though the national news had covered this neo-Nazi activity—I had read about it in California, for example—none of the other students recalled the story, replete with its cross burnings and anti-Jewish and anti-African American leafleting by white supremacists. I took the ignorances of these students as a sign of social privilege and as a sign of their normative whiteness. Their suburbia didn't include discrimination (see Dr. Williams's letter, chapter 1), their whiteness occurred outside of history or even contemporary racial politics. They didn't need to know about things like anti-Semitism and couldn't possibly be motivated by such sentiments or beliefs because their whiteness was supposedly beyond difference and benign. Emily, a girl from a similar community, and certainly a girl who also had been raised to be benignly white, would demonstrate that white supremacy, with its blatant anti-Semitism and racial hatred, is not so far from the heart of suburbia and is certainly challenging its ability to remain racially invisible (white).

Faced with the threat that white supremacy poses to mainstream whiteness, the media take over, and in so doing reveal their true colors, so to speak, as a normative and hence norm-making white institution. Despite Emily's own misgivings about the media, she does turn to them to help her redeem herself, and redeem her they do, with a vengeance. Like Cheryl in chapter 3, Emily becomes the quintessential girl next door who the media need to return to the fold. Normative whiteness needs girls like Emily to discipline and welcome home and hence assert their own supremacy in the larger social order. Emily is an insider, drawn to but not lost to insider-Others. The media itself becomes one of the main characters, along with suburbia and middle-class girlhood, that occupy this chapter in my own unfolding critical narrative on whiteness. Through the spin the media give to Emily's story, they show how invested they are in maintaining certain fictions about whiteness. In establishing a distance between white supremacy and normative whiteness, the media belie an important foundational relationship between these two racial positions. In the end, the lie and the denial turn out to be a kind of truth. Normative whiteness is based on all kinds of social denials.

The Story

Briefly, Emily's story is about a fifteen-year-old girl in the somewhat rural suburbs of Allentown, Pennsylvania, who joined a white supremacist group led by

Christian Identity minister Mark Thomas. In the course of a year, she became intimately connected to the group: she donned the requisite black leather jacket with swastika patch, learned to fire guns, and espoused beliefs in "white power." At one point, after months of fighting with her parents over her connection to the supremacists, Emily moved out of her family's home and into Thomas's. However, within a matter of months, she became pregnant—the father, a slightly older skinhead and intermittent follower of Thomas. Responding to her condition, Emily renounced her white supremacist beliefs, returned home, gave birth to a baby girl, and began talking to the media about her experience—though not necessarily in that order or with equal parts conviction.

Going Public

Emily's media portfolio is long and still in process. By the time I met with Emily in July 1995, she had appeared on *Dateline NBC* in a segment entitled "The Lost Boys" (aired 8 March 1995), which covered the February 1995 murders in Salisbury Township, Pennsylvania, of Dennis and Brenda Freeman and their youngest son Eric, by the family's two older boys, skinheads David and Bryan. She had also been interviewed on National Public Radio by Maria Hinojosa for a *Morning Edition* segment on white supremacy, and she had been quoted as an anonymous background source in a *New York Times* cover story (which I will leave unnamed in order to protect her anonymity). Further, her story had been featured in the *Philadelphia Inquirer* ("Escaping from a World of Hate," Wiegand 1995), the *Washington Post* ("Teen Tells of Her Year as a Skinhead: Onetime 'Big, Bad Nazi Girl' Visits Fairfax School to Offer Warning to Others," Smith 1995), and in numerous smaller newspapers, including *Washington Jewish Week*, *Sun Gazette*, *Jewish Exponent*, and *Klanwatch: Intelligence Report*, a newsletter tracking white supremacist activity and published by the Southern Poverty Law Center in Montgomery, Alabama. She had spoken to high-school students in Washington, D.C., as the above headline suggests, on a local Philadelphia radio show, and before several luncheons sponsored by the Anti-Defamation League (ADL). In other words, Emily and her story garnered more than a little media attention.

As noted earlier, Emily was not entirely satisfied with any of these accounts. But, at the time of our meeting, Emily was more troubled by her recent appearance on a *Montel Williams Show* program featuring present-day and former girl skinheads, bikers, and gang members, "Being in the Cool Crowd Almost Got Me Killed" (aired 3 July 1995). She felt that Montel's producers had misled and betrayed her during both the taping and editing of the program. Emily was disillusioned and angered by this experience, though in the end it didn't stop her from pursuing other media opportunities. Following our conversation, Emily agreed to be interviewed for a made-for-cable-TV-news documentary on the white supremacist movement, *Investigative Reports*'s "The New Skinheads" (aired 6 October 1995) and for an article in *YM: Young and Modern* magazine ("I Was a Nazi Girl" by Emily Heinrichs as told to Andrea Coller, April 1996). Later still, Emily entered into contract negotiations with NBC for an upcoming TV movie-of-the-week based on her story. She agreed to sell the exclusive rights to her story to the network, though as of this writing a film has yet to be produced.[1]

Through all of this, Emily has watched her story and her image go through subtle narrative transformations, some of which she controls, others of which bear the mark of media producers, editors, talk-show hosts, and social agencies with their own agendas. When I asked her about telling her story to high-school kids in Washington, D.C., in May of 1995, Emily spoke about her frustrations.

EH: Every time I say the story it seems like it gets shorter and shorter 'cause, that week in fact, when I was there in Washington, I mean, I had to tell my story like five times a day for three days.

LK: Who brought you down there?

EH: The ADL.

LK: Do they talk to you at all about what they want you to say?

EH: Yeah, they tell me. They are a very selfish organization too. They want it all to be ADL focused. They want me to say, "Well, make sure you mention us, make sure you talk about the anti-Semitism part," that's what they're worried about. They say they are an organization for equality of all races that tries to get rid of discrimination between all races, but they mostly focus on the Jewish part, because they are a Jewish organization. And I like, I was talking to groups of racially mixed kids, and so I more focused on the black-white tensions. So they kept telling me what I should say and I just kept saying what I wanted to say.

In response to the YM article, Emily said quite simply, "I hated it." Furthermore, she explained that she didn't write any of it, in spite of what the byline in her name may suggest. The YM reporter had interviewed her and later called her to do some fact checking. But Emily had neither final approval of the article nor a hand in its drafting. In addition to some erroneous information, the article misrepresented her visually. The editors illustrated the piece with two photographs: one of Emily and her then-toddler, Zoë, in front of an old junked car, and the other of Emily and her two adopted (nonwhite) brothers sitting on this same abandoned vehicle. The car was neither Emily's nor her family's nor was it in the immediate vicinity of either of their houses. The images effectively locate Emily within a "white trash" world. In fabricating these scenes, the magazine drew on existing social prejudices—both about white supremacy as the provenance of the lower class and about Pennsylvania as hillbilly country (for a discussion of hillbillies and white trash, see Hartigan Jr. 1999)—to misleadingly distance white supremacy from the white middle class (the bulk of its readership and a sizable percentage of the people who participate in supremacy groups). Here, visually, Emily is more the exotic Other, somebody else's daughter, than the girl next door. Her whiteness is deliberately classed and not ethnicized as it was in Amy's case. Outside of its Pennsylvania Dutch allure, with its exotic Other Amish, Pennsylvania does not lend itself to the ethnic stereotyping that Long Island does. In the context of Pennsylvania the ethnic Other cannot shield the white mainstream as well as the lower-class white can. So instead of ethnicizing her whiteness, *YM* erroneously portrays Emily as lower class. This speaks more about the history of the region than about the whiteness practiced among its inhabitants. Oddly enough, however, the article also includes an advice column sidebar, "How To Help a Racist Friend," which implies that Emily may be more the girl next door than not. In contradicting rather than illustrating one another, the images and text serve as perfect complements. The photographs of the exotic, white trash Others pique curiosity, while the article and sidebar bring Emily's story home to a captured white middle-class audience. Regardless, neither succeeded in making sense of Emily's story for Emily's sake.

Improving on the Truth

When Emily appeared on the *Montel Williams Show* her worst suspicions about the media were confirmed. The producers orchestrated the entire event, from what the guests wore to how they interacted with one another both on and off screen. The show outfitted the girls who had left "the life" in dresses and pant suits in solid primary colors. Their counterparts appeared in the street wear of their "gangs." Consequently, the active "gang" members looked tough and motley, while the "born-again" girls appeared approachable, not too classy and not too tacky. Emily wore a bright red pant suit and a cross on a chain around her neck.

In describing the "set-up" Emily told me:

> They escorted us. We stayed in hotels. . . . I stayed in the luxury suite. . . . I had such a nice place 'cause I guess I was supposed to be like the "star." I wasn't though, which is probably good. So it was kind of interesting that way.
>
> Oh yeah, they didn't let anyone see each other. . . . Like there were two different hotels, I guess. . . . I didn't even meet anyone until the next morning, but the people who were there, like the gang member was there and the ex-biker was there. And the skinhead girl was in a different hotel and the ex-gang member was in a different hotel 'cause they had to keep us separated. And it turned out that the biker girl and

the ex-biker girl met up somehow before the show and they were getting friendly and the producers were yelling at them saying how they weren't supposed to meet and stuff. And they took them into different rooms so they wouldn't talk. And they were like, "You can't meet each other because you have to be able to yell at each other. You can't like each other. You're supposed to hate each other." That's what they were doing. It was stupid.

In addition to this fairly innocuous manipulation, the producers had a surprise in store for Emily. Minutes before she was to appear on camera, one of the other guests told Emily that there was a "pregnant Nazi chick" in the other room waiting to go on. The pregnant Nazi chick, Emily surmised, was Mark Thomas's "wife," her former white supremacist teenage confidant, Wendy.

I was like, "What?" 'Cause that's when I was still kind of scared to be, like I never want to be on a show against Mark 'cause he would rip me apart if he had to. If I was talking against his cause, or whatever. He just has so much more experience in talking about what he believes in. I would just look like the biggest retard. So I never want to speak with him. And I like flipped out on the producer. I was like there is no way I'm going on the show. I refused. I'm not going on and they had to rip up their tentative script. And I guess they had the ex-gang member go on, and she talked forever, and she was really retarded. So they were yelling at me for wrecking their show and stuff.

Emily ended up appearing after the ex–gang member and the ex-biker. In the end, the producers respected Emily's wishes and did not bring Thomas and Wendy out onto the stage, though the skinhead who did appear—Kym, a girl Emily had never seen before in her life—had apparently been primed with information about Emily by Thomas and the producers.

The skinhead girl called me a slut, and she said that I did four guys in one night, and she started naming people. And I was just like "Whoa." And they wanted me . . . the lady standing off to the side was like, "Say something, do something." And I was getting up ready to walk off, but then I just ended up sitting there not saying anything the rest of the show, and they were all like mad at me, saying, "You didn't do anything. You didn't perform well." They wanted me to be like in a circus.

Most of this altercation between Emily and Kym ended up on the cutting-room floor. Instead, the television audience witnesses Kym asking Emily why she "did" four guys in one night. Emily replies, "I never did four guys in one night." Kym starts naming names as the producers block out the audio. Emily responds, "Not quite." The ex-biker girl asks, "What are these, rumors?" Then the show cuts to Emily and Kym saying simultaneously, "No, they're true," and concludes with

Emily alone saying, "It's true." The edits in this section come fast and furiously. Given that Emily claims that she never "did" four guys in one night, it is not likely that she would have publicly defamed herself. It is more likely that, through a sleight of film, Montel's editors and producers fabricated Emily's seemingly confessional response.

Though Emily had not seen the complete broadcast of the *Montel Williams Show* when I met with her, she knew that they had betrayed her in more ways than one. "They gave me fifty dollars and a little Montel Williams gift bag with a sippy cup thing with a little straw on it and a hand towel. That's what I got for being publicly disgraced," Emily concluded.

Controlling the Discourse

When I went to interview Emily on the heels of all these bad representational experiences, unsurprisingly, she immediately made it clear that our discussion would happen on her terms as much as possible. She showed up several hours late, after her aunt (someone in whom she confides and seems to trust) had put a considerable amount of effort into finding a time when we could meet, and after the aunt and I got up early one Sunday morning to make the four-hour drive from Long Island to Macungie, Pennsylvania, where Emily and her family live. After waiting for about three hours, I got the message and didn't take her interest in talking to me for granted.

At the time, seventeen-year-old Emily and her ten-month-old baby, Zoë, lived in the home of a local minister several miles from Emily's parents' house. She worked at a nearby late-night convenience store, had recently completed high school, and was preparing to enter a local girls' college in the fall on a special scholarship for young mothers.[2] She was also in the process of trying to find an apartment for herself and Zoë through the nearby Housing and Urban Development office. Zoë mostly went to day care while Emily worked or attended school, though on occasion her grandparents agreed to watch her. On the morning of the interview, Zoë was at her grandparents'—having stayed with them the night before while Emily worked late—and Emily's whereabouts were unknown. Phone calls to her house went unanswered. After two or more hours of waiting, her father and aunt got worried enough to drive over to her house, where they came upon Emily fast asleep in bed with the phone turned off. According to her family, her behavior was not in keeping with the way she had conducted her life since Zoë was born in September 1994. I wondered if Emily was consciously, or unconsciously, dreading that she had agreed to talk to me, or perhaps she was just making sure that I understood that she would control the terms of our conversation. I knew that I was nervous about meeting with her and was almost relieved when she didn't show up initially. After all, no matter what the ethnographer in my head said, Emily still was "the big, bad Nazi girl." And in the somewhat anxious hours of waiting, I began to doubt whether my own representational skills would be able to meet the challenge ahead.

Once Emily arrived, we drove off to a local restaurant to conduct the interview over coffee and brunch. At first she was a reluctant, even defensive, interviewee. I began by asking her why she had started talking to the media, and why she wanted her story told. She replied:

> I didn't really. . . . The ADL, the Anti-Defamation League, they're the ones my parents got in contact with while I was living at Mark Thomas's house. They invited me to a luncheon to talk to a big group of people. So there were two media people there, people from the press, I mean. And they interviewed me afterwards too. And I didn't really want to be interviewed. Then just other people started calling me. And that's all it was. Some I'd talk to, and some I wouldn't. But it wasn't like I wanted to.

Again, I got the message, though I proceeded in spite of it.

The conversation between Emily and me became less halting only after I told her a part of my story that related more directly to her recent past. In effect, her hesitancy forced me to shift my position as distant yet interested ethnographer to someone with complicated stakes in her narrative.

LK: So the father of Zoë is part of this group?

EH: Her sperm donor, yeah. [Emily insists on calling the biological father of her child the "sperm donor."]

LK: Were you like girlfriend and boyfriend with him?

EH: I thought we were, he was just . . . [long pause] unfaithful. Let's put it that way.

LK: It was kind of weird, I don't know if [your aunt] told you this, but I actually was pregnant at the same time you were.

EH: Oh!

LK: And I actually made the other decision, to have an abortion, which was not the easiest decision in the world. It was kind of weird 'cause [your aunt] was telling me about you, and I was having the situation of the father not being very supportive.

I mean, I think it took a lot of courage to decide to have Zoë. I just thought it was a really scary proposition to have a kid by yourself. At the time, did you think you were going to be alone when you had her?

EH: I knew I would be alone. I'm too selfish to share. She's mine, and now I'm just trying to raise her. . . . She's mine. She's her own person too. But as far as deciding what she can do, and whatever . . .

LK: So did you decide to have her before you decided that you didn't want to be part of this group anymore, or was it simultaneous?

EH: Oh, I knew as soon as I found out I was pregnant. In fact when I did I was down in Philadelphia like at a two-week-long New Year's Eve party, drunk every day. And that was scary, finding out I was pregnant, 'cause I knew that abortion wasn't an option for me. I mean if I hadn't been involved with them, maybe it would have been an option. But for them, abortion is like . . . I mean, they would have killed me. They really would have if I were to have an abortion. Which doesn't make sense if they are trying to save a life and then they kill two. But I knew I couldn't have an abortion. But I knew I didn't really want to have a baby. I mean, of course I didn't want to. But I knew that I didn't want to raise her, or "it," as soon as I knew I was pregnant, I knew I didn't want to raise it in that group.

In the context of white supremacy, Emily displays none of the moral ambiguity with regard to abortion that the Shoreham-Wading River girls and I exhibited in chapter 1. Unlike mainstream whiteness, white supremacy offered Emily a clear doctrine. Their moral ambiguity, in Emily's eyes, came later, with regard to how they would enforce their beliefs, or at least in how Emily imagined they would act. But even beyond the morality question, the circumstances in which Emily and I made our decisions to go through with and to terminate, respectively, our unplanned pregnancies differed considerably. No one was threatening my life; my pregnancy was not so directly embedded in an organized religious-political context, though it clearly was in a more generalized notion of white middle-class and, to a degree, Catholic culture; and I was not a teenage girl who had left home and who had not finished high school. I was only an ethnographer of teenage girls, temporarily living at home attempting to complete my doctorate. Though Emily seemed to appreciate the fact that on some level we "shared" an experience, she also succinctly underscored our differences in her response to my "confession" when she said, "I knew abortion wasn't an option for me. I mean if I hadn't been involved with them, maybe it would have been an option. But for them, abortion is like . . . I mean, they would have killed me."

I hesitated to tell Emily about my past, in part, because it seemed like too easy a way to make a connection with her, and because it is a past I remember with a mix of pain, shame, hard-earned acceptance, and fear, fear that the person I am speaking to is adamantly and even violently anti-choice. Emily's past and current religious beliefs and affiliations—at the time of our conversation, Emily was involved in a Christian youth group, and before joining Thomas's Christian Identity movement, she had been raised in a strict Christian household since she was about eleven—would seemingly rule out abortion as a viable option for her or any other woman. In our conversation, however, Emily appeared tolerant of the notion of "choice." Instead, her ambivalences lay with what "mainstream" Christianity professed more generally than with the Christian Right's position on abortion.

> I don't agree with Christianity at all. I guess I believe there's a God, but I don't like, I mean, I think Christianity is probably the thing that really screwed me up. Just by constantly being told you are a piece of shit. I don't know, just the way they do it. They make you feel like ashamed of your body and about sex, and look at how I ended up. I mean—I really—like still, Mark Thomas always told me that he thinks that Christianity, mainstream Christianity, Judeo-Christianity is the most corrupt thing in the world. And I think it is too. I think it is a good idea, but . . .

I prompted her to expand on the analysis she left hanging.

> LK: So when you heard him [Thomas] talk, you had already thought about these things in terms of the church that your family was going to and stuff?
>
> EH: Kinda . . . I never really put my finger on quite what it was. He helped me to figure that out.

Making myself even slightly vulnerable to Emily did not make her less vulnerable to me or our relationship one of parity. In fact, on a certain level, it made her more vulnerable to me if it made her open up to me. I was still someone who would once again retell her story, right or wrong (cf. Stacey 1980). But this vulnerability is only half the story. I would also argue that the narrative an informant tells as a result of sharing a more intimate relationship with the ethnographer is not any more truthful or complete than one told more cautiously. To presume otherwise would be arrogant. It would be to assume that the informant is inexperienced in the ways of a conversation- or media-made world. Certainly, Emily is not a representational naif. Consequently, she responded to my "confession" positively but with an appropriate amount of reserve. In the course of working together, Emily and I slowly made our way through the structures of entitlement and obligation, mine as well as hers, that a responsible telling and retelling of her story entails.

I Could Always Say I Didn't Inhale

As a public figure and as the mother of a child whose biological father has ties to the supremacists, Emily cannot simply go on with her own growing up as if nothing out of the ordinary has happened. Her circle of entitlement and obligation is tangible and demanding. Her past is present in the face of her child, as much as it is in her own remembrances and conceptions of herself. In thinking about her future and the difficulty she might encounter getting a job if people know about her past, Emily quipped, "I could always be like Clinton and say I didn't inhale. . . . Well, I didn't really believe. . . . I was just there." But how much Emily "believed" is unclear. Her involvement in Thomas's group ran fairly deep. In discussing who she was as a white supremacist and how she reconciles her past with her current day-to-day life, Emily observed:

EH: Yeah, yeah, I wore like a lot of black and I had "Doc" Martens, big black boots, and I had a flight jacket which had a Confederate patch, upside down American flag, zwas [swastika], an eagle holding a zwas, right here, and, um, I don't know just stuff, iron cross. . . .

LK: Do you have all that stuff still?

EH: I kept some of the patches. I kept the zwas patch 'cause it's like from the actual 1930s, it's like an antique.

LK: Did they give it to you?

EH: Yeah, I got it from Mark. And I kept the flag, just 'cause I didn't want to throw it away. I don't know. Someone else asked that, and they like thought I was so weird 'cause I said, "Yeah." They thought I would want to like burn all parts of my past or something—but why? It is not like it means anything to me. I think it is a very interesting part of history.

LK: What are you going to tell Zoë about any of this? Do you ever think about that?

EH: Well, you see I don't, I don't know. . . . It's just part of my life. It is just like as if I spent a strange summer at camp or something. It's not like a big deal to me, it is just my life and yeah, so I'll be open about it, but it is not gonna be the focus of my . . . I'm not going to be telling her about it all the time. She'll ask questions. Hopefully, even though I just said I'd never get married, hopefully one day there will be a male in my life who is her father. 'Cause she doesn't have a father, she really doesn't. Anyone can be a sperm donor, but people who raise are the father . . . your parents. So hopefully she will have a real father and she won't really care. I mean, I know that she'll want to explore and see what her biological thing . . . She can do that, but she's not going to get much help from me that way. I won't lie to her about anything . . . but . . .

When I asked her what her current friends think about her involvement with Thomas, she said: "They don't really talk about it. They just say, 'Oh yeah, she used to be a Nazi, now she's cool. Yeah, she was on the *Montel Williams Show*.'

They would brag about it that they knew someone who was on the *Montel Show.*" But having gone public has also made Emily's current life more complicated. When the *Montel Williams Show* aired, an Asian friend of Emily's saw the episode by chance. Emily explains: "I was calling up my friend Dave 'cause I was going out with him that night, and he doesn't know anything about my background or past.[3] And I called him, and I was like, 'I'm gonna be coming down now.' And he was like, 'Uh, do you know that you're on TV right now?' And he was like, 'What the hell were you?'"

Emily's friend's bold articulation—"What the hell were you?"—resonates throughout Emily's story. It is the question that fuels media representations of Emily and the question Emily continually faces for herself and her daughter. It is also the question that informs my own work in this chapter. Though I am not so much asking "What the hell were you?" as "Who have the media made you out to be? How do you understand who you were and who you have become? And how does white supremacy figure in the making of 'normal' white middle-class teen girlhood?"

Bringing It All Back Home

In a program like *Investigative Reports*, Emily is a figure we've met before, the girl next door—at least for the program's white middle-class audience—who ran into and out of trouble.[4] With her peaches-and-cream complexion, her long, reddish-blond hair, and her outward displays of maternal affection for and attention to her baby, Emily looks and acts the part.

When the program introduces Emily, the audience sees a pretty white teenage girl walk out of a well-kept, white shingled house. She carries a young child on her hip as she strolls out onto the lawn to sit beneath a nearby tree. The wind blows gently through her hair; a strawberry blond, blue-eyed baby girl plays quietly by her side. The show's narrator tells us: "Emily was just sixteen when she moved out of the house and into a nearby *compound* run by white supremacists." The soundtrack then cuts to Marcia Heinrichs, Emily's mother, talking about her daughter's involvement with the local group: "You think you know your child. I said that I was never afraid of her, but on the other hand you don't, you just don't know."

In relation to the white supremacists, Emily was literally the girl next door. In most media accounts and in Emily's own narration of her life, her white supremacist days began when fifteen-year-old Emily took the family dog for a walk and passed a group of skinhead boys playfully throwing snowballs in a neighbor's yard. Attractive, stereotypically Aryan Emily apparently caught their attention, and they invited her to join them. "So I did," Emily matter of factly told me. For the most part, Emily narrates her involvement with the neighboring supremacists as inevitable: "It was only a matter of meeting them" was how she put it.

BAD NEIGHBORS

The neighbor turned out to be Christian Identity minister Mark Thomas, and the snowball-throwing boys members of Thomas's Christian Posse Comitatus. Christian Identity is the religious arm of the white supremacist movement, which includes Aryan Nations, Posse Comitatus, White Aryan Resistance, the American Nazi Party, and the Ku Klux Klan, among others. Thomas was once grand kludd (chaplain) of the Invisible Empire, Knights of the Ku Klux Klan. Richard Butler, founding father of Christian Identity and Aryan Nations, ordained Thomas an Identity minister and, in August 1994, named him director of Pennsylvania's chapter of Aryan Nations. At his home located about three blocks from Emily's parents' house, Thomas held Bible study sessions, hosted rallies and Hitler youth festivals, taught followers how to use and care for weapons, and published a monthly newsletter, *The Watchman* (Rause 1994; *Klanwatch: Intelligence Report* 1995).[5] In speaking to me about her involvement with Thomas's group, Emily noted with a sense of irony: "[Thomas] has a history of being just a racist fool. Now he says he's found the true light. Like the same as you know how some people get religious and get born again, or whatever. That's just what it is like for him. . . . He says that before he was just an ignorant redneck. Now he's like, he knows why."

The terms white supremacist, white separatist, neo-Nazi, skinhead, and skin identify members of these groups. When I asked Emily to explain the difference between a Nazi, a white supremacist, and a skinhead, the following exchange took place:

EH: Well, I just call them all generically Nazis 'cause I think they are 'cause they look up to Adolf Hitler. They make use of the swastika as part of their whatever, the way they dress and look. And I guess they believe in some of the things that Hitler did. That's just why I call them Nazis 'cause they are against the Jews and stuff.

LK: What do they call themselves?

EH: They call themselves Christian Identity. Now the skinheads, they're kind of like punks. They're just like, like Mark claims he doesn't like them. He likes them if he can use them or teach them about Identity and make them worthwhile. Skinheads are kind of just like, once again, a gang, gang members. They dress the same. They act the same. All they do is drink beer and party and sleep around and get tattoos. So they're just like any other group, like a little black gang, or a little biker gang. You know they are just kind of like that. And . . . what was the third one, white supremacist? Uh, I guess if you're just a white supremacist, you could be a Nazi and a skinhead, but if you're just a white supremacist, then you're just someone who believes that white people are higher than anyone else. And you don't have to necessarily dress a certain way or act a certain way. That's just your personal beliefs.

LK: Aren't there like a lot of skinheads who do it almost like a fashion?

EH: Yeah, that's like the skinheads. 'Cause they're just like a group. They're just like "Be cool, be a skinhead." They don't have beliefs, they're just like racist retards, like rednecks. That's where you find a lot of the younger ones. If you're Christian Identity, then you firmly believe, and you use the Bible. It is like a religion, it is not a fashion statement, or just to be bad, a bad ass, you know. Then you actually, you act religious, which sounds warped and twisted to someone who doesn't understand, but they are very religious people, the people who are Christian Identity. It's just that they're a little wacko.

Thomas and his followers do not call Thomas's twenty-five-acre home a "white supremacist compound," though the media often designate it as such. When I interviewed Emily, she objected to the phrase: "I know Mark [Thomas] and Wendy and they're people. Anyone who doesn't know them has this big scary picture painted of them. And that's one reason why I hate talking to the media and stuff, 'cause they sit there and ask stuff like, "What did you do in the compound?" It's not a *compound*, it's a house. People live there, they socialize there, it is just like a biker lifestyle."

GOOD MOTHERS AND THE GIRL NEXT DOOR

While Emily's descriptions de-escalate the terms of the public discourse surrounding white supremacists, the media tend to fan the flames by bringing the issue closer to home (if home is white middle-class suburban America) and by fashioning a recognizable enemy: the bad seed next door. Here, Emily and her mother serve as model subjects, familiar mothers and daughters. And Mark Thomas fits the profile of the menacing neighbor, an image revived in full force by the media following the 1994 kidnapping, rape, and murder of a seven-year-old New Jersey girl, Megan Kanka, by her convicted sex-offender neighbor, Jesse Timmendequas. Megan's death set off a firestorm of public debates over whether or not neighbors have the right to be notified when convicted sex offenders take up residence among them. The case resulted in what has come to be known as "Megan's Law," a set of controversial New Jersey statutes, which, in part, mandate community notification. President Clinton signed a federal version of the law in May of 1996, declaring, "There is no greater right than a parent's right to raise a child in safety and love. . . . Today America circles the wagons around the children." While the courts consider the constitutionality of such statutes, the media continue to proffer the notion that the quiet, safe, middle-class life suburbanites have taken for granted over the years may indeed be an endangered species falling prey to terrorists of a sort in their midst. To a degree, Emily's story fits this scenario. Mark Thomas is just such a neighbor. And Emily and her family are the perfect everyneighbors. For example, when *Investigative Reports* interviews Emily's mother, they film her flipping through the pages of the Heinrichs's family album and preparing dinner in their identifiably suburban kitchen. Such images make Marcia Heinrichs's statement, "You think you know your child. . . . [B]ut on the other hand, you don't, you just don't know," all the more frightening. They disrupt the audience's ability to think this "can't happen to me or my family"; they put the audience on alert, making them sit up and pay attention to the story that is about to be told.

While *Investigative Reports* portrays Emily's mother as the frustrated good mother, it presents Emily as the girl next door gone bad and then good. Emily is both a disruptive and a stabilizing figure, one that evokes identification, horror, and eventually relief; like her bad-girl suburban sisters, Emily is the prodigal daughter. To this end, Emily's story becomes one of redemption in the face of locally bred evil. Accordingly, she plays a pivotal role in the program's somewhat sensationalist narrative about the rise of white supremacy groups among the nation's youth. She is featured in two of the program's five segments. Emily is "The case of a young teenage girl who suddenly found herself in the center of a white power *compound*" (emphasis mine) and one of "two people who came to reject white-power hatred and why." In addition, the program also includes segments on the 1995 Freeman murders, on the burgeoning skinhead music and magazine industry, and on the 1991 murder in Brooklyn, New York, of a gay man by a gang of skinheads who call themselves DMS (Doc Marten Stompers).

While *Investigative Reports* takes pains to visually mark Emily's narrative status as the girl next door—filming her in nonthreatening, pastorally suburban or domestic settings—the program doesn't stop there or leave much room for interpretation. Instead, it surrounds Emily's interview footage with comments from white supremacist "experts"—representatives from groups ranging from the ADL and the Pennsylvania Human Relations Commission to White Aryan Resistance (WAR), one of the nation's most prominent hate groups—who make it clear that "there but for the grace of God goes *your* daughter." WAR founder Tom Metzger explains that skinheads are

> generally the sons and daughters of white, middle-class, in most cases, sometimes white poor. . . . This is a generation that's been, in a lot of ways sort of been the throwaway generation. While their parents many times were liberals and were afraid to make waves and into p.c., these kids were getting beaten up in school by nonwhite gangs and so forth.

With such proclamations, Metzger offers another, more sinister version of Amy Fisher's Gen X. Here again, middle-class parenting takes the rap. Only this time, it's promiscuity in the guise of liberal social tolerance (see the next chapter for a discussion of the limits of tolerance) that comes under scrutiny.

On the other side of the ideological fence: Barry Morrison, ADL regional director in Philadelphia, states: "the Freeman killings to us say that hatred and bigotry are not isolated incidents." Ann Van Dyke of the Pennsylvania Human Relations Commission notes that "the hate movement in the U.S. has historically been adults, now more and more it is focusing on *sucking in* young people into the hate movement." And the narrator asks: "Was Emily just going through a teenage phase, or was it something more dangerous?" To which I would reply, "Yes, it was something more dangerous, namely, normative white middle-class teen girlhood and its inability to acknowledge how much it depends on and is responsible for the making of its Others."

In portraying Emily as an innocent young thing, the show constructs her as a latter-day Dorothy from *The Wizard of Oz*: a young teenage girl who suddenly found herself—through no volition of her own, according to the script—in the center of the white power movement. Emily's Oz included studying the Bible with Mark Thomas, believing that Jews and blacks are literal devils walking the earth, and learning to shoot guns. As Emily explained to me, "I shot a lot of guns. I learned how to take them apart, put them back together, clean them, and shoot. . . . I like guns, they're scary things, but I think it was the best thing I learned how to do." Like Dorothy, Emily eventually returns home. In the final segment, *Investigative Reports*'s narrator explains: "Despite the rhetoric, not all children who are recruited into the hate movement are doomed to be lifelong converts. Emily Heinrichs was able to break free, but only after she found herself pregnant, the baby's father a hard-core skinhead."

On camera, Emily concurs: "It [her pregnancy] was like a cold splash of water. I just had to leave and get my own life back on track." Reaching out to her daughter, she adds, "And then this new little life."

The Fiction of Public Reality

The casual framing of Emily's pregnancy at sixteen as a solution rather than a problem starkly contrasts with the way the media usually tell the story of teenage motherhood. Emily is not presented as a "welfare queen," a crack addict, or a high-school dropout. Emily's story is not about the horror of "babies having babies" or the so-called teen pregnancy epidemic sweeping the nation. Instead, Emily comes from a large intact family that apparently cares about her well-being. Her mother was not a teenage or single mother, but rather a college-educated woman who chose to stay home to raise her family of two biological daughters, two biological sons, and two adopted, Puerto Rican sons. In telling Emily's story, the media often call attention to the ethnicity of her adopted brothers, in an attempt to demonstrate that Emily's white supremacy is not inherent to her background. Instead, her mother and father are portrayed as the very liberal p.c. parents that Metzger raves against. From the perspective of the mainstream media, this liberalism heightens the tragedy of Emily's racial rebellion and makes her more likely to be potentially everybody's daughter. You don't have to be an extremist to raise a girl like Emily. While *Investigative Reports* doesn't fill in all these details, it doesn't need to. Marcia's and Emily's images as good (white middle-class) mothers speak for themselves.

Given that contemporary media and legislators alike often hold teenage mothers directly or indirectly responsible for most of the nation's woes, including the budget deficit, gang violence, and what some identify as a decaying moral order, this lack of public consternation over Emily's pregnancy warrants attention. *Investigative Reports* actually portrays Emily's early pregnancy and motherhood as socially redeeming. This teenage mother is a sign of hope rather than degradation. Why? Because she is not black, Latina, urban, or poor. This teenage mother is white middle class suburban, and a recovering white supremacist. In the context of the ongoing public dialogue about teenage sexuality, pregnancy, and motherhood, this teenage mother's *white middle-classness* prevail over her sexual and reproductive deviancy because they define her transgression as fully redeemable and, on the level of crafting public narratives about mainstream whiteness, even desirable. As a white middle-class girl, Emily's mistakes—her involvement with the white supremacists and her pregnancy—are just that, aberrations in an otherwise normal life. Moreover, Emily's pregnancy points to the role that girls play in helping the media reinscribe mainstream whiteness. A former white supremacist boy would perhaps be less redeemable; indeed, in my research I did not come across his story. In the context of white supremacy, boys, more often than not, are portrayed as violent and volatile characters. Emily's pregnancy marks her as irrefutably changed and to a degree vulnerable to media manipulation. Boys cannot as easily occupy this position. The media depend on girls' vulnerabilities, their insider-Other status, to continually relocate whiteness on higher moral ground.

Like Cheryl, Emily can be redeemed, so she will be. What happened to Emily is presented as an isolated incident in her life. It has nothing to do with Emily's personal biography (her p.c. parents) or with mainstream whiteness. She can move beyond and learn something from her experience (Tsing 1990, 295). At least, this is how the media profile Emily, even while she herself, in her day-to-day life, still struggles with the moving-beyond part of this equation. For Emily, her story is not so much something to move beyond as it is something to learn to live with, "in the here and now, not quite broken, not quite whole" (Gover 1995, 199).

Moreover, because no one seems particularly concerned that this white girl is having "babies too soon," Emily's story further suggests that redemption narratives have a strong underlying racial component, underscoring the degree to which the public fiction of teen pregnancy in this country turns on questions of race. When the media portray African American single mothers redeeming themselves and their families, more often than not their stories revolve around them pulling themselves up and out of poverty, off welfare, and into the job market. When it comes to a girl like Emily, the media are not interested in her economic status or level of productivity. As *Investigative Reports* demonstrates, it is enough for Emily to be just a white mom, as opposed to a White (read white supremacist, gun-toting, extremist) mom. Though Emily has no visible means of support, none of the media accounts of her story consider her economic status or her plans for the future. In the eyes of the media, Emily is only a former white supremacist, frozen in the moment she became pregnant and left Thomas's group. As Emily noted in our conversation, "No one knew me until I left." And no one cares to consider how this young mother will get by on her own. No one wants to delve too deeply into Emily's story. With the symptom removed—Emily's involvement with the white supremacists—the underlying problem appears to have lost its social import.

GIVING BIRTH TO WHITE PRIVILEGE

In tracking the emergence of teenage pregnancy and motherhood as a sociopolitical issue in the United States, feminist historians have demonstrated how social policy, medical technologies, and public perceptions have fashioned and refashioned teenage pregnancy as a problem fit to accommodate shifting political and economic interests (see, for example, Ladner [1971] 1995; Stack 1974; Ginsburg 1989; Nathanson 1991; Solinger 1992; Lawson and Rhode 1993; and Kunzel 1993). Race surfaces in many of these genealogies as a primary category—a mutable concept serving a host of political agendas and ideological perspectives.

Surprisingly, from a present-day vantage point, teenage pregnancy received little attention until the early-to-mid-1970s when birth control advocates found it politically expedient to put white teenagers at the center of their efforts to make contraception, especially the pill, widely available to U.S. women. Preceding this "discovery" of teen pregnancy, birth control and family-planning advocates focused more broadly on women, nonwhite women to be exact, and not teens. This was in the context of the nation's "War on Poverty," a federal effort launched by President Lyndon B. Johnson in his January 1964 State of the Union Address, when he put "five million poor women," or more specifically poor, urban, black women, at the center of what would turn out to be a decades-long debate over the implementation and later retrenchment of welfare programs. One of the most widely discussed documents coming out of this

"War on Poverty," Daniel Patrick Moynihan's 1965 report, *The Negro Family: The Case for National Action*, inextricably linked black America, poverty, illegitimacy, welfare abuse, rising crime rates, and the disintegration of the American family. Though Moynihan's analysis was not unique, *The Negro Family* received more than its share of attention, influencing public policy and opinion alike. This articulation of black America, with its eugenic undercurrents of managing the black population's reproductive activity, eventually proved too controversial for birth control advocates to use to undergird their own political efforts in the name of poor nonwhite women. Moreover, because the report also fostered welfare spending, it was not an effective political tool for lobbyists to deploy in their campaigns to win over conservative opponents of federally supported family-planning programs. By the late sixties and early seventies, the birth control movement needed a new, more publicly and politically palatable object of concern. They found it in the white teenage girl (Nathanson 1991).[6]

While these political challenges brewed in the public-policy and -service arenas, the business of collecting information about the nation's sexual practices also underwent a major shift. Increasingly, women's and girls' sex lives were becoming everybody's business. With the legalization of abortion in 1973, demographers gained access to information about how many women and teenagers sought to terminate pregnancies in public clinics, thereby allowing family-planning experts to document sexual activity as opposed to just birth rates. Simultaneously, researchers at Johns Hopkins University published one of the first studies tracking teens' sexual experiences and behaviors (Zelnick and Kantner 1980). The numbers showed that though birth rates to women under twenty had been declining since 1957, higher proportions of *single* white women were giving birth (Nathanson 1991, 50–51). White girls, in other words, were flagrantly breaking a mainstream moral code by having sex and babies outside of marriage. In 1976, the Alan Guttmacher Institute (AGI) was the first influential organization to publicly identify adolescent pregnancy as an "epidemic" (Nathanson 1991, 57).[7] By the end of the seventies, through turns of rhetoric, research, and politics, the white middle-class teenage girl emerged as the raison d'être of the family-planning and birth-control movements, occupying a politically expedient role in the public battle over the social control of women's reproduction (Nathanson 1991, 56).[8]

The distinction between the "War on Poverty," which revolved around issues of race (black America) and economics, and the "Epidemic of Teen Pregnancy," which, at least initially, turned on questions of morality, legitimacy, and unarticulated notions of whiteness, crudely delineates a fictional divide between black and white America. In the ongoing public drama of teenage pregnancy, morality is a white thing, about white girls gone astray, while poverty is a black thing, about black girls wantonly reproducing and milking the social welfare system dry. In this model, white girls can be pulled back into the fold, while their nonwhite counterparts can't. Even if they turn their economic lives around, nonwhite girls cannot simply assimilate into the mainstream. The mainstream holds fast to its whiteness. In this context, full redemption becomes racialized as a privilege of whiteness. White girls turned "immoral" can be redeemed. While behavior can be punished and corrected, girls' identities are not as easily subject to the same manipulation. Girls of color and white girls are not playing on the same field when it comes to issues of reproduction and redemption.

In the hands of politicians and the media, the face of the "Epidemic of Teen Pregnancy" did not remain lily white for long. In January 1986, *CBS Reports* with Bill Moyers aired "The Vanishing Family: Crisis in Black America." It gave a "neo-Moynihan construction of adolescent pregnancy," one that drew a cause and effect relationship between teenage pregnancy, nonwhite communities, and welfare dependency (Nathanson 1991, 66; for a discussion of teen pregnancy and media portrayals, see Kenny 1988; for a cogent counterargument to Moyers, see Stack 1974). In the guise of economic concerns, "The Vanishing Family" and other like-minded reports proffered a cultural socioeconomic argument: there is something about black/Hispanic (their vocabulary) culture that encourages teen pregnancy and welfare dependency. At this same historical moment—the age of Reagan ("voodoo") economics—earlier concerns over white morality and teen pregnancy gave way to discussions of psychological distress. White girls having sex early and getting pregnant were deemed psychologically ill; they were falling prey to a medicalized disorder that could be treated. Meanwhile, nonwhite pregnant teens remained trapped in their cultures and the cycle of babies having babies (Phoenix 1993). From this perspective, white teen pregnancy is manageable while nonwhite teen pregnancy is constructed as an intractable menace to (white) society. Sending a girl to a counselor is a lot easier than changing the very foundations (at least as the public discourse defines them) of her culture.

By the time Emily was pregnant in 1994, the "epidemic" had come full circle to a leaner, meaner neo-Moynihanian analysis. The election of a Republican majority to Congress with its anti–New Deal agenda ("Contract with America") and the widely debated publication of *The Bell Curve* put the topic of teen pregnancy once again at the center of national discussions of poverty and welfare reform or what largely amounted to rhetorics of race. *Bell Curve* authors Richard J. Herrnstein and Charles Murray ostensibly peddled a 1990s version of "there's something about nonwhite girls/women that makes them keep having 'illegitimate' babies and going and staying on welfare."[9] This time around, that something was surmised to be "intelligence." "Going on welfare [and bearing illegitimate children]," according to *The Bell Curve*, "really is a dumb idea, and that is why women who are low in cognitive ability end up [single mothers dependent on the state]" (Herrnstein and Murray 1994, 201, 189). Intelligence in *The Bell Curve* is "substantially inherited" and clearly measurable outside of racial, ethnic, and class biases (23). Similarly, Herrnstein and Murray insist that ethnic and racial differences in cognitive ability are not in doubt (269) and demonstrate that women of color are more apt to bear "illegitimate" children and go on welfare (330–331). Readers who add up their arguments are led to conclude that, in general, nonwhite women have an inherently lower cognitive ability than the majority of white women. Though *The Bell Curve* never comes out and crudely states this conclusion, its (racist) message is clearly implied, despite the fact that the book acknowledges in passing that "racism and institutional discrimination" could indeed play a role in the outcomes of women's/girls' reproductive and economic lives (340). As Emily's pregnancy came to term, nonwhiteness was definitely at the forefront of the public anti-teen-pregnancy agenda.

In this context, politicians on Capitol Hill singled out unwed teenage mothers as social and economic liabilities and pushed through legislation that would make teen mothers, eighteen and younger, ineligible for welfare unless they remained in school and lived with an adult. Though President Clinton vetoed two bills that included these provisions, this particular aspect of the legislation had bipartisan support and a nod of approval from the democratic White House. By the summer of 1996, with the presidential election fast approaching, President Clinton, anxious to make good on his 1992 campaign promise to "end welfare as we know it," signed Congress's third welfare reform bill, making federal and state interference in teen mothers' lives the law of the land.[10]

In the midst of all this political and public wrangling, the problem of teen pregnancy and single motherhood was decidedly not constructed as a white girl's issue. As *New York Times* reporter Margaret L. Usdansky notes, "Popular images depict [unwed] mothers as either affluent, white, college-educated and near the end of their childbearing years [e.g., Murphy Brown] or poor, black teen-age high-school dropouts" (Usdansky 1996, 4; see also Sylvester 1994, 4). These images persisted in spite of the fact that in this same period black teenage mothers accounted for less than 12 percent of all unmarried mothers, and teenagers of all races constituted less than a third of all women having babies out of wedlock (Usdansky 1996). The welfare discussions on the floors of the 104th Congress were decidedly not about the Murphy Browns of public perception, but rather her equally fictional counterpart, the urban black teen mother. Numerous media-produced images support Usdansky's claim. For example, in October 1995, PBS broadcast a one-hour documentary, *Sex, Teens, and Public Schools*. The image used to advertise the program was "inner city" and nonwhite. The teen moms in the photo are black or Latina and the one teen dad is black; the kids and their babies stand in a parking lot in front of a graffiti-covered wall; and the title of the program looms above them in tag-style lettering, evoking the streets of South Central Los Angeles or their equivalent in other U.S. cities. Likewise, in the same month that Emily's story ran in *YM*, the magazine's rival, *Sassy*, published a story on teen pregnancy, "Special Report: Teen Moms Tell It Like It Is" (Ziv 1996). The girls who "tell all" here are identifiably Latina, except for "Sabrina" the seventeen-year-old who "terminated" her pregnancy; her racial identity is unmarked. In this racialized "epidemic," a girl like white, middle-class, suburban Emily would not become the poster child for the anti-welfare, anti-teenage-pregnancy crusades of the nineties. Instead, the media pursued her to play the role of informant and shining example of white hope in what they were presenting as yet another epidemic: the rise of white supremacy and white power movements among the nation's youth. In its opening segment, *Investigative Reports*, for example, paints an alarming scenario.

> When they [skinheads] first appeared on the scene in the 1980s with Mohawk haircuts and black leather jackets, they were dismissed as a passing fancy. But now, in the nineties, they are organized, growing, and delivering a frightening message. In this edition of *Investigative Reports*, we examine how thousands of young people in this country are taking that message to heart, how established white supremacist groups have embraced skinheads, and how their voices are becoming louder and louder with each passing day.

This discussion of the history of public perceptions and portrayals of teen pregnancy gives Emily's pregnancy context, while at the same time demonstrating just how white the mainstream media can be. Turning teen pregnancy into a nonwhite problem is a technology of whiteness. It misconstrues reality and protects and legitimizes white racial privilege, by, in part, demonizing the nonwhite Other and letting her white sister off the hook. The way the media handle Emily's teen pregnancy by not rendering *it* the social problem so much as her foray into white supremacy is the flip side of the same coin. Below I explore how Emily's predicament works within the making of white racial ascendancy both from supremacist and mainstream perspectives.

BEING IN A FAMILY WAY: WHAT DIFFERENCE DOES IT MAKE?

In light of the media's inattention to Emily's teen pregnancy and their fascination with her white supremacy, Emily appears caught in a kind of racial contradiction. While her whiteness gets her publicly exonerated in relation to her early pregnancy, her active pursuit of a white identity got her in trouble in the first place; it, and not her unwed pregnancy, is the thing from which she must be redeemed. The contradiction begs the questions: What is the relationship between white supremacy and the white mainstream? And how is that relationship played out on the bodies of teenage girls, specifically through images of the white family and motherhood?

As Emily moves between the radical Right—white supremacy—and the mainstream—white suburbia—the parameters of her narrative remain unchanged.[11] Both camps turn Emily into an example, and both do so in the name of family and family values. For example, as noted earlier, *Investigative Reports* portrays Emily exclusively in the context of her domestic, familial responsibilities and locations. For the mainstream, Emily's pregnancy and turn toward responsible mothering is a godsend. It is the thing that allows them to, even necessitates their desire to welcome her back into the safety of normative whiteness.

But this mainstream manipulation and embrace of images of the family is not so far from how the supremacists respond to Emily's condition or fashion themselves as a community. When Mark Thomas gets on camera, he often speaks of his followers as "one big happy family," an image, Emily explained, he longed to substantiate through her pregnancy and pending motherhood.

Family is not anathema to white supremacists. Instead, a concept of family lies at the core of what they believe and how they structure their lives. When Emily described the religious component of white supremacy, she offered this origin story:

> [Christian Identity] is based on the fact, well they think it's fact, that Adam, the first man created, was a white Aryan man and so was Eve. They had a baby together, Abel. And he is kinda like the father of the white race. And instead of going into the forbidden fruit in the garden, they think that Eve actually had sex with Satan and conceived Cain. He's the father of the Jewish race, and the Jewish race are devils. That's what they think.

Mark Thomas repeats a version of this story in the course of the *Investigative Reports* broadcast, right after he talks about how attractive Emily is and right before he explains that the swastika is biblical.

When Emily became pregnant, Thomas saw an opportunity to replicate the founding-white-family romance of their Bible story. Emily tells the story as follows: "As soon as Mark found out I was pregnant, he wanted me and the sperm donor to get married and live on his land in a little house and start his community. He wants to have a community of people, of white supremacists, living on his land. And he wanted me to be the start of it." Emily and the "sperm donor" were to function as the second coming of the first family; they were to be the parents of a neo-white race, turning the so-called compound into a neo-white Garden of Eden. "Thankfully, that never happened," concluded Emily. Thankfully, because Emily didn't let it happen.

Again, the distance between the mainstream and the extremists here is one of degrees. As the racial and familial history of suburbia has shown and Amy's and Cheryl's stories have legitimated, the reproduction of whiteness has everything to do with keeping white middle-class girls within the confines of the family and the familial, broadly construed as a suburban culture of white homogeneity and avoidance. Privileging the family in this context is a way of privileging whiteness whether you are a white supremacist or just a garden-variety (read greenhouse) suburbanite.

The Contradictions of Whiteness

But what of Emily's quest for a white identity? In its last segment with Emily, the new mother and *former* white supremacist, *Investigative Reports* features clean-cut, visibly upper-middle class, racial separatist Ashley Brown stating: "I always looked at us as kind of being the white blood cells of the white race. When the body has a sickness, the white blood cells come out and attack it. That's what skinheads are: a natural instinctual reaction of the white race."

While *Investigative Reports* doesn't give Brown the airtime to elaborate on his point, the version of Emily's story the program presents evokes similar interpretations of white supremacy. As a tale of redemption, it extends Brown's metaphor. Emily has been cured. Dressed in white jeans and a pastel T-shirt, Emily has discarded her radical whiteness along with her big black boots and her black flight jacket with its skinhead patches for a more socially acceptable form of white identity. This may not have been the defensive cure that Brown had in mind, but it is the message with which *Investigative Reports* concludes.

However, I am left wondering why it takes a brush with extremists, or what I might call "hyperwhiteness"—an extreme, hypersymbolic whiteness—and a plunge into pregnancy and motherhood, a kind of twisted hypernormalness, for a girl like Emily to find her white identity. Emily's story demonstrates the hazards of living in a world where "white culture" is understood to be an oxymoron. By white culture, I mean forms of expression and behavior that are understood to be racially based. Mainstream whites may see themselves as *cultured*, but this is a matter of distinction and taste, not the every day (Bourdieu 1984). White people rarely talk about themselves as acting white, unless of course, they are white supremacists devoting their lives to being and acting white. To be a non-white-supremacist white is to be without a clear identity. It is to be sooo normal and sooo boring. It is to occupy a ubiquitous position—or a position of no position—and ubiquity knows no culture. Normal white racial identity takes on the properties of the color itself: whiteness as the absence of all racial culture. This fiction of white culturelessness leaves girls like Emily to fend for themselves: either they can believe that girls are "born white," end of conversation, or they can seek more tangible expressions of race-based cultures and fill their racelessness with extreme instantiations of white racial culture. White supremacists counter the hyposymbolicness of normal white identity with a hypersymbolic and hyperantisocial whiteness. I use the term *hyperantisocial* to call attention to the fact that while white supremacy is indeed a hypersocial movement, a collective hysteria of sorts, it is also profoundly antisocial in the larger scheme of the world, and therefore it is not normalizing in the way that the SWR girls' collective hysterias were in the previous chapter. White supremacy is only normalizing when taken on by mainstream disciplinary institutions, like the media. The media make Emily part of the technology of mainstream white middle-class femininity when they frame her story as a redemption narrative. Without this framing, her whiteness would linger in the realm of the antisocial.

Unable to believe in the fiction of whiteness as the unnamed norm one is just born into or not, for better or worse, Emily pursued a racial identity, a racial community that recognized itself as such. White supremacists thrive on speaking their own racial name, constructing their own history, and consciously performing their own forms of cultural-racial expression. In this sense, white supremacists do what mainstream white culture cannot do for itself: give girls like Emily a way to define and enact their own racial identity. Having denounced her life with the supremacists, Emily apparently couldn't maintain a belief in the version of whiteness that supremacists espouse. "I guess it was kind of fun to be superior," Emily told me, though the game eventually stopped making sense. Away from the articulated racial culture of white supremacy, Emily once again had to find her own way of naming her whiteness. Only this time, she had a ready-made foil: the whiteness of Mark Thomas and his followers. As Emily says to the skinhead on the *Montel Williams Show* after the girl accuses Emily of being a "race traitor," "I have no respect for the white race if you're representing it." Emily's newfound anti-white-supremacy identity underscores the degree to which normal white culture upholds its silences. While Emily is welcomed back into the mainstream, the mainstream still doesn't provide her with a way of articulating herself as a white girl except in opposition to her own bad-white-girl past. I wonder if, in telling her story over and over, Emily is once again filling this racial void, this time in the context of establishing herself as a former white supremacist.

Emily is not alone in her desire for a white identity. In discussing my research on the racialization of whites with undergraduates at various colleges throughout the United States, I've become accustomed to hearing white students who would identify themselves as antiracist interpret my work as a call for a white-pride movement (c.f. Gallagher 1995). By this, these mainstream students do not mean white supremacy; in fact, I would venture to say that they would be horrified by the thought that their longing for an articulated white identity could be understood as such. They simply mean if black students have

African American clubs then maybe they should have white identity groups. They don't automatically think this position through and realize that because black and white students occupy very different positions in the existing racial hierarchy, white and black identity groups are totally different entities. What comes through in their reaction, however, is again the proximity between the doctrines and instincts of normative whiteness and white supremacy. And the question that remains hanging for these students and for Emily is how to have a white identity that neither denies nor overvalues itself.[12]

Emily's venture into the world of white supremacy was not her first attempt to define herself socially through a racially marked group or activity. In narrating her own history, Emily identifies ninth grade as a turning point in her life.

> See, I was in the gifted classes and I was like kind of in the nerd classes. And I didn't want to be with those people, so I would . . . I don't know how I got hooked up with them [Wiggers]. I guess it started with one guy asking me out. He thought I was cute, and I went out with him, and then I just started hanging out with all his friends and partying all the time. And I just started wearing bigger clothes, big jeans, big shirts, listened to rap, drink, smoke cigarettes, smoke everything else. . . . I mean I hung out with the whole Wigger *culture* in ninth grade. And they liked me. So, I went out with them. [emphasis mine]

"Wiggers" are white kids who emulate black hip-hop culture, or according to Emily, "white kids acting like niggers." "I was such a Wigger; it was sick," Emily told me. When I asked her what she meant by this she replied, "Just like acting black. And that's just sick 'cause why would you want to act like another . . . " Here, she left her thought hanging. Later she explained:

> If skinheads had seen me, they would have said, "Whoa, Wiggers. Let's kick their asses," 'cause they hate Wiggers. They think you . . . like why are you trying to be black when you are white?
>
> LK: They think you're betraying them?
>
> EH: Yeah, and it's true though, because white people are so blessed in this country, and they have so many more advantages, so why would you want to throw that away and try to be black? I mean those are like the trash black people. There are like intelligent black people who do well in school, et cetera, et cetera. And these [Wiggers] are kind of like punks. These are just black trash (laughs). So that's what I gravitate towards . . . all kinds of trash.

What Emily describes as "black trash" she also identifies as "the whole Wigger *culture*," a word she doesn't use to describe any other group. Wiggers, like the white supremacists, are white people with culture, with acknowledged collective symbolic activity (the hypersocial hypersymbolic). Emily was drawn to the fact that these kids had an identifiable style of dress, taste in music, and pattern of behavior. They seemed to fill an emptiness in her that resulted from being a normal white kid in classes for the "gifted," or being one of the blessed, or the people with many more advantages, the people of privilege, or the people "privileged" enough not to have a racial culture. From her current perspective as a former Wigger and former white supremacist, Emily seems to be both struggling with and retreating back into this state of culturelessness. "[Now], I'm just normal. I mean, I'm not like classified as anything. I have a few black friends now, and I have a lot of white friends, and I have . . . different groups of friends. And I don't fit any of the styles of dress. . . . I'm just like . . . " On this note, Emily ends our interview. Unlike the media's portrayals of her story of redemption, Emily's version doesn't end on a definitive note. I leave the interview with a sense that Emily's active pursuit of a white identity, which necessarily now entails living with her white supremacist past, is not yet over.

Waiting to Inhale

What is most threatening about Emily's story is the fact that it announces that the "emperor has no clothes," but doesn't offer many solutions to the predicament of white culture or what is experienced as white culturelessness. If one is not simply born white and one cannot join an extremist group and become white, what does it mean to be a white person, or more specifically a white girl, in a world where race and gender matter? The *YM* article presents Emily, not unlike the college students I referred to earlier, as saying: "After a few weeks, the skinheads started to talk to me about their beliefs. They spoke about Jesus and God and about 'white pride'—the idea that people should be proud of their white heritage. Since black people have black pride, I thought it makes sense for white people to have white pride. It didn't seem like anything racist to me" (Heinrichs and Coller 1996, 56).

Emily learned the hard way that white (or racial) pride is not the answer. In many ways, her story demonstrates that being white is being "not quite broken, not quite whole." It is about learning to live with a past that includes global histories of supremacy (e.g., Nazis, skinheads, and the KKK), exclusion (e.g., suburbia and the cultures of the elite), and neglect (e.g., the unequal distribution of the world's resources across racial, class, and gender differences). In addition, personal experiences of everyday privileges can be isolating and unfulfilling. To be born white, as Emily experienced it, is to live in a world of dubious privilege, to live in a world where you are waiting to discover what it means to be white, to sense that whiteness is laden with culture but to be surrounded by public and private denials of this condition.

Popular notions of race tend to vacillate between taking race for granted and seeing race as a learned cultural practice, with the former largely reserved for white kids and the latter for kids of color. Multicultural curricula, for example, are aimed at either teaching nonwhite kids about their cultural heritages, or teaching white kids about other people's racial and ethnic backgrounds (see chapter 6). Emily's story calls this practice into question, demonstrating that giving white kids no race culture, or at least leading them to believe in their culturelessness, creates a void that some struggle to fill on their own, making them susceptible to the rhetorics and collective cultural-racial performances of groups like Christian Identity. Indeed, perhaps what is most appealing about such organizations to normal, white girls like Emily is that they impart some kind of tangible identity and community. They give girls some kind of story to tell.

When Felipe Luciano—a Latino ex–gang member and ex-convict who is now a reporter on a local New York City news channel—appears on the same *Montel Williams Show* as Emily, he turns to the skinhead, Kym, and tells her that he identifies with her because he used to be a Puerto Rican nationalist. "I needed the identity of race," he concludes. He then addresses the former gang girl, Evelyn, who is half white and half Mexican, and suggests that she needed to get involved with a Latino gang because she was living in a "racial void": "She went to a Catholic school where no one taught her to be Mexican or Latina." While Luciano's comments point to the need for helping kids understand their racial identities as such, his tone rings of morality, suggesting that raising kids within a clear racial and ethnic order is a social obligation, part of what some could construe as a "Contract with America's Children." Through my analysis of Emily's story, I am not advocating for a racial pedagogy that teaches white kids to be white, African American kids to be black, and Mexican American kids to be Latino in some rigid sense of race, ethnicity, and culture. I am suggesting, however, that a fuller presentation of race to all kids, one that includes articulations and understandings of whiteness as a racial category that can speak its history and culture—for better and worse—without reverting to white supremacy, would begin to foreground the intentionally mute foundations of the current racial order.

Like the SWR girls', Emily's travels in the hypersymbolic and the hypersocial ended up being part of a normalizing process, though, as noted earlier, while the media tie up Emily's story in a neat normative familial package, Emily herself continues to struggle with ways to tell her own story and to live a normal life. When it comes to white supremacy, Emily's experience is not necessarily the norm. Emily's normalization took the jolt of the hypernormal—a teenage pregnancy, a kind of real-life parody of white middle-class motherhood—to draw her back into being normal. But Emily's normalness demonstrates even more acutely than the normal SWR girls' collective hysterical performances just how unnormal being normal is. Emily will always be a normal girl with a past and in struggling to live with that past, she continues to search for a hard-won rather than taken-for-granted identity.

I began this chapter concerned that my analysis may not fulfill Emily's expectations for having her story told. In the end, Emily herself has taught me that her racial story, as is true for anybody's, will never be finished or articulated fully. Emily's story makes clear that coming to terms with the racial self is an ongoing process that is best engaged on a day-to-day basis rather than avoided or denied in the here and now, only to be brought to extremes in the future.

Chapter 6 Learning to Tell White Lies

Living with the Other in the Anti-Other America

Disrupting Impressions

NOT LONG AFTER I left Shoreham, my mom called to inform me that there was an iguana perched in a tree in the front yard. "Dad was out mowing the lawn when he saw it," she explained. "We tried to catch it, to bring it to Brian's Aquarium in Rocky Point, but we couldn't. It's been eating our flowers," she added with dismay. She went on to tell of how she and my father had called people on the street to see if anyone had lost their iguana, but no one had. And no one knew anything about it. With that established, they called the Society for the Prevention of Cruelty to Animals (SPCA). But by the time the SPCA sent a van to Shoreham, the iguana was nowhere to be found. Nowhere, that is, until a couple of days later, when it showed up again right outside my parents' bedroom window. This time, instead of calling the neighbors or the proper authorities, my mother called me.

There was fear and excitement in her voice. This intruder was giving her a good story to tell. It was most definitely in-filling her usually very normal life. I too was taken by this image of an iguana up in my parents' tree. What was this creature from a far-off region doing loose in the northeastern suburbs? And how would (my) suburbia cope with this outsider? I started imagining how a photograph of the iguana peering Cheshire-catlike from a branch in my parents' front yard, set against a backdrop of their red colonial house, with its clean white trim, well-tended flower beds, and regularly mowed lawn would make a good image for the cover of this book. Suburbia slightly askew. Not unlike David Lynch's film *Blue Velvet* (1986), which opens with a pan of a picturesque middle-class town replete with white picket fences, glistening red fire engine, and Crayolacolored gardens that ends disconcertingly on a microcosmic view of the colonies of bugs living within the suburban lawn. Later, the bugs reappear, this time to feast on a human ear rotting in a nearby open field. While not as extreme, the sight of an iguana set against a perfectly tame suburban vista would likewise jar a viewer's perceptions just enough to demonstrate the illusiveness of white middle-class domesticity. Unfortunately, the photograph of my parents' iguana never got taken; just the thought of it remains.

The iguana eventually vanished, leaving only some trampled flowers and this surreal, allegorical image behind. In the time since, my father has turned his talk to iguanas on several occasions, mentioning stories he read in the *Science Times* about how iguanas can be vicious, and passing on tales that he has heard about this or that iguana turning on its owner or biting a child. Clearly, the iguana in my father's tree had left a lasting and troubling impression on him. It had become an active part of his imagination, jostling his sense of control over his surroundings and disrupting the predictability he had come to take for granted in his more than three decades in this town. Likewise, it reshaped my own understanding of Shoreham and "home," clarifying just how contrived and hence vulnerable the foundations of suburban life really are.

My parents' iguana story fits into the common suburban trope of wildlife gone out of control in the subdivisions. In this regard, living in suburbia consists of a constant battle with rabid populations, infestations, and overpopulations of various species who either don't belong or only marginally belong in domesticated neighborhoods designed to keep "real" nature at bay. Long Island has a history of such struggles, which include stories about the accidental and careless introduction into the environment of defoliating gypsy-moth caterpillars and Lyme-disease-carrying deer ticks, the spread of rabies among the Island's ravenous raccoons, and the growing menace of deer on the Island's roadways. Stripped of its natural predators and pushed out of its usual out-of-the-way, wildlife habitats by the construction of more and more housing developments, shopping malls, and highways, the Long Island deer population is growing and moving rapidly—to the chagrin of motorists, homeowners, and landscapers alike—deeper and deeper into suburban life. For better or worse, these indigenous "pests" are part of what makes Long Island *not* New York City; hence they are both an asset and a nuisance. At any rate, they are tolerated. The language used to describe these (un)natural migrations and population imbalances echoes the rhetoric used to flame the fires of anti-immigrant and, more generally, anti-Other popular sentiments across the nation.[1] The rhetorical similarities here underscore the investment suburbanites have in maintaining the social greenhouse effect, where a community's equilibrium depends on a closed rather than a permeable system and the known is always more manageable than the unknown. The case of the wandering iguana is a story about a creature who has broken through the greenhouse glass. While suburbanites like their exotic Others, they like them caged and under domestic supervision. Indeed, these fascinating outsiders will only survive in the region if and only if they remain under house arrest and follow house rules. The iguana in my parents' yard had clearly (willfully or not) transgressed the "natural" order of the suburban greenhouse. Unlike that of other intruders, his presence did not threaten the local environment so much as call attention to its parochial limitations. Therefore his fate, rather than the greenhouse's, was clearly in peril.

The winter that followed the appearance and disappearance of the iguana was fairly mild. But even if the iguana had survived the cold and managed to feed itself off of suburbia's discards, surely it had fallen prey to a neighbor's dog (as had, to my grief, our pet rabbit, Freddy, when I was growing up) or to the trash-can-scavenging raccoon, a prominent and aggressive member of the local fauna and a species that had adapted, in spite of its periodic bouts with disease, quite well to living in the interstices of suburbia. I felt a certain amount of compassion for and, like my parents, more than a modicum of fascination with this displaced creature. What could be done for and with such an outsider?

By analogy, the story of the Shoreham iguana demonstrates what happens when suburbanites perceive something or someone as not belonging in their neighborhoods. It is about what happens when suburban tolerance is tested. It is about fear of the unknown, ambivalence, and trying to do what's right under the circumstances (cf. Perin 1988). It is about displaced anxieties that express the unspeakable in other forms, contexts, and vocabularies, making their telling more palatable for the white middle class. Denizens of Shoreham-Wading River rarely speak ill of their Others. In fact, they rarely openly acknowledge differences. Instead, they practice a kind of Other-blindness (or what Ruth Frankenberg identifies as a "color-blindness" or "color/power evasiveness," 1993). It is the polite thing to do in the anti-Other America, a place founded as the antidote to the Other (read nonwhite, poor) America, a place to which anti-Other Americans (read white middle class) fled to escape their perceived Others (new waves of immigrants and the black and Latino urban poor, to be specific). The anti-Other America is the name I give to suburbia: white middle-class America; the middle of the road; the imagined social core of the nation; the places built on social processes of exclusion, on histories and current-day practices that in turn must be erased from the collective suburban memory in order to constitute suburbia as a place without race or difference, a place of whiteness. I use the adjective anti-Other to remember this past and reframe the present within it.

Shoreham-Wading River instantiates the anti-Other America. It is, to a large degree, a place supposedly without difference, at least not the differences that usually count in the racial and social binaries that define what it means to be privileged or not in the United States: for example, black and white, poor and rich, gay and straight, to name three of the most prominent divisions.[2] In a world of social hierarchies, binary thinking is the foundation and dynamic of identity formation. I know I am white because I am not African American, not Latina, not Asian. I know I am straight because I am not gay. I know I am middle class because I am not rich and I am not poor. This is the negative logic of suburbia. It is the way of dividing up and understanding the world that white middle-class communities pass on to their daughters and that their daughters, in turn, learn to manipulate and apply in broad strokes in their lives. Emily, the teenage white supremacist of the previous chapter, exemplifies what happens when that application gets amplified beyond standards of middle-class temperance. But Emily is not so much an anomaly as she is an extreme that proves the norm. SWR girls practice their own versions of binary identity formation, albeit less conspicuously than Emily. And they do so on their own terms, constructing their own Others to complement their self-made and inherited norms.

But to know the Self as a negation of the Other implies that one "knows" the Other. How is this possible in the anti-Other America where the social landscape is built on similarities and not differences? The greenhouse walls are surprisingly effective, especially in a place like Shoreham-Wading River. In the absence of difference, the imagination takes over, fashioning both outsider- and insider-Others. In this sense, despite its best efforts (its history of white flight and its penchant for color-blindness), the anti-Other America is not without its Others. Its public life may look relatively homogeneous, but its imagination is cluttered with thoughts of all those Others it is not or at least the Others it hopes not to be: the welfare mothers with their "retarded" babies and the band of machine-gun-toting Arab terrorists breaking through the ceiling of the local Caldor department store that Tommy spoke of dreaming about periodically, to name two examples from the repertoire of stories SWR students tell about their Others.

In part, these imagined Others come ready-made for them in the media. They are the characters in Disney's *Aladdin* (1992, directed by John Musker) or the gay couple in *Melrose Place* or gangsta rappers on New York City radio. Though very few SWR eighth graders listened to rap music on any regular basis while I was in the field, they certainly knew what it was and what it stood for racially. In contrast, SWR girls most definitely watched shows like *Melrose Place* and *Beverly Hills 90210*, and they flocked to movies like *Aladdin*. Though these media productions were not as clearly racialized for them, they did discuss among themselves the characters that stood out as "different" from SWR's white middle-class heterosexual norm. On the day after a *Melrose Place* episode, for example, girls would begin their day comparing responses to the previous night's story line. They would note with some curiosity a show featuring a gay character, but the trials and tribulations of the school day would soon take over, demonstrating that these imagined and media-fabricated Others do not represent in-your-face, everyday differences for SWR eighth graders. In the day-to-day life of the eighth grade, imagined Others were fairly inconsequential.

When it came to "real" racial Others, SWR kids actively, though somewhat covertly, marginalized them. One day, for instance, two boys, Mike and Brian, were off in a corner talking about the African American basketball player Patrick Ewing. Brian said Ewing "proved the theory of evolution," and they both started making ape noises. This racist construction of a racial Other was not made in reference to their immediate life. Instead it expressed an underlying racist or at least racialized imaginary that rarely saw the light of day among the eighth graders; it rarely needed to. And when it did surface, it rarely did so in a public fashion. It was no accident that on this particular occasion, the students were working in small groups that were scattered about the classroom, the hall, or nearby computer room. The teacher moved among them, spending time with students as needed, making her authority in the room less centralized and less conspicuous. Given that there was no public space in the classroom on this day, no one seemed to hear or notice the two "ape" boys except me, the intently listening ethnographer. The two boys clearly knew that blatant racism in this world of liberal color-blindness would not be tolerated either by their teacher or their peers. I do not know how aware of my presence they were during this particular exchange. Were their ape noises uttered for my benefit? Were they testing the limits of my ethnographic tolerance? Or were they simply absorbed in their own private racial fantasy? Regardless, their actions indicate that these boys knew the codes of subtlety that operated in this anti-Other America, so they minimized the publicness of their racist performance.

When the topic of racial difference was posed to SWR students directly and in a more public context, they made it clear that they thought race was somebody else's issue, one with which they did not need to bother. Here the Other is brought to their attention but it is quickly marginalized, indicating the degree to which the white middle class's Other is less a binary outsider than it is an internally fashioned insider-Other. One day, Mr. R., who often started his morning English-social studies classes by calling attention to something of note in the news, held up a copy of the *New York Post* with its eye-catching cover headline, "L.I. School Gives Peter Pan the Hook," and its inside headline, "Indians Pan Peter: School musical scuttled after L.I. tribe complains." He then proceeded to read the story aloud:

> Peter Pan got the hook this weekend.
>
> It happened in posh Southampton after a group of parents complained that the popular play—scheduled to be performed at a local school—was offensive to Native Americans.

> At issue was a song in the play called "Ugh a Wugha Meatball," said John O'Mahoney, principal of the Southampton Intermediate School.
>
> "Some of the words were offensive. They had 'redskin' in it," O'Mahoney said.
>
> "The song ends with the kids singing 'How,' and the Native Americans said that's not in their vocabulary."
>
> He said that a group of parents from the local Shinnecock Indian reservation also objected to use of the words "squaw" and "brave" and to costumes with feathers—which the tribe allows to be worn only as a special honor.
>
> The whimsical play—about a magical boy who lives in Never Never Land and never wants to grow up—was to have been performed Friday and Saturday night.
>
> But Peter Pan never got off the ground....
>
> [Instead, he] bit the fairy dust....
>
> The school has decided to use the same cast in a production of "The Wizard of Oz."
>
> The play has been approved by a special multi-cultural panel.
>
> The vertically-challenged Munchkins have yet to be heard from. (Neuman 1994, 3; see also Otter 1994, 25)

The article—with its obvious sarcasm when it comes to multiculturalism, effectively trivializing the political claims of the local Native Americans—provoked lots of reactions from Mr. R.'s students, but no disagreement among them. Comments included: "I think they're taking things way too seriously." "It's a fantasy." "Oh, puhleaze!" "It's just entertainment." "Not everything is going to be fair. There's a lot of music that people find offensive." "What if all of a sudden—say, the movie *Boyz 'n the Hood*—they wouldn't stop making that movie just 'cause it offended someone." "I think they're being overly sensitive." And: "In old cartoons they have Indian stereotypes, did they complain then?" Mr. R. asked questions like "Should a school be promoting stereotypes?" And "Do Indians like being called 'redskins'?" To which Christine insistently replied, "Do *we* mind being called white?" The tone of her voice answered her own question: "No, end of conversation." And her choice of pronouns clearly articulated, in both senses of the word, the collective racial identity of the room.

Christine's comment went unchallenged and unexplored by either the teacher or the other eighth graders. Christine did indeed end the conversation. The definitiveness of her observation underscored the degree to which the white middle-class kids in the room did not measure themselves up against their racial Others. In fact, they didn't even consciously register themselves as racialized subjects. Here being white meant being born into the privilege of not having to take one's race too seriously. Instead, whiteness was taken for granted, functioning as a meaningless category in their day-to-day lives. Indeed, when do these kids even find themselves being called white? This is not an epithet, positive or negative, that they use among themselves, nor one they often hear being used to brand them socially. While Christine's statement may once again demonstrate that white middle-classness predicates itself in a kind of racial misrecognition, it also begs the question: If they don't mind being called white, what do they mind being called? In this world of binary identity formation, who are SWR girls' Others?

Name Calling and the Making of Insider-Selves and -Others

If questions of race and racism do not take center stage with SWR eighth graders, what does? While my early experiences in the middle school taught me that gender and its underlying issue of sexuality was an uncomfortable topic in a coed group (see chapter 1), they had not prepared me for just how prevalently sexuality would surface as the framework within which these white middle-class students positioned themselves and their attempts to mark and unmark their social identities. I came to understand sexuality or, more specifically, gayness as the last identity frontier for these young adolescents. In the absence of blackness, for example, gayness became the code word for their white middle-class Other. And like the negative logic of the anti-Other America, the kids' use of gayness taught me much about white middle-classness, tying its production to heterosexuality—as did Amy, Cheryl, Dora, and Emily—and demonstrating that what is not named is just as important as what is named. Since white middle-class decorum did not allow kids to openly racialize themselves, they turned to other means, other ways of naming, and other ways of expressing their anxieties about their social selves. Their near obsessive naming of (homo)sexuality, in turn, called attention to their near obsessive silences around questions of race and class. Gayness in this regard became an indexical marker of white middle-classness; it became the thing that can be spoken in lieu of the thing itself.

Though SWR eighth graders would not and, I suspect, could not articulate a connection between race and sexuality, one only has to turn to the history of antimiscegenation laws in this country to begin to see that social anxieties around sexuality are as much about racializing subjects as they are about sexualizing them (see Domínguez 1986; Spillers 1987). For example, in her study of the legal and social construction of Creole identity in Louisiana, Virginia Domínguez argues that legislation prohibiting interracial marriages was first and foremost concerned with consolidating white property, and hence maintaining a white hegemony, one where race and class are inextricable from each other (see especially chapter 3 in Domínguez 1986). The mixed-race bastard children of white men could not legally inherit their father's white wealth. What at first may appear to be a simple case of a desire for racial purity turns out to be more complex, linking racial hierarchies to economic interests. Work on more contemporary social contexts points to how the race-sex connection continues to flourish. A recent study of suburban mixed-race girls, for example, found that their racial identities as nonwhites did not become an issue until they hit puberty and started dating (Twine 1997). In the context of burgeoning heterosexual identities girls who were once just like everyone else suddenly became African American or Asian American and hence not suitable dating partners for their white classmates. Given suburbia's legacy as a haven for heterosexual families, the place white World War II veterans fled to in order to house and educate their children among other white heterosexual middle-class families, the race-sex-class connection seems unavoidable in a place like Shoreham-Wading River. With this history in mind, it is perhaps not so far-fetched to hear in SWR eighth graders' anxieties around (homo)sexuality a concomitant anxiety about their whiteness and middle-classness, as well as their respective femininity or masculinity. Hence, calling someone "gay" is more complex than simply calling that person's sexuality into question.

Gayness itself took on many forms and served various purposes in the everyday talk of the school. Sometimes it pertained to "real" people often taking the form of rumors about, for example, this or that teacher; other times it identified popular figures or more distant others like the gay athletes one group of eighth graders met on a class trip to New York City during the Gay Games. Though they were not in town to attend the sports competition, the students just happened to have ended up staying in the same hotel that housed some of the Games's participants. The girls who had been on this trip spoke of this serendipitous encounter with a certain amount of pride, as if they had come in contact with an exotic species worth telling their friends about. The gay athletes were giving them a notable story to tell, and girls lie in wait of a good social narrative to traffic among themselves (see chapter 4). I learned of the gay athletes when I overheard two groups of girls exchanging tales about their respective end-of-the-year class trips. One group spoke of their visit to Canada, exclaiming with some glee that they had met some "Canadians," to which girls from the New York City trip replied, "Yeah, well we met some *lesbians*!" Here gayness marked a difference to be cashed in on socially, rather than denounced. These lesbians were apparently exotic and distant enough to call attention to now that the SWR girls were safely back in the cradle of (heterosexual) suburbia. From their nuclear home base, the girls clearly regarded lesbians as one notch above Canadians in the social scheme of teen-girl Others.

More often, however, girls used the word *gayness* to express some form of disgust and to distance themselves from something or someone. The following conversation among three girls represents a more typical SWR response to gayness. Though it includes hints of "tolerance" and ambivalence, the girls quickly collapse these positions back into the more normative, "it's gross" reply. One day during third-period English class when students were working independently, writing their "Letters to Self," they started playing a Depeche Mode CD on the classroom stereo (see chapter 4 for a detailed description of "Letters to Self"). When the male lead singer got to the lyrics "All I want is him here in my arms," Lisa B. explained, "He's gay, so they took it [the MTV video of this song] off the air." When I asked Lisa what she thought of that, she told me it shouldn't have mattered. But then Kelly interjected, "That's [i.e., the "fact" that he's gay is] gross." And Jean added, "That's disgusting." At which point Lisa agreed, "I know, it's weird. He should have just kept it to himself." These kinds of brief exchanges on gayness often peppered eighth graders' conversations. Gayness never really became the main topic of their everyday talk, but it was almost always present as an expression of curiosity or disgust, as in "that's gross," or as a way of marking someone as a social outcast.

In the above exchange, Lisa clearly harbored some ambivalence when it comes to gayness. When not being policed by their friends directly, SWR eighth graders let this kind of on-again, off-again interest in or desire for more knowledge about gayness slip into their talk. In a conversation consisting of "cum-sucking" and semen jokes kids had on a ferry ride from Orient Point, Long Island, to New London, Connecticut, as we were on our way to a conference on Cape Cod (the school's buses were owned by the Seaman Company, which regularly provoked a routine of semen jokes from the kids on field trips), Tommy asked me if I knew any gay people. I told him that I had several friends who were lesbians back in California. "Cool. Wait, really?" he said looking over at me in a kind of surprised yet approving way. Then he asked, "Do they ever come on to you?" Tommy was one of the more socially conscious kids I met at SWR. He was also slightly older than his classmates, having been left back earlier in his education, and he came from a "mixed" marriage: his father was white and U.S. born and his mother was a Cuban-born woman (I'm not sure how she identified herself racially) who, according to her son, "escaped" from the Castro regime via boat to come to the United States, where she married his father and had a family consisting of Tommy and his older, now-runaway sister. Despite his "mixed" background, Tommy did not appear to identify himself as anything but white. More precisely, he didn't identify himself racially at all. Unlike most of his classmates, Tommy kept up with the latest national and world news. For example, Tommy knew the difference between whitewater rafting and Whitewater, the Clinton administration political scandal that was starting to heat up in the media and on Capitol Hill while I was in the field. Consequently, he would make puns accordingly, often duping his peers into revealing their own ignorances. Generally, Tommy's humor ran from subtle turns of phrases and referential asides about politics and popular culture to the utterly scatological: jokes about farts, bodily excretions, and body parts, namely penises. With regard to the lesbian exchange, I felt caught somewhere in between Tommy's fifteen-year-old head and body. He seemed to be coming on to me as much as expressing a desire-disgust for homosexuality. Unlike the girls' exchange on gayness, Tommy's attempted to personalize the issue. I can only speculate about whether this is a gender or age difference. Are adolescent white middle-class boys more threatened and simultaneously more titillated by the idea of gayness than are their female counterparts? Or did Tommy's age and level of social sophistication make him more aware and, to a degree, more in control of how he wields his sexuality in relation to an adult woman who both is and is not an authority in his life? I did not witness girls displaying similar responses to me or the issue of gayness.

In light of my own discomfort in the face of Tommy's "do they ever come on to you," I changed the subject abruptly. In part, I wanted to challenge Tommy's use of a gay stereotype, one that paints gays as oversexed and out to "recruit" straight people (and thereby diminish the procreative white population). But my status as an ethnographer and as an insider of sorts precluded such a pedagogical and direct response. (This particular incident took place late in the school year, so I was more an insider here than not. At the very least, my insider sensibilities were more honed than they were when I first reimmersed myself in this community.) As a retrained insider, I knew how and when not to talk about things. And in this exchange with Tommy, I became more fully the insider than my ethnographic project probably should have warranted. I wasn't going to pursue a conversation about lesbians with this fifteen-year-old boy. Talking about sex (gay or straight) is not something that happens often or comfortably between adolescents and the adults in this town. In fact, a couple of years after I left the field, there was a public dispute over whether or not gay students could be represented during the high school's annual Awareness Day, an event purportedly designed to promote tolerance of social differences. Given the conservative tenor of the community's recent struggles over curriculum and budget reform and the more general national "Don't ask, don't tell" attitude proffered by politicians and the media in relation to gays in the military and in regard to disputes over making condoms available to teens in high schools, I figured it behooved me not to encourage such a potentially volatile discussion. For better or worse, we moved on to other matters. The white middle-class heterosexual culture at SWR prevailed in my conversation with Tommy. We were both caught in the silencing dynamics that circumscribe the idea of tolerance in this community—Tommy tested the limits; I enforced them. "Don't ask, don't tell" is clearly more the rule of thumb here than "I'm okay, you're okay." As will become clearer by the end of this chapter, tolerance is only practiced within restricted parameters in this suburbia.

For the most part, questions of sexuality and sexual orientation located kids (and, at times, this ethnographer) in threatening and unknown territory. They were at the age when their own sexualities were clamoring for their attentions. How much they knew or didn't know, how much they had experienced or hadn't experienced was constantly shifting. This is not to suggest, however, that there is a one-to-one correspondence between their anxieties about their own sexualities and the frequency and vehemence with which they disapproved of gay people or simply used the term *gay* as a marker of difference. Nor is it to suggest that all or even a minority of kids were wondering if they might be gay. Instead, *gay* served as a metonym for the unknown, the Other, the thing that they are not, the thing that they might be, the thing that they know they are but cannot acknowledge openly, the thing that they are drawn to, the thing that repulses them, the Other within the anti-Other Self.

The ambivalences characterized by Lisa's and Tommy's takes on homosexuality give gayness a force among SWR students that blackness or "Indianness" (i.e., Native American), for example, do not. Issues of race, and likewise class and gender, do not call up within them an equivalent uncertainty or love-hate relationship. As Christine has already succinctly underscored, SWR kids do not mind being called white. Moreover, SWR eighth graders are mostly unselfconscious when it comes to class and self-assured, or at least in familiar waters, when it comes to gender. For example, one day in advisory, Lisa B. excitedly announced to everyone present (about tweleve students, a teacher, and myself) that she and her mom were going to buy Karen (a girl of considerably less means than Lisa) a dress for Eighth Grade Night, the end-of-the year graduationlike ceremonies for students and their parents that included dessert, a slide show documenting the students' three years in the middle school, and a final eighth-grade dance that took place for the kids after their parents went home; boys and girls dressed up for the event. Moreover, Lisa warned people not to talk about the dress, not because she was afraid of embarrassing Karen, but because, she said, "It's a surprise." Later in the week, she walked into the same class and let everyone know that they weren't going to buy Karen a dress after all because Karen "is a skank." Here, neither Lisa nor anyone else in the room displayed any discomfort with the way Lisa's pronouncements called attention to their classmate's lower economic status. Of course, Karen was not present on either occasion, and those girls that were were not people whose parents would hesitate to buy them a new dress for the upcoming event. The only eighth graders I witnessed speaking sotto voce about money were the ones who didn't have as much of it, though these were not, by any means, kids who were financially hard up. The economics of this community are relative within a fairly comfortable middle-class continuum, with a few exceptions.

The one time I observed anyone acknowledging class differences as a point of contention within SWR peer groups, the recognition came from an eighth grader who came from a less financially secure situation. However, he privatized his response, internalizing rather than politicizing his feelings of inadequacy. In other words, his reaction was not a social critique so much as it was a display of adolescent embarrassment. Not long after I officially left the field, David, Brad, and Julie came to visit me in my new home in New York City. David wanted to go shopping at Armani Exchange A/X, a fairly expensive and, at the time, chic clothing store in SoHo. David, whose family lived in the "old-money" section of Shoreham, the Village, was accustomed to a lifestyle of a certain distinction. Brad was not. He lived with his divorced mother on the "wrong side" of 25A, in a neighborhood with smaller, sometimes slightly run-down, houses.[3] When I was growing up, my friends and I mostly didn't hang out with anyone from this side of town, nor did we ever discuss why this was the case. We just took it for granted. Though current SWR kids did more class mixing (David and Brad were "best friends," at least in eighth grade[4]), their class differences were not inconsequential for the ones who didn't live in a household with a lot of discretionary income. For example, when David picked up a sixty-five-dollar Armani T-shirt and exclaimed how great it was, Brad pulled me aside and rolled his eyes, looking visibly agitated and uncomfortable. Regardless, he never confronted David, choosing to downplay rather than call attention to his less-monied status.

On the other hand, gender differences were fair game among eighth graders. Even if they didn't like the idea that an adult would be studying these differences, they did not hesitate to negotiate them among themselves. Sexist comments like "She's such a hoochbag," said by one girl about another, rarely went uncontested. Girls would object to or argue about such gendered name calling and could articulate a critique of the idea that if girls have sex, they're "sluts" and if boys have sex, they're "studs." Though such discussions of gender differences hinged on issues of sexuality, they did not call into question the underlying heterosexuality of suburbia. For its part, the media had popularized, perhaps even normalized, gender differences, at least in their heterosexual guise, as a white middle-class issue. For example, the teen magazines that many girls read regularly printed numerous columns on the "battle between the sexes." In some cases the main editorial slant of the magazine hinged on a "what does he think vs. what does she think?" approach to teen-girl culture. Hence, though white middle-class femininity may have been a topic of concern for SWR eighth graders, it lurked in an arena that was already mapped out for them. Their parents and teachers were comfortable talking about it, and it was not a conversation they needed to keep to themselves in the way that they had to with regard to race and, to a lesser degree, class. In the race, class, gender, and sexuality social continuum, sexuality clearly occupied a less subtle and less stable position than did the other three salient categories of difference.

In excessively naming the Other "gay," SWR kids inadvertently call attention to a lack in their own community. However, this supposed absence is imminently present within. One's teacher may be gay, a friend's parent or older sibling may be gay, indeed, just maybe, you're gay. In this sense, gayness becomes a presence more tangible for them than the nonmiddle-class or nonwhite subject who clearly, in their understandings of the world, lives elsewhere, or lives among them with little or no consequence. *Gay* names an insider-Other. And the predominant Others of SWR girls' everyday lives are insider-Others: their peers who remain on the margins, capable of looking and acting the part of full-fledged insiders, but something about them sets them apart. They are not quite white middle-class heterosexual enough. These insider-Others are not the same as the hypernormal girls of chapter 4. Hypernormal girls are *too* white and *too* middle class. They go to the depths of what it means to be an insider. They are alienated from normal girls by their hyperinsider status. They are at the opposite end of the spectrum from the insider-Other. Rather than magnifying insiderness, insider-Others openly reject it or simply have very little access to it, even when they are functioning on a daily basis within it. How SWR girls name and respond to their insider-Others demarcates the boundaries of their own identities. Otherizing some people is a way of fashioning a Self, even if the differences are more elusive than simple binaries allow. Moreover, given their proximity to the center, insider-Others function not unlike the iguana in my parents' tree: they skew what counts as normal and in the process demonstrate the fragility of the white middle-class privilege with which they are almost but not quite juxtaposed.

Inside and Out: Why Insider-Others Matter

Amber, a white lower-class girl living on the outskirts of Wading River with her nonworking, alcoholic mother and two out-of-control older adolescent siblings, was as close as SWR girls came to crossing paths on their own turf with a socially exterior Other. As an economic and cultural outsider Amber landed on the inside by virtue of the somewhat arbitrary mapping of district lines. She could have just as easily attended the lower- to lower-middle-class, racially diverse schools of nearby Riverhead. Having moved into the district only recently, Amber had not "grown up" with her classmates, hence she had not been schooled in their white middle-class ways for long. Rather than pretending she "belonged" at SWR, Amber wore her outsider status as a shield that she would knowingly wield against her peers, distancing them before they could distance her. While the middle-class girls had cliques or tight friendship groups I referred to as clumps earlier, Amber headed the closest thing to a gang that SWR eighth graders seemed to have. Amber and her group of friends—Fran, Sandra, and sometimes

Karen, girls who were also on the edges of SWR life—would travel as often as possible in a kind of pack, copping a "don't mess with us" attitude. Rumors about Amber threatening to "beat up" this or that SWR insider girl were fairly commonplace. In addition, Amber was known to hang out after school with kids—especially older teen boys who drove cars and got into trouble with the law—from the nearby and "rougher" towns of Riverhead or Rocky Point.

By SWR standards, Amber was tough. Amber and her friends were among the few girls in the school whose families were not affluent and whose home lives were visibly far from stable. After finishing eighth grade, instead of attending SWR high school on a full-time basis, Amber would spend part of her day studying at BOCES (Brookhaven Occupational Center and Educational Services), a public vocational secondary school in the area. This was not an option that many students in the district followed (see the introduction for a discussion of the place of BOCES in SWR life). Moreover, by the time high-school graduation rolled around, Amber was the proud mother of a two-year-old daughter, making her even more of an Other in the anti-Other America than she already was (see chapter 1 for a discussion on single motherhood in this community). Despite or perhaps because of her differences, on graduation day, Amber accepted her SWR diploma with an air of accomplishment and belonging, a demeanor I rarely saw her project as an eighth grader, four years earlier. It was as if, as a graduating senior, she no longer cared how much of an outsider she really was; she was going to have the last laugh on her still adolescent (in contrast with Amber who had had to grow up fast), college-bound, upper-middle-class fellow graduates.

Back in eighth grade, SWR insiders didn't know quite what to make of Amber. According to girl talk, Amber's mother bought her alcohol and cigarettes and periodically got out of control, doing things like smashing Fran's brother's car windshield with a brick. According to teacher talk, alcoholism, AIDS, and parental neglect had rendered Amber and her friends' lives difficult to say the least. Insider SWR girls either carefully stayed out of Amber and her gang's way, or they deliberately challenged their somewhat subversive and potentially volatile presence. Amber didn't leave any bruised or broken bodies in her wake, so I don't know for sure how much her reputation was based on hearsay and how much she had actually earned it. I suspect that Amber's toughness was a figment of her classmates' imaginations, up there with the welfare mothers and their retarded babies or the Caldor-invading Arab terrorists. Amber was a partially imagined Other who had to be contended with on a daily basis; hence she became more of an insider-Other than the homogeneous logic of SWR would usually accommodate, or, for that matter, encounter.

Like her SWR classmates, Amber trafficked in the same Otherizing idiom: gayness. But in a move that almost parodied and certainly threatened her middle-class peers, she upped the ante. Instead of matter-of-factly throwing around the term *gay*, she'd walk through the school branding everyone that got in her way as a "fucking dyke!" In a sense, "fucking dyke" was Amber's mantra. Teachers who were giving her a hard time were "fucking dykes"; Lisa B., her sworn enemy and eventual buddy, was a "fucking dyke"; her best friend Fran's grandmother and guardian was a "fucking dyke"; and for talking to Lisa or Mrs. R. or for just doing this ethnography, I'm sure I was a "fucking dyke," though I never heard her call me that to my face. Amber would mutter this epithet under her breath, write it on other girls' lockers, or just say it outright in the middle of an altercation with another girl or adult.

For the most part, Amber managed to carry out the role as insider-Other, consciously or not, in a fashion that mocked the privileges of her classmates' middle-class lives. Her insistent, in-your-face "fucking dyke" refrain made the insider excess "that's so gay" seem impotently normal. Amber was nothing if not defiant against the prevailing middle-class norms of the school. For months, Amber had been coming to school dressed in nondescript jeans and a T-shirt. Her look was more androgynous than anything else—that is, until Eighth Grade Night when Amber arrived not with her parents, as most kids did, but with Fran, who was also not accompanied by an adult. (Fran's mother was dead. Her father lived about an hour west of SWR with his girlfriend. Fran lived with her maternal grandmother with whom she didn't get along very well.) Following tradition, Amber and Fran were dressed up: Amber in a black, lacy, promlike dress, Fran in a tuxedo-like suit. They were, it seemed, in heterosexual drag. It wasn't clear, however, if they were drawing on butch-fem cultural codes deliberately. I wasn't about to ask Amber if she was a "fucking dyke" just so I could clarify the situation. Like SWR insider girls, I avoided pissing off Amber at all costs. Instead, I was left wondering if she was wondering about her own sexuality, and if she and Fran knew from which sartorial vocabulary they were borrowing. It seemed more likely that Amber and Fran were just "fucking" with their SWR classmates' and teachers' expectations and understandings of who the two of them were and how they did or didn't belong in this particular white middle-class, eighth-grade culture. Like Amber's excessive and crude "fucking dyke," her Eighth Grade Night attire was extreme, on the verge of being appropriate and inappropriate at the same time. Consequently, it called attention to her classmates' understated excesses, introducing a tinge of critical social commentary into an event that is otherwise intentionally and unabashedly celebratory of middle-class achievement and decorum.

Amber's "fucking dyke" was clearly more nuanced than it seemed at first hearing (or even at repeated hearings). Unlike her classmates' "he's/she's so gay," it seemed to be spoken from a position of self-awareness. She was not among those privileged enough not to know her own place in this world of middle-class hierarchies. She knew she didn't entirely fit in. Labeling everyone who crossed her path a "fucking dyke" called further attention to her own invasive status. Likewise, unlike the generic "gay," "fucking dyke" was clearly gendered and hence could be understood as a kind of projection that named Amber's own outsiderness. In this sense, Amber was a trickster outsider. She was like the insiders, but not quite. She provoked fear and fascination among insider girls. Someone like Lisa B., for example, an insider who was not entirely comfortable with her insiderness, obsessed over Amber for most of the year. Lisa in-filled her normal life with tales of Amber: stories about public and private fights that involved Lisa's mother, the school's guidance counselors and vice principal, as well as the police and innocent bystanders. But by the end of the year, Lisa's contentious obsession turned to camaraderie. The two girls got together after Amber called up Lisa and basically acknowledged that they both had enough problems without making extra trouble for each other. From that point on, much to her mother's dismay, Lisa began hanging out with Amber and her "white-trash" friends (see chapter 4). Lisa had gotten what she was seeking all along: as near an identification with an Other as she could get in this protected community of sameness. She had, in a sense, in-filled her normal Self with a local Other. And she did it largely in defiance of her mother.

When it came to talking about Amber and acknowledging her difference, SWR kids resorted to euphemisms, though not the obvious "she's so gay"; Amber had already bested them on that front. This was a case, I suspected, of not being able to name an Other for what she was—lower class and underprivileged—because such a bold act would mean articulating one's own privilege and admitting one's own "prejudices" (the operative term in SWR parlance). In a discussion about how the different cliques in the school did or did not get along, Annie explained, "Kerri is trying to kick Amber's butt, but she knows she'll get the crap kicked out of her." Jean interjected, "Amber's nice to me." And Rachel interrupted, "Guys, come on, I like Amber. She's so cute. She's so *big* and *muscular*." To which Annie replied, "She's just got a *mouth*." Amber didn't appear to me to be particularly big or muscular. She was definitely not among the skinniest or most dainty of SWR girls, but she was not exactly beefy either. In reducing Amber to her physicality—imagined or otherwise—SWR girls drew on middle-class stereotypes of the working class as brawny, mouthy, and aggressive, while, ironically, simultaneously trying to avoid appearing to be prejudiced by coming out and directly naming Amber as white trash, which they clearly thought she was. Though I did not ask them why they chose these particular adjectives to describe Amber, I do know that this was not the only time I would hear members of this community use such corporeal terms to name their Others. Hence I understand the girls' evasive vocabulary in the above exchange as more than just local teen-girl talk. As much as they may loathe to admit it, using physical traits to name their Others is a mode of speaking and managing difference that they most likely learned from their parents, the people from whom they struggle to set themselves apart and whom they emulate at the same time.

Policing Adults

Midway through my fieldwork, the girl's high-school varsity basketball team made it to the sectional finals. One eighth-grade girl who was known as a gifted basketball player had been recruited onto the team despite her middle-school standing. So when the team progressed to the finals, I decided to observe the big game. In this first leg of the championship, SWR was matched up against Amityville, a team hailing from a town considerably closer to New York City than SWR is and from a school district whose student population is two thirds African American (Brown 1994, A35). The SWR team was entirely white, while the Amityville team was black. It was an away night game and SWR parents and teachers came out in full force, as did the Amityville community. Consequently, the fans were divided along racial lines, with white SWR fans occupying one section of the bleachers and the black Amityville supporters the other. I sat among the SWR spectators, chatting with the parents, teachers, and district superintendent (and father of one of the players) who had come to cheer the girls on. As both teams were warming up, the talk around me turned to "how *big* the Amityville girls are" compared to "our *skinny* girls." Here big and skinny displaced the obvious: black and white. In this interracial, competitive context, SWR's vocabulary of the body now politely named a racial outsider rather than an economically stigmatized insider-Other. Big, muscular, and skinny are socially slippery and hence useful terms in a culture that prefers to avoid most conflicts and disavow its role in their making.

In a similar vein, one parent also commented on how the Amityville girls all had on the same sneakers, while the SWR girls each wore her own individually selected, parent-bought pair of Nikes, Reeboks, Converses, or what have you. I surmised that the difference marked the teams' class discrepancies. Presumably, the Amityville girls' sneakers were given to them as part of their school-bought uniforms, while the SWR girls supplied their own footwear, no small economic investment, one that parents from a less affluent community could ill afford.

Once the game started, both teams' fans responded vociferously as the girls dribbled up and down the court. The match was charged. Amityville's defense effectively kept SWR girls out from under the basket. As the game progressed, the SWR girls became increasingly frustrated. As a result, they began to slam into the Amityville players and hold onto the ball too long before they attempted to get it by an Amityville girl to an SWR teammate. The refs called foul after foul against SWR, and Amityville kept using their penalty shots to put the ball in the basket, hence increasing their lead over SWR. About halfway into the game, a ref called the first foul on an Amityville girl, bringing the SWR crowd to its feet cheering, and the mother of the best player on the team shouting: "It's about time, ref. I was beginning to think you were *color blind*."

Ostensibly, this mother was referring to the teams' uniforms: SWR in blue and gold; Amityville in red and white. However, the underlying racial connotations of this outburst were hard to ignore. The whiteness and blackness of the two teams stood in starker contrast than their school colors. Regardless, no one around her responded. Instead, her comment hung in the gymnasium air for a split second, while the SWR crowd regained its (white middle-class) composure and got on with rooting for its skinny (read white) daughters. SWR's enthusiasm and ref bullying were to no avail; the girls eventually lost to Amityville by twelve points, forty-six to thirty-four.

As indirect as this racial outburst may have been, in my months in the field I rarely witnessed such a public and direct demonstration of SWR's racial culture at work. This mother's outburst, in many ways, revealed more about the dynamics of race in this community than did the clandestinely muttered ape-noises of the eighth-grade boys described earlier. The "color-blindness" here was not so much the ref's, who was clearly just doing his job, as the SWR parents', who aspired to maintain a kind of social color-blindness while all too obviously remaining deeply color, or more specifically, race conscious. Their race consciousness, however, was not about their own middle-class whiteness—certainly not directly—and the ways they racialized their daughters (and sons), so much as it was about avoiding the topic all together, even when they felt particularly, racially threatened.

To a great extent, SWR girls saw through their parents' color-blindnesses, exploiting the underlying hypocrisies of such a position for their own gain. While among themselves SWR girls may have had little use for racial Others (e.g., "Do we mind being called white?" No, end of conversation.), in relation to their parents girls used race and their parents' prejudices or thinly veiled color-blindnesses to capture their parents' attentions, to differentiate themselves from their families (c.f. Breines 1992, 127–166), and to express the inexpressible: their own fears and hesitations with regard to nonwhite (and, by extension, white) racial identity. Girls told me numerous stories that suggest such an analysis. For example, Lisa insists on dressing hip-hop style, while her mother refuses to be seen with her when she's dressed "black." When I asked her what her mom thinks of Kiwana, her African American friend who came for overnight visits from Connecticut, Lisa told me her mom "loves Kiwana. She [her mom] isn't really prejudice, she's just embarrassed when I dress black."[5] Likewise, Rachel wanted to get her ears pierced when we were at the mall, but said her father would tell her she looks "Puerto Rican. He's soooo prejudice," she added disapprovingly. And one day in English class, Elizabeth turned to me and out of the blue told me that she had a "strange" family. She explained that her cousins in New Jersey were a "bunch of racist jerks. They say stupid racist things, and it really gets me mad. My grandfather in Texas is a racist too, but at least he's trying not to be. He listens to the facts. He listens when I tell him things. My grandmother belongs to some church where they take her money. The preacher gets them to give money all the time. He says he uses it for the church and to help people, but I don't believe him. I went with her once." When I asked her what kind of church her grandmother belonged to, she said she didn't know, but that they speak in tongues, sing a lot, wave their arms in the air, and sway back and forth. In all of these instances, the girls display signs of shame and disgust in relation to their white families' attitudes toward cultural practices understood to be non-white, or in the case of fundamentalist Christianity, having a stigmatized whiteness. But in reacting with such force and at times defending their family's prejudices, the girls also bespeak another concern, "Am I like them?" The adult community either foregrounds for them a fascination with racial Otherness in outbursts like the one I witnessed at the basketball game or backgrounds it for them in color-/power-evasive language, discourses that do not acknowledge histories or present-day circumstances of oppression that constitute race in the United States. Opposing their families allows SWR girls to speak of something that is otherwise an unspeakable issue or a barely perceptible presence in their lives, namely racial difference. In this sense, their relationship to their families' "prejudices" is productively ambivalent. While they admonish their families for their racism, they also depend on them to articulate what they otherwise will not allow themselves to utter: that they are conscious of racial and ethnic differences.

In relation to the adult world, SWR girls were learning to be white in the shadow of, as they saw it, their overly race conscious and "prejudice" parents. As in communities of difference, this world was divided into a them-versus-us structure. However, in this community of similarity, the "them" included insiders, the girls' parents, as well as insider-Others like Amber. Consequently, the lines of opposition and identity for SWR girls were not drawn distinctly along social categories and the Other was not always so clearly different from the Self. As an SWR girl, it would have been difficult to sit in the segregated bleachers and listen to your community yell out, "I was beginning to think you were color blind." Where would your alliances fall? Likewise, it would be difficult to root for the home team, when home included a kind of intolerance for difference that in many respects your middle-class upbringing was also teaching you, at the very least, to keep to yourself or within the privacy of your own home. What was a girl to do?

A Multiculturalism of Inconsequence

Not only was race not supposed to be mentioned in public or in polite company, it was not supposed to be studied or, it seems, in most instances, discussed too extensively or directly at SWR. When the principal asked in his letter opposing my study (see chapter 1), "Aren't girls born white?" and concluded: "The more I think about it, the more inappropriate it seems to conduct racially-based research in a public school setting," he spoke firmly from within the SWR ethos on race and difference. We don't have a problem, so why stir up one? We are race neutral, color blind, equal opportunity providers. Race is of no account or consequence; it has no place in the school district or community. Besides, we aren't in the business of teaching kids to be white or middle class, or, for that matter, girls.

Despite this prevailing attitude, on occasion, teachers did facilitate classroom discussions on race and racism—sometimes as part of a history lesson, sometimes as part of an English assignment, and sometimes as part of a current-events aside—though the subject of SWR's whiteness never came up directly except for the time Christine asked: "Do *we* mind being called white?"

The day after Nelson Mandela won the presidential election in South Africa, Mr. R. held up a full-page advertisement in the *New York Times* for United Colors of Benetton. The image showed a white hand with a black wristband passing a baton off to a black hand with a white wristband. The text, centered above the Benetton logo, read: "We demand our rightful place in the land of our birth. We want one person, one vote in a united, nonracial and democratic South Africa.—Nelson Mandela, April 27, 1991" (*New York Times* 1994, A5). When Mr. R. asked what this was all about, Jean called out, "That's a clothing store, and they're reuniting." Other kids jumped in and explained what had happened politically in South Africa. And with prompting from Mr. R., they collectively cobbled together a sketch of the history of South African apartheid. Then Mr. R. asked, "Why does this sell clothes?" And Tommy replied, "It makes them [Benetton] look good." To which Mr. R. asked, "What's the purpose of the advertisement?" And a voice called out, "It gets your attention." On that note, the discussion of race and racism ended, and the class moved on to tackle the day's assignment: writing an "About the Author" to accompany their Inquiry Projects, collections of essays, poems, and informational pieces on topics of their choosing that they had been working on for the past several weeks.

The one school-based program on race that I observed was part of an extracurricular teaching-tolerance program in which students elected to participate, Bringing Unity to Youth, or BUTY (pronounced "beauty") as the kids and teachers referred to it.[6] BUTY consisted of a "cultural exchange" between the SWR and Riverhead middle schools. Only a twenty-minute drive east of

Shoreham, Riverhead is probably the district closest to SWR with the largest nonwhite population: in 1992–93, of the nearly four thousand students attending Riverhead schools, 30.6 percent were black, 0.8 percent were Asian, 1.9 percent were Hispanic, and 66.5 percent were white (Brown 1994, A35). The economic disparities between Riverhead and SWR are also pronounced. Unlike isolated, virtually commerce-free, and family-oriented Shoreham-Wading River, Riverhead has an extensive commercial center and is a county seat replete with a Department of Motor Vehicles, a New York State Supreme Court building, and a county jail. Until the opening in late 1994 of a complex of outlet stores on the eastern edge of Riverhead, the SWR community did most of its shopping west of Shoreham at places like the Smith Haven Mall, avoiding the Riverhead experience altogether. Now they are drawn to the outlets, but not much further. Likewise, few SWR students, Amber and her friends notwithstanding, have regular contact with Riverhead kids, and those insiders that do, do so to the chagrin of their parents, except when the encounter takes place in the name of multiculturalism and teaching tolerance, under the auspices of an official district program like BUTY. Under these pretenses, in the beginning of May, about thirteen Riverhead kids, almost all of whom were African American, came to SWR, and at the end of the month, about twelve SWR kids (and I), all of whom were white, went to Riverhead. In both settings, kids were paired with an indigenous student and "shadowed" him or her for the day.

At SWR, the preparation leading up to the exchange was fairly perfunctory. About a week before the Riverhead students were scheduled to come to SWR, the community service coordinator in the school, Mrs. F., met with the SWR kids participating in the program to go over the logistics and give them a sense of context for the exchange. For some this would be their second year visiting Riverhead with BUTY. When Mrs. F. asked them what the differences were between the two schools, kids noted that Riverhead has a cafeteria; students have to stay inside during lunch; there are security guards; and there's yellow tape in the hallway, which everyone has to walk to the right of. Then some kids started talking about how Riverhead students reacted to SWR last year: "They thought our school was small and boring." "They kept *axing* us where all the blacks were," a comment that prompted Jean and Jessica to add: "When we were in Brooklyn showing [our slide-show] 'BJ/3,' kids *axed us* that. We said it was our community. It's not that we kick them out."[7] Instead of addressing Jean and Jessica's comment directly, Mrs. F. persisted in her earlier vein of questioning: "What are the differences between you and them?" To which someone replied, "They're *big*," again drawing on a corporeal idiom to misidentify their racial Other. The meeting ended with Mrs. F. trying to get SWR students to think about how to start conversations with their Riverhead visitors, and how to make them feel welcome. Tommy said he'd ask them if they like Pearl Jam (a white grunge band popular at that time). Lisa suggested, "We can pay for their pizza." Both comments could have opened up discussions about whiteness and class, especially in terms of questions of cultural tastes and aesthetics (Bourdieu 1984). How and why, for example, might a band like Pearl Jam appeal to white suburban kids and not African American kids living under less privileged social conditions? These and other questions went unasked; the period was over and everybody moved on to their next regularly scheduled activity.

On the day Riverhead students visited, they walked around SWR saying things like, "This school is like a museum; we don't have couches and stuff"; asking "What can y'all do to get detention?"; and explaining how they get three days detention for having a water pistol, which means they stay after school and sit in a room and can't talk to anyone from 2:30 to 4:00. In a pithy moment, one Riverhead kid went up to the stacks in the library and dramatically ran his hand along the top shelves. "See, you got dust," he said displaying his smudged fingertips, a comment I took to be a biting piece of social commentary; that is, you all may have money and privilege but that doesn't mean you don't have your own "dirt" like everyone else. No one seemed to appreciate or understand his humor. When Riverhead kids passed a black SWR student (all 1.1 percent of them) in the hall, they would say hello. Sue and Lisa noticed this practice, concluding in a somewhat offended manner, "Hey, they're counting the number of black kids in the school."

More significantly, however, SWR kids didn't seem to notice what Riverhead kids knew that they themselves didn't know. In social studies class, Mr. R. just happened to be going over the early 1960s and the civil rights movement, using Billy Joel's lyrics to "We Didn't Start the Fire" and corresponding slides as a basis for the discussion. When Mr. R. asked, "Who defeated the world champion boxer Sonny Liston?" most of the Riverhead kids' hands went up. "Mohammad Ali." No SWR kids had a reply. When Malcolm X's picture came on the screen, again Riverhead kids could tell his story in detail, while only some SWR kids knew anything about him. The Riverhead visit ended soon after this history lesson. Despite the premise of their meeting, as far as I could tell, little was exchanged between the SWR and Riverhead students in the course of that day's visit. To the contrary, much was left unsaid and unanswered.

In writing about her own education in the third world and subsequent transformation into a first-world scholar, Mary E. John notes, "Education is obviously a process by which we learn to avow and remember certain knowledges and devalue and forget others" (John 1989, 55). As a result, John suggests, we forge our subjectivities through a curriculum of "sanctioned ignorances" that at the very least avoid the more difficult questions. Though the context of John's observation dramatically differs from that of the SWR kids' lives, the educational process she identifies travels beyond the obvious borders. Not knowing about the civil rights movement, Mohammad Ali, or Malcolm X may indeed be "sanctioned ignorances" for SWR kids. This was no doubt not the first time they had been "taught" about the civil rights movement. I had seen posters and other educational materials around the school in sixth-, seventh-, and eighth-grade classrooms that illustrated nonwhite histories and white history in relation to nonwhite histories. And I probably would have found similar materials in the district's elementary schools. I knew, for example, that at least one eighth-grade girl understood enough about the history of slavery and emancipation to jokingly call me her "little Harriet Tubman" when I ushered her past the hall monitors into a world of relative freedom from adult supervision in the academic wings during lunch activity one day. The salient questions here are: What and who has sanctioned these white middle-class kids' ignorances? And to what end? In remaining ignorant of nonwhite histories what do they not learn about their own history of whiteness?

Ostensibly, the SWR-Riverhead exchange was designed to counteract such ignorances. To this end, SWR would complete the experience by joining Riverhead students on their home turf. On the morning SWR kids went to Riverhead, Jean said she was sick and that the boy she had been paired with from Riverhead made her uncomfortable when he was at Shoreham. Jessica was convinced she was going to get "jumped." And Lisa G. complained that going to Riverhead was "boring" last year, "You have to sit in class all day long." The SWR boys about to make the trip remained silent, neither expressing nor displaying any apprehension. For the girls, there seemed to be an element of sexuality tied up in the "multiculturalism" (racial differences) of the exchange. Physically, they were more mature than their male counterparts and socially more focused on issues of heterosexual dating, pushing their encounters with "blackness" into the highly charged imaginary of interracial sexuality, with its history of exoticism and white paranoia. In the end, no one got jumped, though some girls clearly had mutually flirtatious—however racially charged they may have been—encounters with Riverhead (black) boys.

The contrasts between SWR and Riverhead couldn't have been greater. Every Riverhead classroom had a set of "rules," "consequences," and "rewards" posted in the front of the room that students were supposed to follow. These included things like: "Be in class and seated when the bell rings." "Always keep your textbook covered." "Do not talk during the lesson." "Remain in your seat." "No food, drink, or candy in class." The science lab had an additional sign: "We are all expected to dress appropriately for school. Weapons, drugs, alcohol, and foul language may not be displayed." In most classes, kids sat in assigned seats in rows. And they rushed between class periods, making sure that they stayed to the right of the yellow line on the floor. For the most part, Riverhead students did not talk in classes, as opposed to the cacophony of SWR life, which also, by the way, often included lots of eating of snacks and lunches and drinking of sodas, boxed juices, and milk during and between classes. Riverhead teachers brusquely reprimanded kids who spoke out of turn, saying things like, "The next person who doesn't behave in class will get detention," while SWR kids often jumped into class discussions on their home turf, with no or few consequences; such independence and initiative was more in line with the pedagogical culture at SWR than not. Lunch at Riverhead was regimented, surveilled, and loud. Sixth graders ate lunch during sixth period (around 10:50 A.M.); seventh graders, during seventh period (around 11:30 A.M.); and eighth graders, during eighth period (around 12:10 P.M.). In the lunchroom, kids sat at metal picnic-style tables with attached benches and talked very loudly while teachers and teachers' aides stood vigil by the exits. At SWR, on the other hand, kids brought food from home, which they could heat up in the microwaves in the various classrooms, or an advisor, another teacher, or I took them out to lunch at the local pizza place or bagel shop or at a fast-food restaurant one town over. When they stayed at school, SWR kids ate in their advisories and had a half hour of free time before eating to catch up on their work or hang out with their friends either inside or outside the school building. Clearly, the white, middle-class SWR students were being disciplined to be individuals, to be their own managers, and to be comfortable with supposedly benign and nearly invisible forms of authority, while their Riverhead counterparts were being taught to stay in line (literally as well as more broadly), to follow orders, and to not question authority.

In addition to the social regulations of Riverhead school life, Riverhead pedagogy was worlds apart from SWR's. In English class at Riverhead, the teacher instructed students to read out loud paragraphs from a textbook on Greek mythology for forty minutes, an activity I never witnessed at SWR. Indeed, few SWR classes used textbooks at all. More often than not, SWR's English classes consisted of students working on individual writing projects. And once a week, teachers devoted a period of class time to silent reading, in which the students, teachers, and any visitors would read for forty minutes from a book of their choosing. SWR eighth-graders kept reading logs and English journals that elaborated on class activities. In art class in Riverhead, everyone worked from kits on the same project. The Riverhead girl I was paired with was making a rabbit pillow, the girl next to her, a heart-shaped one. In SWR art rooms, students worked on elaborate projects of their own design, ranging from ceramic sculptures to silver jewelry to wood furniture. Overall, none of the Riverhead rules, consequences, awards, or activities resembled life at SWR. These differences were not lost on either the SWR or Riverhead students, though their significance remained unexamined.

On the van ride back to Shoreham, the SWR students exchanged stories. Lisa said she got called a "white heifer," a slang, she said, for "white trash," and, I would add, a feminized racial epithet at that. Regardless, she seemed pleased by the fact that she had gotten a lot of guys' phone numbers. Jim had to spend most of the day in detention because his partner kept getting into trouble. Bob fell asleep in social studies. Christine noticed that there was a white side and a black side to most rooms. And they all started imitating how Riverhead kids talk, saying things like "playin," "sweatin," and "Whazup!?" Meanwhile, Mrs. F. continued to drive the van in near silence, choosing not to use the students' spontaneous reactions to their day to facilitate a discussion on the significance of the racial, gendered, and class differences that they had experienced firsthand.

Such was the extent of the "cultural exchange." As far as I knew, there was no follow-up activity. Once the SWR kids got back to Shoreham, some went off to basketball practice, others went home to hang out with friends, watch TV, talk on the phone: the usual. No adult organized a critical conversation about what they had just experienced or about how their perceptions fit into a larger sociohistorical picture. Doing so would have meant facing the SWR kids' whiteness and privilege head on. It would have meant unpacking Jean and Jessica's statement: "We said it was our community. It's not that we kick them [black people] out." It would have meant unsanctioning their ignorances, asking them to look at what they didn't know and to notice patterns in the gaps in their knowledge. Teaching tolerance in this offhand manner more accurately meant teaching evasion, a practice that reinforced rather than disrupted their already learned, culturally prejudiced norms. It meant teaching them to be unconsciously race conscious, to the point where they were learning not to talk about differences, a silence they would most likely only be able to abide under limited greenhouse circumstances. This was, to say the least, a multiculturalism of inconsequence, much like the one Paul Beatty satirically describes in his fictional memoir about growing up black in a white neighborhood:

> I was the only "cool black guy" at Mestizo Mulatto Mongrel Elementary, Santa Monica's all-white multicultural school. My early education consisted of two types of multiculturalism: classroom multiculturalism, which reduced race, sexual orientation and gender to inconsequence; and schoolyard multiculturalism, where the kids who knew the most polack, queer and farmer's daughter jokes ruled. (Beatty 1996, 172)

Instead of teaching SWR students to speak about race—theirs and others'—BUTY reinforces the community's coded racial practices. The only "race" spoken at SWR is found in the utterances that irrupt in the margins of conflicts, in private spaces, or in the euphemisms that in-fill the local race question with negative rather than positive expressions of difference and unexamined rather than critical understandings of whiteness. When SWR kids are taken outside of the greenhouse, they are taught to not recognize their Other. This is a self-serving exercise. Unable to recognize their Other they cannot clearly recognize themselves and the constructedness of their own privilege, which, as a result, remains sacrosanct and naturalized.

Privileged Performances

Back in the greenhouse, the Other once again becomes one of them, an insider-Other they fashion to ensconce themselves within an accepted norm. But even when such otherizing practices are limited to insider-Others, they must be subtle. The torch of white privilege is not successfully passed until SWR insiders learn to publicly appear to incorporate and embrace difference, if only for a brief moment.

During my fieldwork, that moment came late in the year. The setting was Eighth Grade Night and the Other was once again one of their classmates, Penelope, or Penny as she was called. Penny is the oldest daughter of a single mother. Like Amber, Penny is white, though not middle class. Unlike Amber, Penny has an unassuming presence. At times she is painfully shy, retreating into herself. At others, she is cautiously social. Through most of her eighth-grade year, Penny lived with her mother and two toddler brothers in one of the small, once-army, now temporary public-assistance houses located across from the high school. In Penny's "About the Author" section of her end-of-the-year magazine for English class, she penned a poignant biography of herself:

> When Penelope Johnson was born she had a heart problem which was corrected with two major surgeries, one of which she almost died from.
>
> Penelope likes to sing and hang out with her friends. Her favorite foods are chicken, fruits and vegetables. Her least favorite food is red meat. In April of this year when Penny moved to Patchogue, that was the eighth time she has moved in her almost fifteen years on this planet.
>
> Penny has two brothers—Jerry and Matt. In the future Penelope would love to major in astronomy at the University of Minnesota.

As an insider-Other, Penny represented a different kind of whiteness and a different kind of girlness. In many ways, Penny was a loner in the school, though I sensed that she was a fairly gregarious person. She liked to talk about her life when given the opportunity, but her peers didn't seem to give her much of a chance. On numerous occasions I watched other girls move away from her or shut her out of a conversation. For example, one day at lunch activity, I watched

Penny come into Mrs. R.'s room, sit down next to Kelly, and blurt out, "I'm moving tomorrow." Kelly replied, "Are you serious?" A few awkward moments passed between them until Kelly picked up her stuff and relocated across the room; at which point Penny turned to me and said, "I'm moving tomorrow." This latest move was very unsettling to Penny. She had only been in the school since September, and it had taken her a number of months to begin to make a place for herself at SWR. Mrs. R., her advisor and English-social studies teacher, had spent a lot of time with Penny, supporting her through various family and personal crises. Unlike most of the SWR girls, Penny's crises were not self-fabricated or particularly social. They were not part of girl culture, and they were not part of a hypernormal or false normal life like the one Tracey leads (see chapter 4). In dealing with her problems with a responsible and caring adult, Penny was facing her life circumstances in an appropriate and productive manner. Her troubles were not hypersymbolic and hypersocial. They weren't about creating a community so much as taking care of her life so that she could participate in girl culture more freely at some point in the future. For Penny, girl culture was a luxury, not a foundation for a normal life. This, however, did not make Penny abnormal in the sense in which I used this concept in relation to the storytelling practices of insider SWR girls in chapter 4. Rather, Penny's life had pushed her beyond girl culture too soon, and she was handling things accordingly. Mrs. R.'s efforts and attentions seemed to be starting to make a difference for Penny. She appeared happier and made more attempts to establish relationships with her peers, and some girls were responding positively to her friendly overtures. When her mother moved in April, the district allowed Penny to finish out the school year, but she would go to high school in her new town the following September. Understandably, Penny seemed anxious about this change. She was beginning to know what she would be losing, for better and worse, by leaving SWR, while her new home remained more or less an unknown.

In contrast to most of her peers at SWR, Penny carried herself with a certain "grown-upness" or a "grown-up-too-fastness." She had had to grapple with things that fourteen-year-old white middle-class girls are not supposed to experience. Most SWR kids didn't know all the details of Penny's life, but they knew that her life was not like theirs, as did Penny. In her end-of-the-year-magazine, which she called *Face Your Fears Head On*, Penny seemed to foreground her difference. On the cover, she drew a road sign that announced: "Caution Fear Ahead 2 yards." Inside, she included poems entitled "Scared," "No One Knows," "Surgery," and "Fear"; an essay about her younger brothers; and a short story about a fictional mom telling her daughter that she is planning on remarrying in a month and that she is pregnant. In her poem "Fear," Penny offers a somewhat philosophical understanding of her position in life:

> Fear. This is something we all have. From a child to a grown up, we all have it. As a baby fear is usually of falling. A child might be afraid of the Boogie Man or of the dark. Some are even afraid of Santa Claus.
>
> A teen is afraid of rejection, of not fitting in, of wearing the wrong clothes, having the wrong hairstyle. Adults' are afraid of everything: of not being good parents, not getting a job. Elders are afraid of illness and death. Fear is something we grow up with and have to live with for the rest of our lives.

Penny's not fitting in went deeper than her clothes or her hairstyle. In spite of this, or perhaps as a consequence of this, Penny's life at SWR would end on a different note. In the darkened auditorium on Eighth Grade Night, as kids sat next to their families viewing the eighth-grade slide show—a kind of multimedia yearbook—basking in the carefully fabricated aura of nostalgia and promise that fills the room at such events, the SWR community publicly embraced Penny for a second and then let her go. At one point in the slide show, an image of Penny appeared on the center screen of the three-screened extravaganza; the outer screens were dark. In the slide, Penny sits alone on one of the cement benches out in front of the school. Presumably she is waiting for the minibus to pick her up and take her back to her out-of-town new home. I had seen Penny sitting alone, often for more than an hour, in that very spot on numerous occasions. Sometimes I would join her, and she would tell me story after story about her family, about what she would do on the weekends, and about her dreams for her future. Her stories were never about the difficulties in her life. She did not need to in-fill her life as her insider peers did. When she was anxious about something, she would talk around it, as if she were trying to allay her own fears and convince herself that everything would be all right. Mostly she would talk about more mundane things, about dyeing her hair with her cousin, about Elizabeth warning her that if she dyes her hair blond now she'll be dyeing it pink sooner than later (a friendly warning against the Other within), about something cute yet annoying that her brothers did, or about her crush on a certifiably insider eighth grader, Mike, and what he did or didn't do. Most of the SWR community didn't know this side of Penny, but with her image projected larger than life, the kids and their parents gave her a long, heartfelt round of applause.

I was struck by how the already affect-filled room swelled with emotion at the sight of Penny, and as the applause subsided, how quickly she was forgotten. If part of living with the Other in this community of near sameness was denying her existence and absolving oneself of any responsibility (a multiculturalism of inconsequence, the "it's our community, it's not that we kick them out," "aren't they just born white" school of middle-class whiteness), then SWR had just staged a winning performance. In disavowing difference in the public company of their parents, the SWR eighth graders clearly displayed that they had learned to wear their cloaks of white middle-class privilege well, even if only for that moment or that evening. Though their lives will not always be as clear as they were on Eighth Grade Night, they will always have these skills of privilege—the mental and emotional capacity to disavow difference—on which to fall back or, at the very least, with which to get by.

White Lies

When Eighth Grade Night is over, a multiculturalism of inconsequence finishes going through the motions of cultural exchange, and girls like Amber move on to being young single mothers on the fringes of suburbia, insider girls are left with an anti-Other Self that still can't speak its name and knows all too well that some things are better left unsaid in this community of similarity. The Self here is built on a series of "white lies," a vocabulary of euphemisms and a system of disavowals that shelters the anti-Other Self from effectively living with differences both within and without. These white lies are passed on to girls sometimes by what is said directly, sometimes by what is embedded in the silences that constitute public discourse at SWR, and sometimes by what is implied in the community's halfhearted efforts to embrace its Others through tolerance curriculums or fleetingly sincere displays of empathy for someone who leads a less privileged life. But like a normal life that is "sooo boring," a life built on white lies ensnares the anti-Other Self in a conundrum. If one cannot know the Self without also knowing the Other, and if knowing the Other means having to recognize the Self as part of a deliberate history of exclusions and carefully calculated, as opposed to natural, privileges, then knowing the anti-Other Self means undoing its foundational white lies. A multiculturalism of consequence would ask the Self to take responsibility in some form or another for the life it was handed and the life it has made. White lies, at best, fall short of this task, and at worst refuse to engage the process.

Moreover, the cultural practices at SWR demonstrate that the Self and the Other are not so far apart, that one doesn't have to venture too far from home to encounter difference. Here, the anti-Other America keeps running into its own limitations. Girls need more than white lies to grow up in a community of similarity as much as in a community of difference. Differences come in many forms, cutting across and ultimately breaking up landscapes of intentional similarity. Pretending we are all the same, when we are obviously not, does not help a girl understand the Self, regardless of whether she is an insider or an outsider. Girls need life skills that do more than conceal ambivalences or feign an unconsciousness about difference, one epitomized in the basketball mom's outburst. Facing differences head-on, as Penny articulates in her end-of-the-year magazine and, in many ways, exemplifies in her life, would be one way to initiate a multiculturalism of consequence and to begin to undo the many white lies that constitute this community and the whiteness it engenders in its daughters.

Conclusion

Listening to White Girls' Stories

DAUGHTERS OF SUBURBIA tells many stories—the girls', the community's, the media's, and my own. Read together these stories are meant to fill the suburban greenhouse with critically productive rather than self-replicating, self-consuming narratives. They are meant to begin to tell a story that is, by design, not supposed to be told: the fiction of white, middle-class privilege as it emerges in all its culture-filled glory in the lives of teenage girls.

Girls like Emily, Cheryl, Dora, and Amy Fisher aptly demonstrate just how terrifying and volatile a storyless life can be. In search of her own white-girl story, Emily joined a violent and hate-filled white supremacist group; caught in a "deadly silence," Cheryl could envision patricide as her only way out; positioned as a pawn in her father's love life, Dora began to speak her own story through physical symptoms; and looking for a Hollywood-sized life, Amy was willing to go way too far to get what she wanted (ironically, a Hollywood-sized life is exactly what she got, though presumably not quite in the form she imagined).

The SWR girls, on the other hand, struggle with just how "boooring" and confusing a storyless (normal) life can be. Some search for their stories, and consequently themselves, in their cultural Others, while some fear or ward off the Others within themselves. Likewise, they fill their lives with collective serial dramas, with stories of entitlement and obligation, infectious stories, and stories that make sense of things from their own perspective. *Daughters of Suburbia* offers a different kind of story, one that places the "sooo boring" lives of white, middle-class, suburban girls in a broader cultural landscape. It does so with the hope that one day girls like Lisa B., Lisa G., Rachel, and Caitlin, for example, can use their already honed story-making skills to disengage the white lies that sustain their privileged yet isolated lives and perpetuate larger social inequalities.

Not surprisingly, when it comes to white-girl stories, the media love an unlovable subject. Amy's, Cheryl's, and Emily's cases suggest, however, this is not a love to be trusted or the responsible love I looked for throughout this book. Through close analyses of suburban bad girls writ large by broadcast and print media, *Daughters of Suburbia* lays bare the white middle-classness of this industry's story-making practices. The media thrive on larger-than-life ready-mades. They talk in stereotypes, rely on conventional narrative plots, and conduct their business in headline-packed sound bites—the "Pistol-Packing Lethal Lolita," the "Homeroom Hit Man," and the "Big, Bad Nazi Girl." They like a story with a happy heterosexual ending, a moral message, or a narrative twist that redeems the status quo. Without critical intervention, none of these approaches help girls out of their storyless predicament. Sure, media stories may enthrall girls or give them fodder for their own story making, but this only adds to the cacophony that in the end makes a normal life possible; they are part of the white lies girls are being taught to live with and fashion for themselves.

In analyzing media stories and, in the case of Emily, talking back to media distortions, *Daughters of Suburbia* makes these popular stories do the critical work of telling what indeed makes a story a *white-girl* story. The mainstream becomes nervous when white girls don't follow the rules about not making a spectacle of themselves and their cultureless culture, and when their actions call into question basic middle-class social institutions like the heterosexual family, the suburban community, and legal, religious, and educational authorities. The problem with unlovable girls' stories is that their narratives reveal too much about white middle-class life. Mainly, they demonstrate the ways in which identity categories like race, class, and gender are fundamentally overlapping storied (not natural) phenomena, and as such, how they might be revised to tell a story that gives the lie to normative privileges.

While *Daughters of Suburbia* could have just told the SWR girls' stories, such an ethnography would have had a harder time analyzing what was white and middle-class about their lives. By situating the girls' stories in relation to national media stories and within their town's and the region's histories and public life, this book looks at how the SWR girls' cultural practices and poetics are more than just local girls' talk. The stories of privilege being waged in the surrounding community were largely about disavowing difference and telling white lies. The town believes itself to be multicultural and absolves itself of any responsibility when it comes to racializing its children. According to the prevailing nonstory, girls are, after all, just born white. However, when the unmaking of the Shoreham Nuclear Power Plant undermined the foundations of this community's privilege, neighborly decorums and community fictions began to break down. Having to make hard choices between their children's educations and their own economic well-being ran counter to and hence made tangible this community's middle-class sensibilities, the same ones that had allowed them to believe in the power plant in the first place, the ones that didn't ask hard questions or look too far into the future. For years this community had taken the power plant and its tax base for granted. And the solvency of the district had allowed the community to keep its conflicts to a minimum. However, taking things for granted, as the community at SWR has found out the hard way, is a dubious privilege, one better examined than gambled against.

As an autoethnography, this book seeks to analyze the things taken for granted in my own and my subjects' lives. I have attempted to do my "homework" and to undo the white lies with which I had grown up and with which I continue to live, sometimes more consciously and critically than others. I have told my own growing-up stories alongside the girls' ethnographic stories. I have situated myself in the field as both an insider and an outsider and as a Self with a past and a present that do not always remain distinct from each other and cannot always be distinguished from my subjects' present-day lives. The autoethnographer cannot feign dispassionate interest in her subject. By definition, I am intimately connected to the many daughters of this book. The partiality and trajectory of my perspective demonstrate that cultural practices are always in process, that they have a history and social context, and like the SWR girls' stories, they need to be engaged with and elaborated on in order for them to have social and cultural currency. In the spirit of my subjects' storytelling habits, I hope this book invites its own retellings.

While *Daughters of Suburbia* does not tell the whole story or the only stories about growing up white, middle class, and female in a place like Shoreham-Wading River or suburbia more generally, it does tell the stories that helped me make sense of the greenhouse world I (re)encountered. Though whiteness, middle-classness, and girlness can't be reduced to its stories—its parodies, movies-of-the-week, lies, rumors, serial dramas, headline news, diary entries, or escalating social narratives—these stories begin to give this intentionally identityless identity substance, texture, and context. By reading these stories responsibly—acknowledging and following through on my own stakes and obligations toward my subject—*Daughters of Suburbia* gives white, middle-class girls a different set of stories to grow up with, exchange, and build upon.

Epilogue

On Writing Behind Girls' Backs

"SHOULD I SAY IT?" Jessica asks as she sits among a group of girls during lunch activity. "Do you know what I'm thinkin' about, you guys?" she wonders, looking around at Rachel, Jean, Lisa, and Annie. "Do you know, Rachel?" "Say it, say it," shouts Jean. "She's a whore," Jessica finally lets out. To which Rachel responds in an apologetic whine, "I think she's nice, you guys." And Jean adds, "So do I, that's why I'm not saying anything. She's always been nice to me." Annie explains, "She'd always be nice to your face and then behind your back she'd talk about you. That's why I'm not friends with her anymore. We used to be best friends in sixth and seventh grade." Annie's comment reminds Jean: "Yeah, we went upstate, and her and Myra and all them were all best friends, and she was like talking about Annie and, no, she was tellin' Annie about how much she hates Myra. And then the next day, she was like tellin' Myra how much she hates Annie."

As the story unfolded about why two groups of girls in the school were feuding, or "in the middle of a war," as Jean suggested, the group telling their version of the story to me sat playing with each other's hair, interjecting comments about each other's clothing like, "Rachel, I like really like that jacket, where did you get it?" and generally speaking over each other, competing for the position of main social narrator. The girl with the louder and more insistent tone usually won, though that didn't stop other girls from telling their version of the story simultaneously in quieter voices that would trail off as they struggled to listen to their friend, the primary narrator. As the main audience at this scene, I was having a hard time following the story; the girls' multiple talk jumped from topic to topic and speaker to speaker, pulling me in various directions all at once.

In the end, however, I was left knowing that talking behind someone's back was both a major social faux pas and a major pastime among SWR girls.

In the midst of talking behind someone's back by talking about how this person talks behind other girls' backs, at least one member of every group, the collective social conscience, would periodically come to the defense of the maligned party, "You guys, she's nice to me. . . . " Typically, someone else would agree, and someone else would go on to elaborate on the original offending story. Apologizing for "not being nice" (i.e., talking behind someone's back or disagreeing with someone) allowed the speaker to continue to not be nice. In writing this autoethnography, I have been tempted to make my own periodic apologies. For in writing about the SWR girls, I am, in a sense, writing behind their backs. Though in my eyes I have not been speaking badly about them, a key component of talking behind someone's back, I fear that they will perceive my observations and analyses as indictments of who they are and what their community stands for. For this I apologize in true Long Island girl form, "Like you guys were nice to me. . . . "

Notes

Introduction **Truth or Dare**

1. Throughout this book all names of students and adults at SWR Middle School have been changed. In addition, any writing by students or SWR adults has been presented in its original form, with all spelling and grammatical errors preserved. Likewise, I have attempted to reproduce my subjects' speech verbatim in order to give the reader a sense of the sounds and cadence of life among these suburban daughters.
2. Interestingly, *My So-Called Life* (MSCL) was about a normal, pretty typical, white middle-class girl, who, like the SWR girls, thought her life was terribly boring (which essentially means a life without a story to tell). In pulling the drama off the air after only two seasons, apparently the executives at ABC agreed. The viewing public, however, did not. The cancellation of the show provoked an outpouring of support for the show and its stars, largely via the Internet. The show catapulted its main actor, the then-thirteen-year-old Claire Danes, into a serious movie career. Five years later, there were still very active Web pages on the show and MSCL marathons on cable TV. Perhaps ABC was wrong to conclude that there is no story to be told in a normal girl's life. Unfortunately, the viewing public never got the chance to find out; the powers that be never brought the show back into production.

Chapter 1 **Raising Teenage Girls**

1. However, word had already gotten out among the eighth graders. Throughout my stay at SWR, one boy, a student in the wing that housed the students I had least contact with, kept trying to persuade me to convene a group of boys so I could study teen masculinity. He posed this as an equal rights issue and teased me that I was discriminating against the boys. I would appease him by telling him my next book would be about boys.
2. In 1992, the *New York Times* recorded a $103,000 average household income in Shoreham and a $70,000 one in Wading River (*New York Times* 1992a).
3. According to *Statistics for Public School Districts: February 1993 Report to the Governor and the Legislature*, this rate is actually higher, at 96.6 percent (Table 1, 18).
4. Unidentified newspaper clipping, 23 April 1971.

5. Unidentified newspaper clipping, "Suburban Home for Retarded Planned," 11 November 1977.
6. McMullan 1971. A 1995 brochure lists Leisure Country property, which includes Leisure Village among other retirement housing complexes, at $150,000–200,000 with monthly maintenance fees of $140–250 and yearly property taxes of $1300–2880.
7. SWR students had more contact with elderly people living in a privately operated adult home, Perkins, in Riverhead than they did with people living in the neighboring Leisure Village. As part of her English-social studies curriculum, Mrs. R. took her classes to Perkins one afternoon a week for two semesters (half her classes went one semester, the other half participated the second semester). Students worked one on one with residents on special projects and kept journals about their experiences. Many SWR students developed close ties with their Perkins partners, and some even pursued relationships outside of this school-sponsored community service unit. The program culminated in the late spring with the "Sr. Prom," a party that SWR kids attended with their Perkins partners. Kids and residents alike got dressed up and danced away an evening together, with generally a good time being had by all. I can only wonder if a similar program would have been possible at Leisure Village or if the social proximity of Leisure Village elders would make this too threatening a proposal for the mostly youthful communities of Shoreham and Wading River.
8. In 1991, SWR was listed as the highest spender per student among school districts with at least 1,000 students in the New York Metropolitan region, with a rate of $17,435 per student. The lowest spender, also a district in Suffolk County, Patchogue-Medford, spent $8,493 per student (*New York Times* 1991).
9. The *Community Journal*'s partisan politics in favor of cutting school programs and instituting more conservative educational approaches became increasingly clear in light of the closing of the Shoreham plant. Consequently, in 1994, a group of SWR teachers and their allies living in the district got together and started another local paper, the *Sound Observer*, in an attempt to present a more school-friendly perspective to the community, counterbalancing the *Journal*'s coverage.
10. This was also the meeting at which the middle-school staff exchanged rumors about Joey Buttafuoco buying a house in Wading River as they tongue-in-cheekly speculated about having the Buttafuoco kids in their classes next year (see chapter 2 for a discussion of the role Joey Buttafuoco plays in the cultural imagination).
11. The amalgam of the familial and the technological here is not simply coincidental. In "From Theatre to Space Ship: Metaphors of Suburban Domesticity in Postwar America," Lynn Spigel traces the degree to which the language of the space race and middle-class domesticity came together in U.S. discourses of the family and suburbia in the late fifties and early sixties. Such metaphors, Spigel argues were both symptomatic of and responsible for the homogeneity and insularity of middle-class suburban culture. She writes, "In one utopian sense, these metaphors of . . . space travel have come to stand for the dream places people wish to inhabit; in another way these metaphors have been used to defamiliarize the 'lived' suburban spaces that are oppressive in their homogeneity and rigid social expectations; and finally these metaphors have been deployed in blatantly racist, classist, homophobic, and sexist ways to keep the suburbs clean of those 'aliens' that won't or can't play the 'roles' required of them" (1997, 235–236). The metaphors of nuclear power that circulated in the seventies and eighties—an era that saw the revival of conservative discourses on the nuclear family—offer more recent instantiations of how the metaphors of suburbia and science can act as strange and consequential bedfellows.
12. After the closing of the plant, the amount of taxes LILCO owed SWR became a point of legal contention, with LILCO claiming that the plant had been overassessed and the school district contending that the power company had to pay school taxes on a permanent basis regardless of its current operating status. In part the battle lines

were drawn over a 1984 county law that mandated that school districts could not be held liable for overassessed property unless they had a nuclear power plant in their jurisdiction. Given that Shoreham was the only district on Long Island that fell into this "special category," the law was obviously drafted with the closing of Shoreham in mind and with the power company's best interest at heart. At the time the legislation passed, the district challenged the law on the grounds that it violated a 1960 law that says states will pay localities "payments in lieu of taxes," or PILOT payments, to offset the loss of revenue if the state acquires taxable land. The judge presiding over this original challenge ruled that since the district did not face any imminent penalties or consequences from the new law, the district's complaint was irrelevant, and he dismissed the case. The issue, however, was far from over. The fiscal fallout from the Shoreham plant amounted to a twenty-year tax dispute involving the power company and Nassau and Suffolk Counties, the Town of Brookhaven, the North Shore Library District, the Wading River Fire District, and last but not least, the Shoreham-Wading River School District. After an extremely protracted and complex legal battle, the parties reached a $620 million settlement in January 2000. As part of this deal, LIPA agreed to continue to make on a declining basis through March 2002 the PILOT payments it had been paying since 1992 to the SWR School District (McQuiston 2000a, 2000b).

13. While I was doing fieldwork, Grumman was bought out by the Los Angeles-based Northrop Corporation. I knew of only one eighth grader, Bill, an aerospace and airplane aficionado, who followed the takeover. For a brief history of Grumman, see Lambert 1996.
14. On 31 March 1994, while I sat in the SWR classrooms, a fire damaged a physics experiment at the Brookhaven National Laboratory, releasing radiation inside and outside a nuclear reactor building and contaminating seven workers (Wald 1994, B5; Pleven and Cooke 1994, A5, A61).
15. This is not to say that no individuals nor local organizations objected to the plant. For example, Citizen's Lobby Opposing Shoreham (CLOSE), mainly composed of SWR residents, formed over the plant's lifespan and argued that "Shoreham is a mistake" (*Pennysaver* n.d.). However, the pronuclear or, at the very least, indifferent side of the debate constituted the local mainstream.
16. Largely as a result of the Shoreham plant debacle, Long Islanders paid the highest electrical rates in the contiguous United States, until LILCO officially merged with Brooklyn Union Gas Company in 1998.

Chapter 2 **Amy Fisher, My Story**

An earlier version of this chapter appeared in *Socialist Review* 24, no. 3 (1994): 81–127. Thanks to David Trend for his editorial work on the original article.

1. In announcing that Barrymore was to play Amy in *Beyond Control*, *Newsday* locates her in her blue-blooded yet tragic Hollywood background. "Barrymore, a descendant of the famous acting family whose name she bears, became a child star at 7 in *E.T.—The Extra-terrestrial.* She has said she began drinking when she was 9, smoking marijuana at 10, snorting cocaine at 12 and going through rehab at 14. She recently posed in the nude for the cover of *Interview* magazine. She's 17, a year younger than Fisher" (Kubasik n.d.). Barrymore recently had made her comeback by starring in teen bad-girl movies like *Poison Ivy* (1992, directed by Katt Shea Ruben and Andy Ruben) and *Gun Crazy* (1992, directed by Tamra Davis). See also Barrymore with Gold 1990.
2. When Amy's story broke in 1992, the Internet was not yet a household word. By 1999, the year she was released from prison at the behest of Mary Jo, there were numerous web pages devoted to Amy, including one sponsored by Aimee: The Official Amy Fisher Organization (Aimee was the way Amy had her name decaled onto her

car) and several porn-related sites, asking questions like, "Would you sleep with Amy now that she's out of jail?"

3. Amy has come to represent a certain kind of bad girl: young, relatively privileged, white women who go too far to get what they want. In an irate letter to *People* on their coverage of another notorious bad girl, Hollywood Madam Heidi Fleiss, a reader calls Fleiss "the new Amy Fisher. Another dysfunctional spoiled brat elevated to celebrity status through (alleged) criminal behavior. Wonder how many TV movies your new lover girl will generate" (*People* 1993, 4). Later, in reference to the Tonya Harding-Nancy Kerrigan debacle, Tony Kornheiser, a syndicated columnist for the *Washington Post*, writes, "There's going to be a market for Tonya Harding in the same way that there is going to be a market for Amy Fisher, when she gets out of jail. That's who Tonya is now: Amy Fisher on skates" (Kornheiser 1994).
4. I am arguing here for the need to study "normal" white middle-class teen girls as much as marked teens: teen moms (Nathanson 1991; Solinger 1992; Kunzel 1993; Lawson and Rhode 1993), gang girls (Campbell [1984] 1991; Taylor 1993; Sikes 1998; Fleisher 1998), and nonwhite inner-city girls (Ladner [1971] 1995; Leadbeater and Way 1996). The glut of academic and nonacademic material, especially in education, psychology, and deviance studies on nonwhite urban kids points to how much these communities are stigmatized and made to appear to be *the* problem. As noted in the introduction, the recent shootings in white middle-class suburban and exurban high schools throughout the country suggest that becoming normal may not be such a seamless activity. While these events present a crisis in white middle-class masculinity, Amy is the feminine version. In my discussion of Emily in chapter 5, I also develop this theme. Taking whiteness and privilege for granted can produce stark gender-specific consequences. I am not advocating that we teach kids to be better whites, rather I am suggesting that we help them examine whiteness and social privilege in a critical and historical context that will help them create a more racially just world.
5. Amy received $8,000 for the article. *Newsday* reported that she planned on using most of the money to establish a "victim's fund" (Forrest 1994, A35).
6. While black, Asian, and Latina girls also have reputations for being difficult, they are depicted as teen moms, high-school dropouts, and gang members, for example. As such, they are not portrayed as unlovable subjects so much as social problems. Neither the media nor outspoken congressional representatives exhibit a lot of affection for teen moms (i.e., welfare queens in the making), for example. These girls are definitely held outside the norm. Their threat is exterior. Therefore, they are simply not loved, and nobody appears to be taking any responsibility for them or their lives.
7. I use this and similar terms—somebody else's daughter, nobody's daughter—with a certain amount of irony. My analysis is about how she is portrayed by the media and how these constructions also fabricate audiences. It is not about who she is or who the viewing public actually is. It is about media assumptions and manipulations.
8. Later tabloid megastories that took the genre even further include the O.J. Simpson case and the President Clinton–Monica Lewinsky affair.
9. In less than four months following the publication of Rosenbaum's article, Long Island once again gained prominent national news status following the December 2d double suicide of two Long Island High School girls. The two Suffolk County honors students (i.e., not "at risk" kids) laid themselves down on the tracks of the Long Island Railroad one afternoon and were run over by a commuter train.

   On the heels of this incident, Long Island became the object of national horror once again when a gunman, Colin Ferguson, a Jamaican immigrant, opened fire on the 5:33 P.M. commuter train out of New York City bound for Eastern Long Island.

Five people were killed, many others were seriously wounded. According to notes found in Ferguson's possession, the shootings were supposedly motivated by his rage against "whites and Asians and 'Uncle Tom' blacks." He obviously knew that the Long Island Railroad would be a place to find a concentrated number of middle-class whites and some middle-class people of color. (See Rabinovitz 1994, 10.) In February 1994, a Nassau County judge took under advisement a request by Ferguson's defense team to change venues so that he could be tried by a jury of his peers. They argued that the jury pool in Nassau County was too white and too middle class (National Public Radio, 1994; see also Garvey 1996).

The Long Island Railroad massacre became the focus of the gun-control debate over the Brady Bill that Congress and the White House were embroiled in at the time. It also prompted Carolyn McCarthy—a Long Island wife and mother whose husband died in the train shooting and whose son survived with permanent injuries—to wage a public campaign against gun violence by running for a vacant seat in the U.S. House of Representatives in 1996. She won as a Democrat in a heavily Republican district. She was reelected in 1998.

10. There is a history of folk and consumer-culture representations (decorative maps and tchotchkes) of Long Island that emphasize its whale-like shape. In part, this is a nostalgia for Long Island's early days as a collection of whaling villages. My own family has acquired a few such items over the years.
11. See also the growing identification of Long Island with a rise in breast cancer rates among women in the United States. Long Island is the home of the "1 in 9 Club," a group of women activists, lobbying for more money for breast-cancer research, forming support groups for women with breast cancer, and organizing educational campaigns to promote early detection and increase public awareness.
12. The Venerable John A. Greco, Archdeacon of Nassau County for the Episcopal Diocese of Long Island, as quoted in *Newsday* 1993, 47.
13. Dr. Mary Rose Paster, psychologist specializing in teenagers' problems, Glen Cove, Long Island, as quoted in the *New York Times* 1992b, 16.
14. Herbert J. Gans, professor of sociology, Columbia University and noted "expert" on the early history of suburbia (see Gans 1982), as quoted in *Newsday* 1993, 41.
15. Molly Ivins, columnist for *Fort Worth Star-Telegraph*, as quoted in *Newsday* 1993, 47.
16. Given the popularity of women-in-prison "lesbian" fantasies in pornography and in B-movies, it is not surprising that Amy the "lesbian" surfaces again in the media after she is in jail. At first, the reports are that Amy and her mother fear she will be sexually assaulted by the other inmates. The *National Enquirer* quotes a prison guard as stating, "We estimate that 70 percent of our female prisoners are lesbians. One fine day, just to show her [Amy] that she's no better than everyone else, Miss Amy Fisher is going to be ganged up on when the guards aren't close by—the women will do nasty, unspeakable lesbian things to her" (Bolton 1993, 22). Almost a year later, the *Star* gleefully published Amy's love letters from jail to her alleged female lover, "Lizsette" (Burton 1993, 27, 29).
17. Carolyn Warmus is the white upper-class high-school teacher who brutally killed her lover's wife in suburban Westchester County, N.Y., in 1992. The Warmus story also garnered the media's attention; they deemed it worthy of two network television movies that aired only months before the Amy movies.

According to a *New York Times Magazine* article on Amy's incarceration, Warmus and Amy have actually crossed paths in prison. "Once held briefly at Bedford Hills, in Westchester County, [Amy] shared Yom Kippur supper [a rare reference to Amy's Jewishness] with the 'Brinks ladies,' Kathy Boudin and Judy Clark, who seemed highly intelligent, although her dinnermate Carolyn Warmus was [according to Amy] a 'serious nut case' who never changed her shirt" (Israel 1996, 18).

Chapter 3 **Justify My Love**

1. "Dora" is the pseudonym Freud gave his patient, Ida Bauer, in writing her case history. Bauer was born in 1882 in Vienna and died in 1945 in New York City. (See Bernheimer and Kahane [1985] 1990, 34.) When I refer to Dora and for that matter Cheryl Pierson, as with Amy Fisher, I am talking about the representations of them and not the girls themselves.
2. Cheryl's class status is a bit more ambiguous than the SWR girls' or Amy's. Cheryl's father, James Pierson, was an electrician (a typical working-class job). The family lived in a modest ranch-style home, and yet Kleiman reports that James Pierson had become a wealthy man, though "no one quite knew how. There was the cable television business he was running on the side. There were the real estate deals from time to time. But these days he had more money than he knew what to do with. He had just bought his wife a Lincoln Continental with the license plate CATHLEEN. He had just totally redecorated a new house and bragged to friends he had more money than he thought he would ever need" (1988, 15). Later, Kleiman also notes that Pierson's estate was estimated after his death to be worth about one million dollars (111). Cheryl's, her brother's, and her friend's appearances, with their long hair cut short and shag-like on top, marked them as more lower-middle to working class. Theirs was the kind of "big hair" that became part of the stereotype of the trashy, lower-middle-class side of Long Island in the 1980s.
3. I use the term modern here in its historical sense. Broadly speaking, modernity refers to a time period commensurate with the French, American, and Industrial Revolutions (eighteenth century), the expansion of European colonialism in the late nineteenth century, and the founding of nation states throughout this era and into the early twentieth century. These events and practices precipitated phenomena like the rise of the middle class, new concepts of race and racial differences, the spread of global capitalism, the implementation of democratic as opposed to aristocratic rule, the consolidation of the nuclear family, the rise of social-scientific and bureaucratic forms of analyzing and classifying "populations," the introduction of public education, the development of extensive penal systems, and the widespread distribution of news and information, among other salient features (for useful sources regarding modernity, see Foucault (1970; 1972; 1973; 1979; 1980; 1985; and 1988) and Stoler's critique (1995); Anderson [1983] 1991; and Balibar and Wallerstein 1991). Psychoanalysis is itself a modern institution, as is adolescence. In his social history of childhood, Philippe Ariès notes that there was a glimpse of the idea of the adolescent in the eighteenth century, which eventually grew into the adolescent as hero in the twentieth century, or what Ariès deems as the "century of adolescence" (Ariés 1962, 29–30). I am arguing here that Dora is part of the discovery and making of that century of adolescence, but more specifically, she is its feminine middle-class version.
4. Dora's story captivated Freud's analytic attention throughout the latter part of his career. Though, in January of 1901, he wrote up the case in the month immediately following Dora's departure from analysis, he didn't publish his findings until five years later, and he continued to amend the manuscript with footnotes over the course of the following three decades. For these and related reasons, Dora's story also garners the attention of present-day scholars, especially academic feminists working with psychoanalytic theory. Within these studies, Dora has became an archetype of the resistant female hysteric, and the convoluted history of her case has become the ground for symptomatic readings of Freud's practice. (See McCall et al. 1981; Hertz 1983; McCaffrey 1984; Bernheimer and Kahane [1985] 1990; Decker 1991; Roof 1991; Lakoff and Coyne 1993; Kahane 1995; Morrissey 1995; Mahony 1996. This is only a partial list of the books available, and does not include the numerous journal articles, which are beyond the scope of this chapter. My point is simply that there is a

veritable academic industry centered around Dora.) In my own interpretation of Freud's Dora, I am not so much interested in reading Freud or, for that matter, Dora, as I am in naming how the narrative defines what it means to be an adolescent girl with regard to questions of sexual desire and familial relations.

5. The founding of suburbia, after all, was based on the proliferation of the nuclear family at the expense of extended families with their strong ethnic identities. In turn, these new families in their new homes opened up a wide new market for consumer items, tying conjugal heterosexuality to the economic well-being of the country.
6. See also Stoler's discussion of how the disciplining of childhood sexuality, the relations between children and (lower-class and nonwhite) servants, and the discourse of middle-class parenting in the eighteenth century worked together to produce white bourgeois subjects (1995, especially chapter 5). While neither Dora's nor Cheryl's story discusses the girls' sexualities in relation to nonwhite Others, Dora's does consider the role of her lower-class governesses in her upbringing.
7. Though Cheryl's story predated my ethnographic work by eight years, some SWR girls still maintained a curiosity about her. One day during a silent reading period, I noticed Karen poring over Charles Patrick Ewing's *Kids Who Kill*, which devoted an entire section to Cheryl Pierson (Ewing 1990).
8. For example, one often overlooked fact about teen pregnancy is that men over twenty impregnate two-thirds of all teenage mothers (see Males 1994, A27).
9. In her own discussion of this same excerpt, Teresa de Lauretis finds Foucault unable to account for class or gender, and ultimately history, in his analyses of the relationship between power and resistance in this narrative (de Lauretis 1984, 94). Judith Butler offers a similar critique in *Gender Trouble*; she points to the farmhand story as a moment when Foucault slips into articulating a primary emancipatory sexuality that is positioned before and outside of culture. Like de Lauretis, Butler catches Foucault undermining his own analysis of the productive, mutually constituting relationship between sex and power (Butler 1990, 97).
10. I am arguing throughout this book that the prototypical adolescent is bourgeois/middle class and white. Being an adolescent is in a sense one of the privileges of modern middle-class whiteness. Not every fifteen-year-old has the opportunity (as dubious as it may seem at times) to be a teenager. Adolescence is intertwined with practices of race, class, and gender.
11. Though Freud refuses to connect Dora's venereal disease to her father, he does draw a causal relationship between her father's venereal disease and Dora's hysteria. He writes: "I was careful not to tell her that, as I have already mentioned, I was of opinion, too, that the offspring of [male] leutics were very specially predisposed to severe neuro-psychoses" (93). It is not entirely clear, however, who Freud protects by not sharing this hypothesis with Dora.
12. In all likelihood, these "humanly dramatic television shows" also featured stories on incest and murder. Moreover, most accounts of Cheryl's story contend that she got the idea to have her father killed from an article that appeared in *Newsday* about a local woman who hired hit men to murder her abusive husband. Cheryl and Sean, in the same homeroom by virtue of the fact that both their last names begin with "P," supposedly discussed this nearby murder, which led Cheryl to think about hiring Sean to kill her father. *Newsday* reconstructs their conversation as follows: "'Who would be crazy enough to do that?' Cheryl said. 'Anything can be done for money,' Sean said. 'I know someone who might be interested,' Cheryl said. According to Sean, Cheryl brought up the subject again a few days later in the yellow-walled homeroom, where the only decorations are a few Shakespearean posters. She said she hated her father and wished he were dead. Cheryl told Sean she needed a hit man. Sean told her he would do it. 'How much?' Cheryl asked. '$1,000,' Sean said" (Perlman and Durkin 1990, 169).

13. Judge Sherman's decision, delivered on 5 October 1987, came after nearly two years of court proceedings involving the three defendants: Cheryl, Sean, and Rob. After Cheryl's and Rob's arrests on 13 February 1986, and Sean's the following day, the case went before a grand jury on 20 February. The court handed down two counts of second-degree murder and second-degree conspiracy against Cheryl and Sean. It did not indict Rob on the original conspiracy charges at that time, but left his role in the murder open for further investigation. Cheryl and Sean were subsequently released on bail, and a pretrial hearing began on 16 September to determine whether or not Cheryl's and Sean's confessions could be used as evidence in their upcoming trial. Judge Sherman ruled in early November that the confessions were admissible and that Cheryl and Sean should be tried together. In March of 1987, during a plea-bargaining session before Judge Sherman, Cheryl and Sean both admitted their separate roles in the murder. The plea forfeited their right to a trial by jury and set the maximum sentence for Cheryl at 2 to 6 years and for Sean at $8^{1}/_{3}$ to 25 years, or less for either if the court later granted them youthful offender status. The judge revoked Sean's bail and remanded him to jail to await sentencing in April, at which time he rejected Sean's request for youthful offender status and sentenced him to 24 years in prison with no eligibility for parole before 8 years. Cheryl and Rob were both granted youthful offender status, hence, in part, Cheryl's reduced sentence. On 8 October 1987, Rob received 5 years probation for his part in the murder.

Chapter 4 **Among Friends**

1. Being a native in this regard did not help. Either I had lost most of my sensitivity to a Lawn Guyland accent over my fifteen years of living elsewhere, or the accent itself as well as the linguistic velocity that seems to accompany it, at least among teen girls, had intensified during the same period. I suspect a little of both is at work here.

   I was reminded of how difficult their talk is to understand when, in preparing to write a draft of this chapter in May 1996, I rewatched a video I and the adult son of one of the teachers had recorded over a two-day period in May 1994. There is some talk among the girls on the video I can no longer fully understand. My SWR ear is out of practice.
2. Versions of this observation persisted. Three months into my field research, I wrote, "Everyone seems to be on speed today. They rush in in a burst of energy, blurt things out, and run out."
3. Canguilhem directly takes up the question of the normal and the pathological vis-à-vis the social in a section written twenty years after the original essay, "New Reflections on the Normal and the Pathological (1963–1966)."
4. The "Trenchcoat Mafia" of Littleton, Colo., is perhaps the exception that proves the rule. As members of this group, Dylan Klebold and Eric Harris did not seem to catch too many people's attentions. Their dress and antisocial, albeit gang, behavior fit within the realm of normal middle-class teen culture. That is until they took their style beyond the symbolic and into the realm of the literal by killing themselves, twelve classmates, and one teacher on the anniversary of Hitler's suicide, 20 April 1999. Whether or not there were warning signs that Dylan and Eric were more false normal than not is up for investigation and beyond the scope of this study.
5. See also a favorable review of many of these texts in Long Island's widely read daily newspaper, *Newsday* (Oleck 1996, B1–B3). It became apparent to me that Ann had read about or read some of these texts, since it was not uncommon for her to pepper her conversations with me, someone she clearly perceived as a liberal feminist, with references to popular theories of gender and self-esteem.

   In a brief critique of the self-esteem industry, Joseph Adelson attests to the popularity of these theories when he reports: "Recently, I dropped in at my local library to see what they had on a subject, self-esteem, that now commands enormous attention in our everyday discourse. I thought I would find a few titles. There were *41*, mostly quite recent. Then I went to the bookstore—really a megastore—across the street from my psychotherapy office. There I expected to find at most a shelf-ful. There were 49 shelves, each three feet long, holding altogether at least 1,000 separate titles. Almost all were less than five years old . . . " (1996, 34).

6. Second period took place immediately following advisory at about 8:30 A.M. First period took place before advisory and was reserved for things like band rehearsal, one-on-one advisory conferences, and teachers' meetings.
7. Jessica was quite proud of her familial connection to Mariah Carey. The fact that Carey is African American never figured into Jessica's conversation either because she didn't know light-skinned, straight-haired Carey is black or she was intentionally filling her own "white bread, bland" existence with a little racial color and a lot of untouchable fame and fortune. (See Frankenberg 1993, 199.)
8. I say "most" because some girls had firsthand experiences of losing a friend or relative to suicide, but such immediate knowledge was not common or talked about openly. One girl, Terri, wrote a short story about the death of a friend of hers two years earlier. Her friend, who had just finished fifth grade, had hung herself in her backyard on a swing set. Terri ends her written account of the incident wondering if her friend's death was indeed a suicide as she had been told by another friend's mother or if it was just an accident as the girl's playmates suggested. This story, however, was not a public, traveling narrative among eighth-grade girls.
9. By using *wazup*, Mr. R. employed one of Lisa's favorite expressions, one she borrows from hip-hop culture. This is a racially marked cultural appropriation that in-fills Lisa's whiteness. See below more on Lisa's use of marked racial categories to resist and fashion her own whiteness.
10. Not to mention numerous cult and popular teen films like Todd Solondz's *Welcome to the Dollhouse* (1995) or Amy Heckerling's *Fast Times at Ridgemont High* (1982), and others of this genre.
11. Lisa was one of the few SWR girls who would openly acknowledge race. I attribute this to her transitional status in this community and to her earlier experiences growing up in a more urban and more racially diverse area in Connecticut. See chapter 6.

Chapter 5 ***I Was a Teenage White Supremacist***

1. This chapter does not violate the spirit of that contract because I am not telling Emily's white supremacy story so much as critiquing the media representations of it.
2. Emily was graduated from the same school in the spring of 1999.
3. All names that have not already appeared in published stories about Emily have been changed.
4. In the context of mainstream programming that both reflects and constitutes its audience, by definition "the girl next door" is the white middle-class girl.
5. On 30 January 1997, Mark Thomas was charged with conspiracy to commit bank robbery and receiving stolen money in connection with seven bank robberies that netted over $112,000. The money was supposedly used to stockpile weapons to be used by Thomas and his followers in the impending race war that he foretold. Thomas pleaded guilty to these charges less than a month later and, after cooperating with Federal authorities and apologizing for his involvement with hate groups, he was sentenced to an eight-year prison term.
6. Anna Tsing makes a similar observation about the deliberate use of the image of the vulnerable pregnant teen by pro-choice feminists. "When feminists first used this imagery to counter anti-abortion forces, it was intended to inspire commitment to equal rights and opportunities for young women" (Tsing 1990, 290).

7. This moniker persists despite the fact that between 1990 and 1996 the overall U.S. teen pregnancy rate declined 17 percent. To put this decline in perspective, however, it is important to remember that teen pregnancy rates in the United States remain much higher than those in other developed countries: twice as high as in England, Wales, or Canada, and nine times as high as in the Netherlands or Japan (Alan Guttmacher Institute, 1999).
8. I am not arguing that teens of color were no longer on the reproductive control agenda, but that historically white and nonwhite girls have figured differently in the national debate on this issue. Sometimes, in certain contexts, white girls make for better poster children, while at other political moments, African American and/or Latina girls fit the bill. By teasing out how white girls have appeared and disappeared in this regard, I am hoping to make clear what is and is not white about teen pregnancy, and hence why Emily does, or does not, fill out the profile within her historical moment.
9. Herrnstein and Murray (1994, 177) insist on the term "illegitimacy" as opposed to "'out-of-wedlock births' or 'births to single women,' because [they] think that, in the long run, the word illegitimacy will prove to be the right one." To substantiate this claim, they speciously turn to Malinowski's early-twentieth-century, cross-cultural research on kinship structures in which the anthropologist set out "a universal sociological law" pertaining to the "principle of legitimacy."
10. As the third congressional bill made its way to the president's desk, its detractors seemed to abandon teenage moms as their cause célèbre and replaced them with the less politically volatile image of the four million children who would go without "clothing, diapers, cribs, medicine, and school supplies" if the bill became law (DeParle 1996). Kids, it seems, make for better sound bites in a presidential election year than teen moms.
11. I use the terms "radical Right" and "mainstream" with the understanding that they are defined in relation to and against each other.
12. The journal *Race Traitor* and its editors, Noel Ignatiev and John Garvey (1996), advocate for the abolition of whiteness. This is a polemical way, as I read it, of calling for the end of a racial order based on racial hierarchies. Mainstream whiteness and white supremacy are both products and producers of this racial order. While I agree with the basic premise of this analysis, I think the racial system is more complex than such a solution takes into account. For example, posing the problem as solely an issue of whiteness does not consider in any meaningful way the role that class or gender may play in the construction of many kinds of whitenesses. In place of the abolition of whiteness, I am proposing a critical study of whiteness.

Chapter 6 **Learning to Tell White Lies**

1. I am referring to the discourses surrounding recent affirmative-action and immigration-reform initiatives raised at the state and federal levels. See especially California's Proposition 187, which aimed to block illegal immigrants from obtaining any state-supported "benefits" like public education and prenatal or emergency health care. The proposition passed by popular vote in the fall elections of 1994, but was held by the courts to be unconstitutional. Proposition 209, otherwise known as the California Civil Rights Initiative, effectively ended statewide affirmative action programs after it passed by popular vote in 1996. This time the courts did not enjoin the law.
2. By invoking these binaries, I am not suggesting that they operate in such a simple fashion. Not all blacks are poor, not all gays are discriminated against in all contexts, not all whites are privileged. Instead, I am calling attention to the imaginary framework that undergirds U.S. social hierarchies. In practice, the machinations of

social privilege are much messier. To a great extent it is this morass that this book attends to overall.

3. With the recent introduction of new, expensive subdivisions on the south side of 25A, this distinction, between the right- and wrong-side of the tracks, is beginning to change. However, Brad's neighborhood is fairly established and hence includes no room for any new development. Consequently, the economic tenor of this section of Shoreham is likely to remain less affluent than surrounding neighborhoods, new and old.
4. When I ran into David two years after I had officially left the field, he took offense when I asked him about Brad. Apparently they had had a major falling out. I can only speculate about the role, however direct or indirect, their class differences played in this breakup.
5. As noted in chapter 4, SWR kids say "She/He isn't prejudice," not the proper "She/He isn't prejudiced." When I asked an SWR teacher if she thought the kids said "prejudice" instead of "prejudiced," she confirmed my suspicion and said that kids will write "she/he is prejudice" even after she points out their mistake to them. "It's a hard thing to correct because they hear 'prejudiss'," she explained.
6. Before I knew exactly what BUTY was, I thought the kids were referring to some kind of school-sponsored cosmetology program, a club that would have seemed out of place in this middle-class community that prided itself on sending 95 percent of its graduates to college.
7. "BJ/3," otherwise known as "The Fire Burns On," is a slide show set to the tune of Billy Joel's "We Didn't Start the Fire," a popular song covering world history between 1949 and 1989. As part of a social studies unit in Mr. R.'s class, kids rewrote the lyrics to "Fire" to chronicle historical events occurring in their lifetime (1979–1993) and then compiled a slide show visually representing the same period. Throughout the year, Mr. R. took kids to present "BJ/3" at different schools and teacher conferences.

Bibliography

Abu-Lughod, Lila. 1986. *Veiled Sentiments: Honor and Poetry in a Bedouin Society*. Berkeley: University of California Press.

———. 1991. "Writing Against Culture." In *Recapturing Anthropology: Working in the Present*. Ed. Richard G. Fox. Santa Fe, N.Mex.: School of American Research Press.

———. 1993. *Writing Women's Worlds: Bedouin Stories*. Berkeley: University of California Press.

Adelson, Joseph. 1996. "Down with Self-Esteem." *Commentary*, February: 34–38.

Alan Guttmacher Institute (AGI). 1976. *Eleven Million Teenagers: What Can Be Done about the Epidemic of Adolescent Pregnancies in the United States*. New York: Alan Guttmacher Institute.

———. 1994. *Sex and America's Teenagers*. New York: Alan Guttmacher Institute.

———. 1999. "Facts in Brief: Teen Sex and Pregnancy, 1999." Available from http://www.agi-usa.org/pubs/fb_teens_sex.html.

American Association of University Women (AAUW). 1992. *The AAUW Report: How Schools Shortchange Girls*. Washington, D.C.: AAUW Educational Foundation.

Anderson, Benedict. [1983] 1991. *Imagined Communities*. New York: Verso.

Appadurai, Arjun. 1996. *Modernity at Large: Cultural Dimensions of Globalization*. Minneapolis: University of Minnesota Press.

Ariès, Philippe. 1962 . *Centuries of Childhood: A Social History of Family Life*. Trans. Robert Baldick. New York: Vintage Books.

Balibar, Etienne, and Immanuel Wallerstein. 1991. *Race, Nation, Class: Ambiguous Identities*. New York: Verso.

Barrymore, Drew, with Todd Gold. 1990. *Little Girl Lost: A Child Star's Descent into Addiction and Out Again*. New York: Pocket Books.

Baumgartner, M. P. 1988. *The Moral Order of a Suburb*. New York: Oxford University Press.

Beatty, Paul. 1996. "Taken Out of Context." *Granta* 53 (spring): 167–194.

Behar, Ruth, and Deborah A. Gordon, eds. 1995. *Women Writing Culture*. Berkeley: University of California Press.

Bernheimer, Charles, and Claire Kahane, eds. [1985] 1990. *In Dora's Case: Freud—Hysteria—Feminism*. New York: Columbia University Press.

Blee, Kathleen M. 1991. *Women of the Klan: Racism and Gender in the 1920s*. Berkeley: University of California Press.

Blodgett, Nancy. 1987. "Self-Defense: Parricide Defendants Cite Sexual Abuse as Justification." *American Bar Association Journal*, 1 June.

Bolton, Bennet. 1993. "Bitter Long Island Lolita: I Should Have Shot My Lover Instead of His Wife." *National Enquirer*, 12 January.

Bourdieu, Pierre. 1984. *Distinction: A Social Critique of the Judgment of Taste*. Trans. Richard Nice. Cambridge, Mass.: Harvard University Press.

Breines, Wini. 1992. *Young, White, and Miserable: Growing up Female in the Fifties*. Boston: Beacon Press.

Brodkin, Karen. 1999. *How Jews Became White Folks: And What that Says about Race in America*. New Brunswick, N.J.: Rutgers University Press.

Brown, Lyn Mikel, and Carol Gilligan. 1992. *Meeting at the Crossroads: Women's Psychology and Girls' Development*. New York: Ballantine Books.

Brown, Peggy. 1994. "On LI, Race Looms Large." *Newsday*, 20 May.

Buhr, Jenni. 1990. "Levittown as a Utopian Community." In *Long Island: The Suburban Experience*. Ed. Barbara M. Kelly. Interlaken, N.Y.: Heart of the Lakes Publishing.

Burton, Alex. 1993. "Amazing Story of Love Behind Bars: I Was Amy Fisher's Jailhouse Sweetheart . . . And She Sent Me These Passionate Love Letters." *Star*, 7 December.

Butler, Judith. 1990. *Gender Trouble: Feminism and the Subversion of Identity*. New York: Routledge.

Campbell, Anne. [1984] 1991. *Girls in the Gang*. Cambridge, Mass.: Basil Blackwell.

Canguilhem, Georges. [1966] 1991. *The Normal and the Pathological*. Trans. Carolyn R. Fawcett. New York: Zone Books.

Casey, Robert. 1983. "Risk from Shoreham Is Infinitesimal." *Newsday*, 10 November.

Chambers, Marcia. 1986. "Children Citing Self-Defense in Murder of Parents." *New York Times*, 12 October.

Cixous, Hélène. 1983. "Portrait of Dora." *Diacritics* 13, no. 1 (spring): 2–32.

Clifford, James. 1988. *The Predicament of Culture: Twentieth-Century Ethnography, Literature, and Art*. Cambridge, Mass.: Harvard University Press.

Clifford, James, and George E. Marcus, eds. 1986. *Writing Culture: The Poetics and Politics of Ethnography*. Berkeley: University of California Press.

Community Journal. 1979. "Shoreham Costs Investigated," 18 July.

———. 1994. "Letters to the Editor," 4 May.

Coupland, Douglas. 1991. *Generation X: Tales for an Accelerated Culture*. New York: St. Martin's Press.

———. 1992. *Shampoo Planet*. New York: Pocket Books.

de Certeau, Michel. 1984. *The Practice of Everyday Life*. Trans. Steven Rendall. Berkeley: University of California Press.

Decker, Hannah. 1991. *Freud, Dora, and Vienna 1900*. New York: Free Press.

de Lauretis, Teresa. 1984. *Alice Doesn't: Feminism, Semiotics, Cinema*. Bloomington and Indianapolis: Indiana University Press.

———. 1987. *Technologies of Gender: Essays on Theory, Film, and Fiction*. Bloomington and Indianapolis: Indiana University Press.

DeParle, Jason. 1996. "The New Contract with America's Poor." *New York Times*, 28 July.

De Witt, Karen. 1994. "Suburban Expansion Fed by an Influx of Minorities." *New York Times*, 15 August.

Didion, Joan. 1993. "Letter from California: Trouble in Lakewood." *New Yorker*, 26 July: 46–50, 52–60, 62–65.

Domínguez, Virginia R. 1986. *White by Definition: Social Classification in Creole Louisiana*. New Brunswick, N.J.: Rutgers University Press.

Dorst, John D. 1989. *The Written Suburb: An American Site, An Ethnographic Dilemma*. Philadelphia: University of Pennsylvania Press.

Dyer, Richard. 1988. "White." *Screen* 29 (fall): 44–64.

Eckert, Penelope. 1990. *Jocks and Burnouts: Social Categories in High School.* New York: Teachers College Press.

Eftimiades, Maria. 1992. *Lethal Lolita: A True Story of Sex, Scandal, and Deadly Obsession*. New York: St. Martin's Press.

Ehrenreich, Barbara. 1989. *Fear of Falling: The Inner Life of the Middle Class*. New York: Harper Perennial.

Ewing, Charles Patrick. 1990. *Kids Who Kill*. New York: Lexington Books.

Ezekiel, Raphael S. 1995. *The Racist Mind: Portraits of American Neo-Nazis and Klansmen*. New York: Viking Press.

Fabian, Johannes. 1983. *Time and the Other: How Anthropology Makes Its Object*. New York: Columbia University Press.

Fanon, Frantz. 1967. *Black Skin, White Masks*. New York: Grove Press.

Fisher, Amy. 1994. "Without Boundaries." *mouth 2 mouth*, spring: 72–75.

Fisher, Amy, and Sheila Weller. 1993. *Amy Fisher: My Story*. New York: Pocket Books.

Fishman, Robert. 1987. *Bourgeois Utopias: The Rise and Fall of Suburbia*. New York: Basic Books.

Fleisher, Mark S. 1998. *Dead End Kids: Gang Girls and the Boys They Know*. Madison: University of Wisconsin Press.

Foley, Douglas E. 1990. *Learning Capitalist Culture: Deep in the Heart of Tejas*. Philadelphia: University of Pennsylvania Press.

———. 1995. *The Heartland Chronicles*. Philadelphia: University of Pennsylvania Press.

Forrest, Susan. 1994. "A Jailbird No Longer: Buttafuoco Welcomed Home." *Newsday*, 24 March.

Foucault, Michel. 1970. *The Order of Things: An Archaeology of the Human Sciences*. London: Tavistock.

———. 1972. *Archaeology of Knowledge*. Trans. A. M. Sheridan Smith. New York: Pantheon.

———. 1973. *Birth of the Clinic: An Archaeology of Medical Perception*. Trans. A. M. Sheridan Smith. New York: Vintage Books.

———. 1975. *I Pierre Rivière, having slaughtered my mother, my sister, and my brother . . . A Case of Parricide in the Nineteenth Century*. Trans. Frank Jellinek. New York: Random House.

———. 1979. *Discipline and Punish: The Birth of the Prison*. Trans. Alan Sheridan. New York: Vintage Books.

———. 1980. *An Introduction*. Vol. 1, *The History of Sexuality*. Trans. Robert Hurley. New York: Vintage Books.

———. 1985. *The Uses of Pleasure*. Vol. 2, *The History of Sexuality*. Trans. Robert Hurley. New York: Pantheon.

———. 1988. *The Care of the Self*. Vol. 3, *The History of Sexuality*. Trans. Robert Hurley. New York: Random House.

Fox, Richard G., ed. 1991. *Recapturing Anthropology: Working in the Present*. Santa Fe, N.Mex.: School of American Research Press.

Frankenberg, Ruth. 1993. *White Women, Race Matters: The Social Construction of Whiteness*. Minneapolis: University of Minnesota Press.

———, ed. 1997. *Displacing Whiteness: Essays in Social and Cultural Criticism*. Durham, N.C.: Duke University Press.

Freud, Sigmund. 1963. *Dora: An Analysis of a Case of Hysteria*. New York: Collier Books.

Fussell, Paul. 1983. *Class: A Guide Through the American Status System*. New York: Touchstone.

Gaines, Donna. [1990] 1991. *Teenage Wasteland: Suburbia's Dead End Kids*. New York: Harper Perennial.

———. 1992. "An American Girl: Amy Fisher's Teenage Wasteland." *Village Voice*, 13 October.

Gallagher, Charles A. 1995. "White Reconstruction in the University." *Socialist Review* 24, nos. 1 & 2: 165–187.

Gans, Herbert. 1982. *The Levittowners: Ways of Life and Politics in a New Suburban Community*. New York: Pantheon.

Garbarino, James. 1999. *Lost Boys: Why Our Sons Turn Violent and How We Can Save Them*. New York: Free Press.

Garvey, John. 1996. "Panic, Rage, and Reason on the Long Island Rail Road." In *Race Traitor*. Ed. Noel Ignatiev and John Garvey. New York: Routledge.

Ginsburg, Faye D. 1989. *Contested Lives: The Abortion Debate in an American Community*. Berkeley: University of California Press.

Ginsburg, Faye, and Anna Lowenhaupt Tsing, eds. 1990. *Uncertain Terms: Negotiating Gender in American Culture*. Boston: Beacon Press.

Gover, Paula K. 1995. *White Boys and River Girls*. Chapel Hill, N.C.: Algonquin Books.

Gray, John. 1995. *Men Are from Mars/Women Are from Venus*. New York: HarperCollins.

Gurian, Michael. 1998. *A Fine Young Man: What Parents, Mentors, and Educators Can Do to Shape Adolescent Boys into Exceptional Men*. New York: Putnam.

Hall, Stephen S. 1999. "The Bully in the Mirror." *New York Times Magazine*, 22 August: 31–35, 58, 62, 64–65.

Haraway, Donna J. 1991. "Situated Knowledges: The Science Question in Feminism and the Privilege of Partial Perspective." In *Simians, Cyborgs, and Women: The Reinvention of Nature*. New York: Routledge.

Harding, Susan. 1987. "Convicted by the Holy Spirit: The Rhetoric of Fundamental Conversion." *American Ethnologist* 14, no. 1: 167–181.

Hartigan, John Jr. 1992. "Reading Trash: *Deliverance* and the Poetics of White Trash." *Visual Anthropology Review* 8, no. 2 (fall): 8–15.

———. 1999. *Racial Situations: Class Predicaments of Whiteness in Detroit*. Princeton, N.J.: Princeton University Press.

Heinrichs, Emily, as told to Andrea Coller. 1996. "I Was a Nazi Girl." *YM* April: 56–59.

Henneberger, Melinda. 1993. "Long Island, Like Ya Nev-ah Seen It, in Amy Fisher TV Movies." *New York Times*, 3 January.

Henry, Jacqueline. 1994. "Teen-Age Pregnancy Rate Puzzles East End." *New York Times*, 24 April.

Herrnstein, Richard J., and Charles Murray. 1994. *The Bell Curve: Intelligence and Class Structure in American Life*. New York: Free Press.

Hertz, Neil, ed. 1983. "A Fine Romance: Freud and Dora." *Diacritics* 13, no. 1 (spring).

hooks, bell. 1992. "Representing Whiteness in the Black Imagination." In *Cultural Studies*. Ed. Lawrence Grossberg, Cary Nelson, and Paul Treichler. New York: Routledge.

Howe, Neil, and Bill Strauss. 1993. *13th Gen: Abort, Retry, Ignore, Fail?* New York: Vintage Books.

Hunter, Latoya. 1992. *The Diary of Latoya Hunter*. New York: Vintage Books.

Hymes, Dell, ed. 1969. *Reinventing Anthropology*. New York: Random House.

Ignatiev, Noel. 1995. *How the Irish Became White*. New York: Routledge.

Ignatiev, Noel, and John Garvey, eds. 1996. *Race Traitor*. New York: Routledge.

Israel, Betsy. 1996. "Amy Fisher's Time." *New York Times Magazine*, 21 July: 18–21.

Jackson, Kenneth. 1985. *Crabgrass Frontier: The Suburbanization of the United States*. New York: Oxford University Press.

Jacobson, Matthew. 1998. *Whiteness of a Different Color: European Immigrants and the Alchemy of Race*. Cambridge, Mass.: Harvard University Press.

John, Mary E. 1989. "Postcolonial Feminists in the Western Intellectual Field: Anthropologists and Native Informants?" *Inscriptions* 5: 49–73.

Kahane, Claire. 1995. *Passions of the Voice: Hysteria, Narrative, and the Figure of the Speaking Woman, 1850–1915*. Baltimore: The Johns Hopkins University Press.

Kellerman, Vivien. 1994. "Welcome Retirement from the Limelight." *New York Times*, 31 July.

Kelly, Barbara M., ed. 1989. *Suburbia Re-examined.* New York: Greenwood Press.

———. 1990. *Long Island: The Suburban Experience.* Interlaken, NY: Heart of the Lakes Publishing.

———. 1993. *Expanding the American Dream: Building and Rebuilding Levittown.* Albany: State University of New York Press.

Kenny, Lorraine. 1988. "The Birds and the Bees: Teen Pregnancy and the Media." *Afterimage* 16, no. 1 (summer): 6–8.

———.1990. "Are You Sure I'll Still Be a Virgin?" *SF Camerawork* 17, no.2 (summer): 8–14.

Kindlon, Daniel, and Michael Thompson. 1999. *Raising Cain: Protecting the Emotional Life of Boys.* New York: Ballantine Books.

King, Larry. 1990. *Larry King Live* (20 April). New York: Journal Graphics, Inc.

Klanwatch: Intelligence Report. 1995. "Skinheads Charged in Family Murders." March: 1–2.

Kleiman, Dena. 1986. "Murder on Long Island." *New York Times Magazine*, 15 September: 52, 56, 58, 62, 64, 66.

———. 1987. "Girl Says Hiring Father's Killer Seemed 'Like a Game' at First." *New York Times*, 15 September.

———. 1988. *A Deadly Silence: The Ordeal of Cheryl Pierson: A Case of Incest and Murder.* New York: New American Library.

Kondo, Dorinne K. 1990. *Crafting Selves: Power, Gender, and Discourses of Identity in a Japanese Workplace.* Chicago: University of Chicago Press.

Kornheiser, Tony. 1994. Untitled. *Los Angeles Times.* 8 February.

Kubasik, Ben. n.d. "Barrymore Will Play Fisher in TV Movie." *Newsday.*

Kumar, Nita. 1992. *Friends, Brothers, and Informants: Fieldwork Memoirs of Banaras.* Berkeley: University of California Press.

Kunzel, Regina G. 1993. *Fallen Women, Problem Girls: Unmarried Mothers and the Professionalization of Social Work 1890–1945.* New Haven, Conn.: Yale University Press.

Ladner, Joyce A. [1971] 1995. *Tomorrow's Tomorrow: The Black Woman.* Lincoln: University of Nebraska.

Lakoff, Robin Tolmach, and James C. Coyne. 1993. *Father Knows Best: The Use and Abuse of Power in Freud's Case of Dora.* New York: Teachers College Press.

Lambert, Bruce. 1996. "From the Heights of Space to the Fall of an Industrial Empire." *New York Times*, 5 May.

Lawson, Annette, and Deborah L. Rhode, eds. 1993. *The Politics of Pregnancy: Adolescent Pregnancy and Public Policy.* New Haven, Conn.: Yale University Press.

Leadbeater, Bonnie J. Ross, and Niobe Way, eds. 1996. *Urban Girls: Resisting Stereotypes.* New York: New York University Press.

LeBlanc, Adrian Nicole. 1999. "The Outsiders." *New York Times Magazine*, 22 August: 36–41.

Levine, Judith. 1994. "The Heart of Whiteness: Dismantling the Master's House." *Voice Literary Supplement*, September.

Limón, José. 1991. "Representation, Ethnicity, and the Precursory Ethnography: Notes of a Native Anthropologist." In *Recapturing Anthropology: Working in the Present.* Ed. Richard G. Fox. Santa Fe, N. Mex.: School of American Research Press.

———. 1994. *Dancing with the Devil.* Minneapolis: University of Minnesota Press.

Lipsitz, George. 1995. "The Possessive Investment in Whiteness: Racialized Social Democracy and the 'White' Problem in American Studies." *American Quarterly* 47, no. 3 (September): 369–387.

Long Island Almanac 1993. 1994. Ronkonkoma, N.Y.: Long Island Business News.

McCaffrey, Phillip. 1984. *Freud and Dora: The Artful Dream.* New Brunswick, N.J.: Rutgers University Press.

McCall, Anthony, Claire Pajaczkowska, Andrew Tyndall, and Jane Weinstock. 1981. "Sigmund Freud's Dora: A Case of Mistaken Identity." *Framework*, nos. 15–17: 75–81.

McGinn, Susan. 1994. "After School Bounty, Shoreham Retrenches." *New York Times*, 24 July.

McMullan, Penelope. 1971. "Village Designed to Exclude Worry." *Community Journal*, 13 April.

McQuiston, John T. 1999. "Amy Fisher Is Released After Almost 7 Years in Prison." *New York Times*, 11 May.

———. 2000a. "Suffolk Spared and Nassau Helped as LIPA Settles Tax Case." *New York Times*, 14 January.

———. 2000b. "School District Still Suffering after Settling L.I. Tax Fight." *New York Times*, 15 January.

Maeroff, Gene I. 1990. "Getting to Know a Good Middle School: Shoreham-Wading River." *Phi Delta Kappan* 71, no. 7 (March): 505–511.

Mahler, Sarah J. 1995. *American Dreaming: Immigrant Life on the Margins*. Princeton, N.J.: Princeton University Press.

Mahony, Patrick J. 1996. *Freud's Dora: A Psychoanalytic, Historical, and Textual Study*. New Haven, Conn.: Yale University Press.

Males, Mike. 1994. "Why Blame Young Girls?" *New York Times*, 29 July.

Mani, Lati. 1989. "Multiple Mediations: Feminist Scholarship in the Age of Multinational Reception." *Inscriptions* 5: 1–23.

Marcus, George E., with Peter Dobkin. 1992. *Lives in Trust: The Fortunes of Dynastic Families in Late Twentieth-Century America*. Boulder, Colo.: Westview Press.

Moffatt, Michael. 1989. *Coming of Age in New Jersey: College and American Culture*. New Brunswick, N.J.: Rutgers University Press.

Moreno, Joëlle Anne. 1989. "Killing Daddy: Developing a Self-Defense Strategy for the Abused Child." *University of Pennsylvania Law Review* 137, no. 4 (April): 1281–1307.

Morrison, Toni. 1992. *Playing in the Dark: Whiteness and the Literary Imagination*. New York: Vintage Books.

Morrissey, Kim. 1995. *Dora: A Case History*. London: Nick Hern Books.

Morson, Gary Saul. 1989. "Parody, History, and Metaparody." In *Rethinking Bakhtin: Extensions and Challenges*. Ed. Gary Saul Morson and Caryl Emerson. Evanston, IL: Northwestern University Press.

Moynihan, Daniel Patrick. 1965. *The Negro Family: The Case for National Action*. Prepared for the Office of Policy Planning and Research of the Department of Labor. Washington, D.C.: U.S. Government Printing Office.

Mulvey, Laura. 1992. "Pandora: Topographies of the Mask and Curiosity." In *Sexuality and Space*. Ed. Beatriz Colomina. New York: Princeton Architectural Press.

Narayan, Kirin. 1993. "How Native is a 'Native' Anthropologist?" *American Anthropologist* 94, no. 3: 672–686.

Nathanson, Constance A. 1991. *Dangerous Passage: The Social Control of Sexuality in Women's Adolescence*. Philadelphia: Temple University Press.

National Public Radio. 1994. *All Things Considered*. 10 February.

Neuman, William. 1994. "Indians Pan Peter." *New York Post*, 7 March.

Newman, Katherine S. 1988. *Falling from Grace: The Experience of Downward Mobility in the American Middle Class*. New York: Vintage Books.

———. 1994. *Declining Fortunes: The Withering of the American Dream*. New York: Basic Books.

Newsday. 1992. "What Amy Says about America." Editorial, 15 November.

———. 1993. "Amy: The Phenomenon." 18 January.

———. 1994. "Mr. Suburbia: His Houses Were Sturdy and Affordable: He Built the American Dream." Special Section, 30 January.

New York Times. 1991. "How Much New York Districts Spend." 6 May.

———. 1992a. "Path to Higher Status: Coveted Zip Codes." 4 October.

———. 1992b. "Amy Fisher Case: Parable or Aberration? Long Islanders Consider the Implications." 18 October.

———. 1994. United Colors of Benetton ad, 26 April.

Oleck, Joan. 1996. "Sinking Feeling: In Adolescent Girls Self-Esteem Often Disappears into What One Expert Calls the Bermuda Triangle." *Newsday*, 6 April.

Ong, Aihwa. 1987. *Spirits of Resistance and Capitalist Discipline: Factory Women in Malaysia*. Albany: State University of New York Press.

Orenstein, Peggy. 1994. *School Girls: Young Women, Self-Esteem, and the Confidence Gap*. New York: Doubleday.

Ortner, Sherry B. 1991. "Reading America: Preliminary Notes on Class and Culture." In *Recapturing Anthropology: Working in the Present*. Ed. Richard G. Fox. Santa Fe, N.Mex.: School of American Research Press.

———. 1993. "Ethnography Among the Newark." *Michigan Quarterly Review* 32, no. 3 (summer): 411–429.

Otter, Jack. 1994. "Flight Canceled for 'Peter Pan.'" *Newsday*, 8 March.

Pennysaver. 1984. "Shoreham and the Persian Gulf." 26 May.

———. n.d. "Anti-Shoreham Residents Protest Legislator's Visit."

People. 1993. Letters to the Editor. 13 September: 4.

Perin, Constance. 1988. *Belonging in America: Reading Between the Lines*. Madison: University of Wisconsin Press.

Perlman, Shirley E., and Laura Durkin. 1990. "A Homeroom Murder Pact." *Newsday: Celebrating Fifty Years of Newsday and Long Island*, 14 October.

Phoenix, Ann. 1993. "The Social Construction of Teenage Motherhood: A Black and White Issue?" In *The Politics of Pregnancy: Adolescent Pregnancy and Public Policy*. Ed. Annette Lawson and Deborah L. Rhode. New Haven, Conn.: Yale University Press.

Pipher, Mary. 1994. *Reviving Ophelia: Saving the Lives of Adolescent Girls*. New York: Ballantine Books.

Pleven, Liam, and Robert Cooke. 1994. "Radiation Leak." *Newsday*, 1 April.

Podd, Roger. 1994. "Who Knows What Lurks in the Mind of Teens? Lorraine Kenny Might." *Village Beacon*, 6 January.

Pollack, William S. 1999. *Real Boys: Rescuing Our Sons from the Myths of Boyhood*. New York: Owl Books.

Rabinovitz, Jonathan. 1994. "Lawyer of Defendant in Train Killings Seeks Review of His Client's Sanity." *New York Times*, 11 December.

Rause, Vince. 1994. "The State of Hate." *Philadelphia*, August: 66–71, 141–148.

Roediger, David R. 1991. *The Wages of Whiteness: Race and the Making of the American Working Class*. New York: Verso.

Roof, Judith. 1991. *A Lure of Knowledge: Lesbian Sexuality and Theory*. New York: Columbia University Press.

Rosaldo, Renato. 1989. *Culture and Truth: The Remaking of Social Analysis*. Boston: Beacon Press.

Rosenbaum, Ron. 1993. "The Devil in Long Island." *New York Times Magazine*, 22 August: 21–27, 36–38, 42, 44.

———. 1995. "Staring into the Heart of Darkness." *New York Times Magazine*, 4 June: 36–45, 50, 58, 61, 72.

Sacks, Karen Brodkin. 1994. "How Did Jews Become White Folks?" In *Race*. Ed. Steven Gregory and Roger Sanjek. New Brunswick, N.J.: Rutgers University Press.

Schembari, James. 1996. "Once Bitten, Twice Shy: Jumpy Suburbanites See Rabies Lurking All Over." *New York Times*, 25 May.

Schemo, Diana Jean. 1994a. "Persistent Racial Segregation Mars Suburbs' Green Dreams." *New York Times*, 17 March.

———. 1994b. "Suburban Taxes Are Higher for Blacks, Analysis Shows." *New York Times*, 17 August.

Shakespeare, William. [1959] 1974. *The Tempest*. Baltimore: Penguin Books.

Shuman, Amy. 1986. *Storytelling Rights: The Uses of Oral and Written Texts by Urban Adolescents*. New York: Cambridge University Press.

Sikes, Gini. 1998. *8 Ball Chicks: A Year in the Violent World of Girl Gangsters*. New York: Doubleday.

Smith, Leef. 1995. "Teen Tells of Her Year as a Skinhead: Onetime 'Big, Bad Nazi Girl' Visits Fairfax School to Offer Warning to Others." *Washington Post*, 25 May.

Solinger, Rickie. 1992. *Wake Up Little Susie: Single Pregnancy and Race before Roe v. Wade*. New York: Routledge.

Spigel, Lynn. 1997. "From Theatre to Space Ship: Metaphors of Suburban Domesticity in Postwar America." In *Visions of Suburbia*. Ed. Roger Silverstone. New York: Routledge.

Spillers, Hortense J. 1987. "Mama's Baby, Papa's Maybe," *Diacritics* 17, no. 2 (summer): 77–80.

Stacey, Judith. 1980. "Can There Be a Feminist Ethnography?" *Women's Studies International Forum* 11, no. 1: 21–27.

Stack, Carol B. 1974. *All Our Kin: Strategies for Survival in a Black Community*. New York: Harper & Row.

Stewart, Kathleen. 1991. "On the Politics of Cultural Theory: A Case for 'Contaminated' Cultural Critique." *Social Research* 58, no. 2: 395–412.

———. 1996. *A Space on the Side of the Road: Cultural Poetics in the "Other" America*. Princeton, N.J.: Princeton University Press.

Stoler, Ann Laura. 1991. "Carnal Knowledge and Imperial Power: Gender, Race, and Morality in Colonial Asia." In *Gender at the Crossroads of Knowledge: Feminist Anthropology in the Postmodern Era*. Ed. Micaela di Leonardo. Berkeley: University of California Press.

———. 1995. *Race and the Education of Desire: Foucault's* History of Sexuality *and the Colonial Order of Things*. Durham, N.C.: Duke University Press.

Strathern, Marilyn. 1992. *After Nature: English Kinship in the Late Twentieth Century*. Cambridge: Cambridge University Press.

Swinburne, Algernon Charles, Michael Apice, and Eddie Cornbury. 1993. *The Amy Fisher Story/The Joey Buttafuoco Story*. New York: First Amendment Publishing.

Sylvester, Kathleen. 1994. *Preventable Calamity: Rolling Back Teen Pregnancy. Policy Report*, no. 22. Washington, D.C.: Progressive Policy Institute.

Talty, Stephan. 1996. "The Method of a Neo-Nazi Mogul." *New York Times Magazine*, 25 February: 40–43.

Tannen, Deborah. 1990. *You Just Don't Understand: Women and Men in Conversation*. New York: Morrow.

Taylor, Carl S. 1993. *Girls, Gangs, Women and Drugs*. East Lansing: Michigan State University Press.

Treen, Joe, and Maria Eftimiades. 1992. "Treachery in the Suburbs." *People*, 29 June: 32–37.

Tsing, Anna Lowenhaupt. 1990. "Monster Stories: Women Charged with Perinatal Endangerment." In *Uncertain Terms: Negotiating Gender in American Culture*. Ed. Faye Ginsburg and Anna Lowenhaupt Tsing. Boston: Beacon Press.

Twine, France Winddance. 1997. "Brown-Skinned White Girls: Class, Culture, and the Construction of White Identity in Suburban Communities." In *Displacing Whiteness: Essays in Social and Cultural Criticism*. Ed. Ruth Frankenberg. Durham, N.C.: Duke University Press.

Usdansky, Margaret L. 1996. "Single Motherhood: Stereotypes and Statistics." *New York Times*, 11 February.

Visweswaran, Kamala. 1994. *Fictions of Feminist Ethnography*. Minneapolis: University of Minnesota Press.

Wald, Matthew L. 1994. "7 Exposed to Radiation in U.S. Lab Accident." *New York Times*, 1 April.

Ware, Vron. 1992. *Beyond the Pale: White Women, Racism, and History*. New York: Verso.

Wasserman, Elizabeth. 1993. "Reel Crime Stories: Fact More Entertaining than Fiction in Hollywood." *Newsday*, 3 January.

Wiegand, Virginia S. 1995. "Escaping from a World of Hate." *Philadelphia Inquirer*, 5 April.

Willis, Paul. 1977. *Learning to Labor: How Working-Class Kids Get Working-Class Jobs*. New York: Columbia University Press.

Winerip, Michael. 1983. "Pro-Shoreham Group: Voice Now Heard." *New York Times*, 3 July.

Winner, Langdon. 1986. *The Whale and the Reactor: A Search for Limits in an Age of High Technology*. Chicago: University of Chicago Press.

Wolcott, James. 1994. "The Clash of Cheekbones." *New Yorker*, 25 July: 74–76.

Wray, Matt, and Annalee Newitz, eds. 1997. *White Trash: Race and Class in America*. New York: Routledge.

Zelnick, Melvin, and John F. Kantner. 1980. "Sexual Activity, Contraceptive Use and Pregnancy among Metropolitan Area Teenagers, 1971–1979." *Family Planning Perspectives* 12 (September/October): 230–237.

Ziv, Laura. 1996. "(Un)Planned Parenthood: Teenage Moms Tell All." *Sassy*, April: 76–79.

Index

About the Author

Lorraine Delia Kenny is Public Education Coordinator for the American Civil Liberties Union's Reproductive Freedom Project. She received her Ph.D. from the History of Consciousness Program at the University of California, Santa Cruz, in 1996. She is the former coordinating editor at the National Council for Research on Women and former associate editor for *Afterimage*, a journal of media arts and cultural criticism, and has taught anthropology at Sarah Lawrence College and on the Graduate Faculty of the New School for Social Research.